Chains of Fortune: Linking Women Producers and Workers with Global Markets

Commonwealth Secretariat

Published by the Commonwealth Secretariat

Commonwealth Secretariat
Marlborough House
Pall Mall, London SW1Y 5HX, United Kingdom

Designed and published by the Commonwealth Secretariat
Cover pictures by Brian Moody and Abdullah Zuberi, *The New Age*
Printed in Britain by Formara Ltd.

Wherever possible, the Commonwealth Secretariat uses paper sourced
from sustainable forests or from sources that minimise a destructive impact
on the environment.

ISBN 0-85092-798-6   Price: £11.99

Web site: http//www.thecommonwealth.org

Contents

Foreword   v

Introduction   1
Marilyn Carr

Case Studies

From Tree-minders to Global Players: Cocoa Farmers in Ghana   11
Pauline Tiffin, Jacqui MacDonald, Haruna Maamah and Frema Osei-Opare

Tradition, Trade and Technology: Virgin Coconut Oil in Samoa   45
John Cretney and Adimaimalaga Tafuna'i

Cashing in on Cashew Nuts: Women Producers and Factory Workers in Mozambique   75
Nazneen Kanji, Carin Vijfhuizen, Carla Braga and Luis Artur

National Labour Legislation in an Informal Context: Women Workers in Export Horticulture in South Africa   103
Stephanie Barrientos, Andrienetta Kritzinger and Hester Rossouw

Rags, Riches and Women Workers: Export-oriented Garment Manufacturing in Bangladesh   133
Naila Kabeer and Simeen Mahmud

On the Threshold of Informalization: Women Call Centre Workers in India   165
Swasti Mitter, Grace Fernandez and Shaiby Varghese

The Trade Policy Context   185
Sheila Page

Lessons Learned   197
Marilyn Carr

About the Contributors   217

Foreword

Global trade and investment policies are having a dramatic impact on employment relations and work arrangements around the world. But there is no single meaning of increased liberalization for the global workforce. The impact can be both negative and positive and differs by geographic location, by industry and trade, and by employment status.

At the Sixth Meeting of the Commonwealth Ministers responsible for Women's Affairs (WAMM) in New Delhi, India in April 2000, globalization, and specifically trade liberalization and privatization, were seen as having transformed the social, economic and political landscape of the Commonwealth. Ministers saw globalization as presenting new opportunities and challenges to policy-makers who should take steps to ensure that women and men benefit equally from liberalization and are protected equally from its negative effects.

To date attention has tended to focus on the negative effects of globalization, particularly on weak and vulnerable economies, and on the women and children within them. However, there is also a need to take steps to ensure that weak societies and weak groups of people are enabled to take advantage of the new economic opportunities which arise from globalization.

It was with this intention that a project was initiated jointly by the Commonwealth Secretariat's Social Tranformation Division and its Economic Affairs Division to develop this book, *Chains of Fortune: Linking Women Producers and Workers with Global Markets*. Its focus is on the positive experiences of women producers and workers in the informal economy who, in many parts of the world, comprise the majority of the economically active population and who could contribute much more to growth of output and exports if they were enabled to do so.

This book contributes to the 2003 Commonwealth Aso Rock Declaration's vision of a Commonwealth that is committed to a more equitable sharing of the benefits of globalization. It explores practical examples from Commonwealth countries of how governments have supported (or could support) the economic and export efforts of informal women producers and workers, and of the complementary roles that other institutions – such as membership associations, local and international NGOs, private corporations, consumers' associations and fair trade organizations – can play in this process.

This publication complements another book that is simultaneously being published in the Commonwealth Secretariat series on gender mainstreaming in critical development issues, *Mainstreaming Informal Employment and Gender in Poverty Reduction: A Handbook for Policy-makers and Other Stakeholders*. It represents the growing recognition of the need for governments to focus on employment, and especially informal employment, as a path to achieve both gender equality and poverty reduction.

The development of this book has been a collective effort of many groups and individuals. It contains contributions from 20 authors from nine Commonwealth countries. Of these, we would particularly like to thank those who led their research teams. These include: Jacqui MacDonald, Pauline Tiffen, Adimaimalaga Tafuna'i, John Cretney, Nazneen Kanji, Stephanie Barrientos, Simeen Mahmud and Swasti Mitter. We also would like to thank Chris Stevens of the Institute of Development Studies, University of Sussex for providing early inputs on trade policy, including guidelines for authors, and Sheila Page of the Overseas Development Institute for providing an overview of the case studies from a trade policy perspective.

Dr Margaret Snyder made very helpful comments on the many versions of the introduction and 'lessons learned' chapters of the book.

Thanks are also due to the Commonwealth Secretariat team who reviewed the book, especially to Sarojini Ganju Thakur, and to Rawwida Baksh, Maryse Roberts, Ivan Mbirimi, Roman Grynberg and Rupert Jones-Parry for their contributions. Further thanks to Christabel Gurney for her careful editing of the manuscript.

And last, but not least, we would like to specially thank the editor of the book, Dr Marilyn Carr, who not only guided and coordinated the project, but also inspired us by her commitment and dedication to the wider cause of recognition of the rights and potential of women in the informal economy.

Indrajit Coomaraswamy
Director
Economic Affairs Division
Commonwealth Secretariat

Nancy Spence
Director
Social Transformation
Programmes Division
Commonwealth Secretariat

Abbreviations

ADPP	Assistance to Development for the People by the People
AGOA	African Growth and Opportunity Act
ATO	Alternative Trading Organization
AMODER	Association for Rural Development
BCEA	Basic Conditions of Employment Act
CDE	Centre for Development of Enterprise
CII	Confederation of Indian Industries
CMB	Ghana Cocoa Marketing Board
CMC	Ghana Cocoa Marketing Company
Cocobod	Ghana Cocoa Board
COSATU	Congress of South African Trade Unions
CRMG	Commodity Risk Management Group
DfID	Department for International Development
DME	Direct Micro Expelling
EEA	Employment Equity Act
ENOWID	Enhanced Opportunities for Women in Development
EPZ	Export Processing Zone
ETI	Ethical Trade Initiative
FAO	Food and Agriculture Organization
FDI	Foreign Direct Investment
FLO	Fair Trade Labelling International
FOB	Free on Board
GDP	Gross Domestic Product
ICCO	International Cocoa Organisation
ICT	Information and Communications Technology
IIED	International Institute for Environment and Development
ILO	International Labour Organization
IMF	International Monetary Fund
INCAJU	Institute for the Promotion of Cashew
ITES	Information Technology Enabled Services
KKFCU	Kuapa Kokoo Farmers' Credit Union
KKFT	Kuapa Kokoo Farmers' Trust
KKFU	Kuapa Kokoo Farmers' Union
KKL	Kuapa Kokoo Limited
LBC	Licensed Buying Company
MDGs	Millennium Development Goals
MFA	Multifibre Arrangement
NASAA	National Association for Sustainable Agriculture Australia

NAFTA	North American Free Trade Association
NASSCOM	National Association of Software and Services Companies
NGO	Non-Governmental Organization
NIC	Newly Industrializing Country
OECD	Organisation for Economic Cooperation and Development
PAMSCAD	Programme of Action to Mitigate the Social Cost of Adjustment
PBC	Produce Buying Company (part of CMB)
PCOC	Pure Coconut Oil Company
PIIDS	Pacific Islands Industrial Development Scheme
QCD	Quality Control Division (part of CMB)
R&D	Research and Development
RMG	Ready-Made Garment
SDO	Society Development Officer
SNV	Netherlands Development Organization
TDCA	Trade Development and Cooperation Agreement
TWIN	Third World Information Network
UNDP	United Nations Development Programme
UNIDO	United Nations Industrial Development Organisation
WIBDI	Women in Business Development Incorporated
WTO	World Trade Organization

Introduction

Marilyn Carr

Much has been written about the impact of globalization on the world's poor and especially on low-income women producers and workers. It is generally accepted that the impact can be both negative and positive and differs by country, industry or trade and employment status. Some women find new jobs or new markets for their products, while others have lost jobs or markets. In addition, many have seen their wages decline, their working conditions deteriorate or their workloads increase.[1]

While recognizing that negative effects do occur, the focus of this book is to show that globalization, and especially trade liberalization, open up new economic opportunities and that low-income women can take advantage of these if enabled to do so. The six case studies commissioned on this theme have been written by teams of international and national experts from various Commonwealth countries. In recognition of the fact that conditions and needs of women in different types of employment vary considerably, the studies cover a range of employment types including smallholders in traditional export commodities, wage workers in non-traditional export crops and wage workers in labour-intensive export industries.

The women upon whom the case studies are based are representative of those who make up the majority of the world's 550 million working poor (ILO, 2004). If the Millennium Development Goal (MDG) of halving the number of those living in poverty by the year 2015 is to be met, then women like these must be enabled to adequately contribute to and benefit from export-led growth. Trade liberalization will not automatically result in a reduction in poverty. This book hopes to contribute to our understanding of how this linkage can be strengthened by giving a detailed account and analysis of a range of strategies that have been developed and implemented in order to make sure that liberalization benefits those who are most in need.

Purpose of the Book

The research undertaken in the preparation of the case studies had four major purposes. First, it aimed to provide activists and researchers in Commonwealth countries with the opportunity of examining their experiences of working with women within the context of trade liberalization. Thus, the case studies have been written by people who have been very closely involved in the initiatives described.

Second, it aimed to contribute to the current debate about women and trade policy in developing countries with a focus on the informal economy.

Third, given the complexity of the strategies needed to overcome the constraints which women face in benefiting from trade liberalization, it aimed to provide information that would be useful to a range or actors and institutions in developing successful strategies. The institutions involved include international agencies, government agencies, non-governmental organizations (NGOs) and the private sector, including companies, cooperatives, membership associations and trade unions.

And finally, given the important role that trade and other government policies play in the way in which benefits from trade and market liberalization are distributed among different segments of the population, the research was intended to be of use to governments. It aimed to provide government policy-makers in Commonwealth countries with concrete examples of how policies and programmes which accompany trade and market liberalization can enable and have enabled a shift of access, power and returns in favour of low-income women producers and workers within global value chains.

Research Questions

The overall research question posed in the book is: to what extent can women producers and workers in developing countries benefit from new economic opportunities arising from trade and market liberalization?

More specifically, the book looks at:

- the nature and content of the strategies which have successfully linked women producers with global markets or created jobs for women in export markets;
- the role of government and other actors in successful strategies;
- the replicability and sustainability of achievements.

Selection of Case Studies

All the case studies in the book include the common premise that low-income women producers and workers can benefit from trade liberalization if they are enabled to do so. However, they were also selected to provide a range of contexts, strategies and experiences which can add to our understanding of the complex issue of spreading the gains of trade and market liberalization to poorer sections of the population. Therefore, they include:

- different regions of the Commonwealth and economies of different sizes;

- different types of local producers/workers, including independent producers, employees in small-scale factories, and wage workers in large farms, factories and companies supplying export markets through global value chains; existing members of the workforce are involved as well as new entrants;

- different economic sectors, including unprocessed and processed traditional commodities, non-traditional agricultural commodities, labour-intensive manufactured goods and labour-intensive services;

- different strategies/approaches to maximizing trade-related employment opportunities, including alternative trade, traditional business development services, social entrepreneurship, corporate social responsibility/labour legislation, female-led industrialization and technology-driven globalization;

- different types of actors (international agencies, governments, international and national NGOs, and the private sector) involved in different combinations in assisting local women producers and workers to take advantage of new economic opportunities arising from trade and market liberalization.

Summary of the Case Studies

Of the six case studies included in the book, three are from Africa (Ghana, Mozambique and South Africa), two are from South Asia (Bangladesh and India) and one is from the Pacific (Samoa). Several of the case studies also involve developed countries within the Commonwealth, including the UK, Australia and New Zealand, which are linked to producers and workers in the South through various marketing arrangements and commodity or production chains. The size of the economies involved varies from very tiny (Samoa) to very large (India).

In terms of work involved, three of the case studies focus on independent producers/smallholders (Ghana, Samoa and Mozambique), one involves employees of small factories (Mozambique) and three involve wage workers in large enterprises (South Africa, Bangladesh and India). Those involved in Ghana, Samoa, Mozambique and South Africa are existing members of the workforce, while the women in Bangladesh and India tend to be new entrants. All the women in the case studies are either self-employed or wage workers without contracts and are thus part of the informal economy. The only exception is the India case study, where the women do have contracts, but are working under conditions which bear many of the characteristics of the informal economy.

Three of the case studies involve traditional commodities (cocoa in Ghana, coconuts in Samoa and cashew nuts in Mozambique), although in all cases strategies have included moving into value-added processed commodities (chocolate, organic virgin coconut oil and processed cashews). One study involves non-traditional agricultural exports (deciduous fruits in South Africa). The Bangladesh case study looks at labour-intensive manufactured goods (ready-made garments) and the India case study looks at labour-intensive services (call centres). The relationship between trade policies and these various economic sectors is explored in a separate chapter.

In terms of strategies, there are examples of fair trade (Ghana); traditional business development services/niche market (Samoa); small enterprise development/social entrepreneurship (Mozambique); ethical trade/labour legislation (South Africa); female-led industrialization (Bangladesh); and technology-driven globalization (India). These strategies are all set within the context of global value chains and the way in which analysis of these chains has informed their development.

Finally, while most of the case studies involve a range of actors, there are usually one or two dominant players. These include: fair trade organizations/ international NGOs (Ghana); a national women's NGO (Samoa); social entrepreneur/government (Mozambique); Northern supermarkets/government (South Africa); international agencies/private sector (Bangladesh); and multinational companies/national companies (India).

Obviously, not all countries and not all the different types of employment undertaken by low-income women could be included. One important category which is not covered is that of homeworkers or industrial outworkers who work from their homes under informal arrangements within global value chains. This category, which is fast growing as employers try to reduce costs by contracting out work, has, however, been covered in other recent publications (Lund and Nicolson, 2003; Oxfam, 2004). In addition, while the case studies are very detailed, not all issues of importance to low-income women could be covered within them. One important subject that is not covered is that of the extension of social protection to low-income women who work informally. Again, this has been covered in another volume of case studies (Lund and Nicolson, 2003).

Some of the main characteristics of each case study are presented in the brief summaries below as a guide to the main section of the book.

Kuapa Kokoo Cooperative, Ghana

The Kuapa Kokoo cocoa cooperative in Ghana buys cocoa from its members for onward export and sale through the Ghana Cocoa Marketing Company (CMC). It has a membership of 45,000 farmers in 890 villages, of whom 70 per cent are smallholders and 30 per cent are women. The cooperative was established in 1993, with the assistance of Twin Trading, UK and the Netherlands development organisation, SNV, in response to the liberalization of the cocoa sector, and has grown very rapidly from its original membership base of 2,000 farmers. The output of the cooperative represents about 8 per cent of total world sales of cocoa. Of this, about 3 per cent is separated and tagged for the fair trade market which guarantees a 'floor' price per tonne and a 'premium' of US$150 per tonne for investment in community projects which meet women's priority needs in their everyday lives. In addition, Kuapa Kokoo members own the Day Chocolate Company in the UK which moves producers up the global value chain from production to retailing. The case study shows how smallholders were helped to seize the opportunities which arose following the abolition of the Ghana Cocoa Board (Cocobod) and were thus able to take control of their own livelihoods.

Virgin Coconut Oil Cooperatives, Samoa

The second case study is from Samoa, where a local NGO, Women in Business Development Incorporated (WIBDI), has introduced an improved production technology to 13 cooperatives to enable them to produce organic virgin coconut oil for export markets – primarily Australia and New Zealand. Each cooperative has about 50 members, all of whom belong to the same extended family. Women manage all but three of the cooperatives and women's status has increased as they are seen as having brought income opportunities to their communities. The project was started by WIBDI in 1996 as part of its micro-finance and micro-enterprise scheme, and has enabled women and their families to improve their incomes as well as reviving coconut production and contributing to export earnings. Exports have increased significantly since organic certification was obtained. The study shows how a local NGO can assist women to enter export markets through provision of traditional business services including credit, training, improved technologies, and marketing research and assistance.

Cashew Nut Producers and Processors, Mozambique

The third case study focuses on women smallholders and factory workers involved in efforts to regenerate the cashew nut production, processing and export industry in Mozambique. Following the collapse of the large state-owned processing factories in the 1990s, several smaller-scale factories have been established by the private sector with government support. A particularly interesting experiment is the setting up of 'satellite' processing units around one of these factories. This is seen as a way of adding more value locally, shortening the supply chain by eliminating middlemen and providing more employment for rural people, including women. This innovative model revolves around a social entrepreneur in partnership with government and an international NGO, Technoserve.

Deciduous Fruit Workers, South Africa

The fourth study looks at the introduction of national labour legislation and private sector codes of conduct and their impact on women working in the fruit industry in South Africa. At the end of apartheid in 1994, there were an estimated 102,000 permanent workers on South African fruit farms (of whom 26 per cent were women) and 181,000 temporary workers (of whom 69 per cent were women). While these numbers have increased, there has also been a restructuring of the workforce and of employment relations as a result of liberalization, which disbanded the government-regulated marketing channel for fruit exports and opened fruit growers up to the direct forces of global competition and international quality and labour standards. Enactment of national legislation, backed by international codes of conduct imposed by UK supermarkets, means that women's labour rights are being addressed for the first time and that they are now entitled to contracts in their own right. However, the combination of government legislation and increased global competition has prompted many growers to shed on-farm labour – mainly women – who then work as casual labourers without access to a contract. Thus, although labour protection has shifted in a more equitable direction, further progress is needed if it is to be consolidated for all women workers, including the most vulnerable.

Women Garment Workers, Bangladesh

The fifth case study examines the export industry for ready-made garments (RMG) which has been a major result of liberalization in Bangladesh. The industry currently employs 1.5 million workers, the majority of whom are women, and is a prime example of female-led, export-led industrialization. This was promoted by the introduction of international quotas and export-oriented national policies, which supported the transfer of production and marketing expertise from Korea, and by the drive of local entrepreneurs. Women workers in export industries, and especially in Export Processing

Zones (EPZs), receive more benefits, higher wages and better working conditions than those in domestic industries. Exports have provided much-needed employment for women in the poorer section of the rural population and raised their visible significance as economic contributors to their families. However, there are queries about the long-term sustainability of the industry, partly as a result of the phasing out of the Multifibre Arrangement (MFA) in 2005.

Women Call Centre Workers, India

The last study looks at the relocation of jobs in the information technology-enabled service (ITES) industries, such as call centres, from high wage to low wage countries. India has been a major recipient of such work and is expected to have a US$57 billion annual export industry in information services by 2008 employing four million people, of whom at least 40 per cent will be women. Call centres already employ more than 160,000 people, of whom between 45 and 70 per cent are women. Although these jobs are located in the formal sector, they display many characteristics typical of informal employment. These include lack of security as a result of companies moving to countries with lower wage rates than India, and the cancelling of work contracts as a result of pressure in the North to limit the outsourcing of jobs.

The book concludes with two overviews. One looks at the overall trade policy context within which the case studies are situated, while the other draws out the main lessons learned from them and highlights some of the good ideas for policies and programmes to be considered for future action.

Note

1   For some of the recent literature on trade and gender, see N. Catagay, 2001; M.
    Fontana *et al.*, 1998; S. Joekes, 1999; M. Williams, 2003; M. Carr and M. Chen,
    2002.

References

Carr, Marilyn and Chen, Martha (2002). 'Globalization and the Informal Economy:
    How Global Trade and Investment Impact on the Working Poor', Working Paper
    on the Informal Economy, No. 1, ILO, Geneva.
Catagay, Nilifur (2001). *Trade, Gender and Poverty*, UNDP, New York.
Fontana, Marzia, Joekes, Susan and Masika, R. (1998). *Global Trade Expansion and
    Liberalization: Gender Issues and Impacts*, BRIDGE Report, No. 42, Institute for
    Development Studies, University of Sussex, Brighton, UK.
Joekes, Susan (1999). 'A Gender-Analytical Perspective on Trade and Sustainable
    Development', in *Trade, Sustainable Development and Gender*, UNCTAD, New
    York and Geneva.
ILO (2004). *Global Employment Trends 2004*, International Labour Organization,
    Geneva.
Lund, Francie and Nicholson, Jillian (eds) (2003). *Chains of Production, Ladders of
    Protection: Social Protection for Workers in the Informal Economy*, School of
    Development Studies, University of Natal, Durban, South Africa.
Oxfam International (2004). *Trading Away Our Rights: Women Working in Global
    Supply Chains*, Oxfam, Oxford.
Williams, Mariama (2003). 'Free Trade or Fair Trade? An overview of the WTO and
    the myths surrounding it', DAWN (Development Alternatives with Women for a
    New Era) Special Supplement.

Case Studies

From Tree-minders to Global Players: Cocoa Farmers in Ghana

Pauline Tiffen, Jacqui MacDonald, Haruna Maamah and Frema Osei-Opare

1 Background

Ghana has experienced one of the fastest poverty reduction rates in Africa, with extreme poverty falling from over one-third to about one-quarter of the population and the economy growing at an average rate of 4.3 per cent during the 1990s.

Economic liberalization has been undertaken rapidly under pressure from the World Bank and the IMF, significant efforts by the aid community have sustained levels of development assistance and Ghana is a major recipient of foreign direct investment (FDI). Despite this, the manufacturing sector contracted during the 1990s and although there has been some success with horticultural and fruit exports, the economy remains dependent on three traditional export commodities – gold, timber and cocoa – the prices of which fluctuate considerably, making the country vulnerable to external shocks. As a result, doubts have been expressed as to whether Ghana will reach the Millennium Development Goals in a number of key areas, including halving the number of people living in poverty by 2015.

Women in Ghana have a significant and socially accepted role in local trading, and are also involved in informal food production and processing activities. Although some government programmes (for example the PAMSCAD-ENOWID[1] programme (up to 1996), the Rural Finance Scheme (1996) and the Emergency Relief Fund (2001)) have focused on women's economic activities, they have reached relatively few women and women are virtually excluded from mainstream banking and credit systems. Similarly, programmes imple-

Opposite: *Divine Chocolate Bar from the Day Choolate Company.* PICTURE: THE DAY CHOCOLATE COMPANY

mented by NGOs have reached women in more depressed areas of the country on a limited scale, but have failed to have a significant impact on poverty.

Cocoa: Cocoa is a 'traditional' cash crop and export commodity. First grown in Central America, cocoa products have featured in the European and, later, 'New World' economies for more than 150 years. Like many such conventional commodities, the market has been mediated for most of the post-war era by an international body, the International Cocoa Organization (ICCO), based in London, which operates as a negotiating platform between nation states denominated as producers and consumers. Like most raw materials cocoa is not taxed on entry to G-8 countries unless it is processed into the next ingredient stage, butter, powder or cocoa liquor which are derived from grinding the dried, fermented cocoa beans. In this sense the traditional call to achieve 'value added' at source has not been realized on any scale.[2] Cocoa, a strictly tropical crop, is not grown in the European Union or the US, so there is no direct subsidized competition. However, chocolate and, by default, cocoa are sensitive to sugar and milk trade policy – these latter ingredients far outweigh the cocoa content in a typical chocolate product – and are affected by labelling regulations, i.e. when cocoa butter may be substituted for other subsidized and cheaper fats.

Globally, including in West Africa, plantation and large-scale production of cocoa is widespread. Ghana is somewhat of an exception with cocoa farms typically less than three hectares. These are worked on by the whole family, extended family and some tenant or hired assistance under traditional land tenure systems called *abunu* and *abusa*.[3] There are no large farms or plantations with traditional, salaried farmworkers and no mechanized production or intensive forms of agriculture. Cocoa is also socially important – for both men and women. Many women own cocoa farms and work them in their own right. Often women receive cocoa farms as inheritance gifts from their husband's or father's extended family lands to ensure that they have an income and are protected from destitution, especially in old age. Tenant or share-cropper families, many from the poorer northern regions of Ghana, frequently take up cocoa farming, the *abunu* and *abusa* systems offering some social mobility (including the future opportunity to buy some of the land) or a chance to send remittances to families left behind at home. In common with many cash crops in sub-Saharan Africa, it is cocoa that provides most rural families in Ghana with the means to enter the cash or formal economy, to buy medicine and other basic goods and to pay for school uniforms and fees.

Ghana was the leading world exporter of cocoa from the 1920s until the 1970s. Tax levied on cocoa has contributed significantly to overall government revenues, contributing between 4 and 14.7 per cent of tax revenue between

1995 and 2000. More than 1.5 million people are now involved in production and transportation up to export. Prior to liberalization in 1992–93, the numbers were greater, with a vast army of employees of the state marketing board and related cocoa bodies (quality, agronomy, buying and transportation) almost matching the number of farmers and eroding the growers' income to a low of 29 per cent of the Free on Board (FOB) price in 1983. Perhaps unsurprisingly, volumes fell with poor incentives and disease problems, culminating in a very low production in 1983–84 of 154,000 tonnes.

IMF and World Bank pressure to liberalize internal and external commodity marketing functions in West Africa generally, and in Ghana in particular, aimed to end the role of marketing boards and the significant waste, economic rent-seeking and corruption that they fostered. Pro-liberalizers can point to a rising share of FOB price going to farmers in Ghana and elsewhere as a result. Equally, anti-liberalizers can point to the chaos, losses, quality deterioration and loss of market value across the region caused by the collapse of many ancillary and important services provided to farmers such as equipment and input supply and quality control. In Ghana, liberalization has been more successful than in many neighbouring countries as it has been partial, with quality and export functions retained under the control of the state.

Since the reforms in the cocoa sector from the mid-1980s, and the partial liberalization of internal marketing in 1992–93, volumes of cocoa production and exports have begun to grow again – although Ghana has not reached its earlier overall levels. In an attempt to overcome this problem, the government has committed itself to passing on at least 70 per cent of the FOB price to farmers by the 2004–2005 cocoa year to improve their returns. Cocoa still accounts for 45 per cent of Ghana's exports, but the bloated Ghana Cocoa Board and its subsidiaries and divisions are a thing of the past.

The free market can lead to significant changes in farmers' experiences of marketing cocoa. First, they normally face fluctuating market prices more directly and second, they may suffer greater exploitation at the hands of private traders instead of the state with little or no recourse to protection. To try to avoid these problems, the government of Ghana, both previous and current, has resisted full liberalization of cocoa in the face of considerable pressure from multilateral institutions; although since 2000 regulations for the liberalization of external marketing have been drawn up, they have not yet been implemented. The government maintains full control of exports and offers a guaranteed 'minimum' internal price, called the 'producer price' in local currency. But in the early 1990s the internal organization of production and marketing did change fundamentally in Ghana and it is this that opened up 'space' for new initiatives in the sector.

2 Kuapa Kokoo Cooperative

History
Liberalization of the internal market for cocoa in 1992–93 meant the end of the state-owned buying company's monopoly role as purchaser of cocoa from farmers. This represented both a threat and opportunity to cocoa farmers in Ghana. Many farmers understood this conjuncture; they hated the old system, characterized by significant levels of cheating (fixed scales, underpaying), cheques that bounced, systematic bribery and considerable harassment of those who complained of misdeeds by the government buying clerks called 'Kookoo Krakye', but they also feared the arrival of new private buyers who would not be accountable at all.

Local organization
Older farmers in Ghana had had considerable success in organizing cocoa collection, transportation and sales prior to independence. The British colonial authorities even encouraged this, because it reduced the need for investment in the 'interior'. In newly independent Ghana, the farmers' cooperatives were nationalized. Over the subsequent decades farmers' status, opportunities and remuneration declined: the price they received for their cocoa reached a nadir of 29 per cent of the FOB price in 1983. Control of the sector through the Cocoa Marketing Board of Ghana, later named the Ghana Cocoa Board, was comprehensive: all purchases, all inputs, all quality control, all exports and cocoa research. More than just complaining about falling income, however, many farmers interviewed in 1993 expressed frustration and rued their loss of dignity during this stifling period, feeling themselves reduced to the status of 'tree-minders'.

When the government of Ghana published the new regulations on liberalization in 1992–93, a number of leading farmers, including a visionary farmer representative on the Ghana Cocoa Board, Nana Frimpong Abrebrese, came to realize that they had the opportunity to organize, as farmers, to take on the internal marketing function. This would mean they could set up a company to sell their own cocoa to the Cocoa Marketing Company, the state-owned company that would continue to be the single exporter of Ghana cocoa. No official support was offered to would-be licensees, as it was believed that this would constrain free and fair competition and the emergence of a new private sector in cocoa trading. There were considerable obstacles to overcome to comply and obtain a licence to trade. For example, in order to qualify new licensed buying companies had to:

• operate in at least three cocoa growing regions from the outset;

Women's soap-making enterprise funded through the fair trade bonus.   PICTURE: THE DAY CHOCOLATE COMPANY

- provide collateral and financing for operations (i.e. there were no advances from CMC for future deliveries);

- set up fully-equipped operational buying centres – with scales, sacks, tarpaulins and grates on which to store cocoa professionally; and

- pass inspection by the Quality Control Division of Cocobod.

By mid-1993, when the regulations were due to be implemented in the upcoming main season (October 1993–February 1994), farmers attempting to start a new, collectively organized company had been effectively thwarted in their efforts. While they were looked on favourably by some in Cocobod, they lacked capital and credibility. At this point, the Kuapa Kokoo founding Chairman, Nana Frimpong, linked up with two development NGOs, SNV in the Netherlands and Twin Trading in the UK. Each of these organizations was prepared to support the local efforts to get a new, farmer-owned, company off the ground. After a short and intense mobilization – consisting of awareness raising and village-level discussion about the historic change in the trading regime and the idea of starting a new farmer-owned company – there was an upsurge of interest in joining the initiative. Around 2,000 farmers from 22 villages volunteered to organize their facilities to satisfy the authorities and committed to deliver at least 100 tonnes of cocoa beans per village.

At village level these new emerging groups were called Kuapa Kokoo village 'societies'. The company was formed, named Kuapa Kokoo Ltd. ('Good Cocoa Farmers' in Twi, the local language), with a handful of 'founding father' farmers representing three regions, staking the title to their land as collateral and with financial backing in the form of a loan guarantee by Twin Trading. Kuapa Kokoo presented its case in the form of a modest business plan to obtain a licence to trade to the special independent commission established by Cocobod for this task.

'Cooperative means coming together and caring about each other's welfare. All of the profit comes to farmers, we're not just producers. Compared to other buying agencies, Kuapa is unique.'[4]

Growth

The Board issued the licence and Kuapa began to trade. The start-up was painful, with problems including:

- confusion throughout the sector on the ways the new regime should work, with differing interpretations of the new regulations in the regions;

- delayed payments to new licensing companies by Cocobod, causing extreme cash flow crises;

- re-emergence of some 'bad habits' from the previous regime, especially among the recorders (the Kuapa version of 'clerks' or Kookoo Krakye) trusted by the farmers to manage their books at village level;

- the sudden death of the founding chairman and the chief accountant during the first season.

However, farmers rallied around the 'idea', if not the first season's performance, which resulted in a sudden and significant operating loss and debt to Twin Trading (although not to the local banks which were paid off in full). By the second season, the 'light crop', with significant effort and further mobilization, Kuapa Kokoo started to become a standard setter for quality, prompt payment, and 'honest scales'.[5] It even recorded a small operating profit and promptly distributed this as a bonus. In the words of one delegate to the first Kuapa Kokoo farmers' annual general meeting in 1994, 'seeing became believing'. The subsequent growth in sales (see Table 1) demonstrates clearly the rise of Kuapa's presence and market share.

Twin Trading, an alternative trade organization, and the UK charity TWIN (Third World Information Network), Kuapa Kokoo's business and

---

Box 1: Certified Fair Trade Cocoa – Terms

Fair trade is about development and trading standards that stipulate that buyers must:

- Buy from registered groups which are democratically organized;

- Pay a price to producers that covers the costs of sustainable production and living – namely not less than US$1,600 per tonne;

- Pay a 'premium' that producers can invest in development – namely US$150 per tonne;

- Make partial advance payments when requested by producers;

- Sign contracts that allow for long-term planning and sustainable production practices.

An independent body, Fair Trade Labelling International, monitors and inspects producers and buyers to ensure confidence in the guarantees being offered behind the claim of 'fair trade'.

More information is available at: *http://www.Fair trade.net/pdf/sp/english/cocoa.pdf*

---

development partners, facilitated Kuapa Kokoo's introduction and acceptance on the Fair Trade Labelling International cocoa producer register in 1993. This enabled importers, chocolate companies and The Body Shop International to source beans from Kuapa under fair trade conditions (see Box 1).

The fair trade terms celebrate Kuapa Kokoo's structure and its dedication to its members and offer a minimum price and social premium. Only a small percentage of Kuapa Kokoo's cocoa beans have been sold each year on fair trade terms because of the low market demand. However, the contact Kuapa Kokoo has with the outside world – with companies and activists of all kinds – has been attributable to its fair trade links. The fair trade social premium fosters a wider programme of support to members and the communities in which they live.

As can be seen in Table 1, while the bulk of Kuapa Kokoo's sales go through the conventional marketing channels of the CMC, a significant proportion is separated and tagged to the fair trade market.

Table 1: Growth – Kuapa Kokoo Performance Indicators since 1993

	Fair Trade Cocoa Sales (mt); % of Total		Number of Village Societies	Total Tonnage of Cocoa	Number of Cocoa Growing Regions
1993–1994	50	3	22	1,540	3
1994–1995	550	21	41	2,629	3
1995–1996	792	17	57	4,620	3
1996–1997	598	8	95	7,811	3
1997–1998	600	5	182	12,500	4
1998–1999	450	2	275	19,000	5
1999–2000	850	3	462	32,350	5
2000–2001	400	1	672	34,000	5
2001–2002	650	2	937	37,000	5
2002–2003	1,300	3	890	38,700	5

Source: FLO International; the Day Chocolate Company; Kuapa Kokoo

Structure

In late 2003, when several thousand farmers from Kuapa Kokoo came together to celebrate the tenth anniversary of the organization, more than 45,000 farmers in 600 villages could boast of being 'organized' in a democratic union and 'owners' of a successful cocoa trading company, a farmers' trust (or non-profit foundation), a credit union and a chocolate company (the Day Chocolate Company) in the United Kingdom (founded in 1997).

The growth of the cooperative and its complex structure (Figure 1) reflects the special circumstances and needs of farmers in Ghana as much as the

Figure 1: Structure of Kuapa Kokoo Cooperative 'Group'

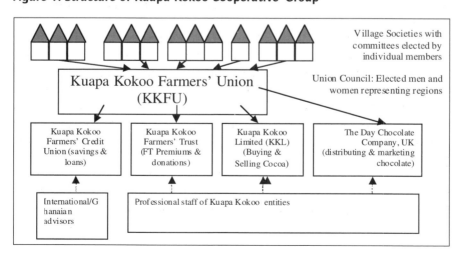

organizing efforts of the leaders and NGO supporters. For example, the existence of the CMC meant that Kuapa Kokoo was always guaranteed a market for all the good quality cocoa ('good fermented quality') collected from members for a predictable price. Full liberalization would have plunged them immediately into a turbulent and cut-throat international market, dominated by some of the largest multinational corporations in the world. Structured finance, possible only because of the 'single conduit' into the international market via the CMC, made it possible, although not easy, for Kuapa Kokoo to obtain working capital. This was via the financing arrangements through local commercial banks offered to all licensed cocoa buying companies by the Cocoa Marketing Board, called 'seed funds' (Figure 2).

Figure 2: Flows of Credit to Kuapa Kokoo Farmers' Union Members

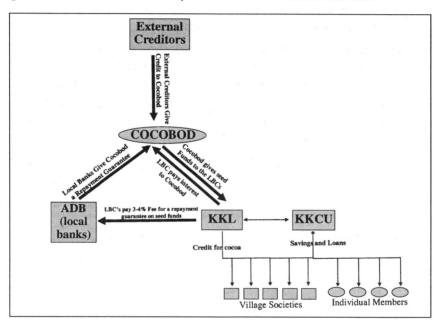

Source: Commodity Risk Management Group, World Bank

Key: KKFU – Kuapa Kokoo Farmers' Union; KKL – Kuapa Kokoo Limited; KKCU – Kuapa Kokoo Credit Union

The rising numbers of farmers who want to join Kuapa, and their determination, reflects their 'relief' at an honest and accountable buyer in the market after years of degrading and exploitative treatment at the hands of the employees of the Produce Buying Company and the local banks. In addition, over time there have been growing and palpable benefits – cash bonuses paid from profits and fair trade premiums, community projects, for example drinking water wells, scholarships, prizes for societies and individuals for achievement and women's income-generating projects. Kuapa representatives have toured the UK, Germany and the US, and have participated by invitation in many international events, including a symposium sponsored by the International Cocoa Organisation. In turn, there have been many visitors – journalists, writers, students and officials – to Kuapa Kokoo village societies from the US, Europe and other West African countries. The full range of reasons for the growth of Kuapa Kokoo membership is outlined in Box 2.

Box 2: Reasons for the Rapid Growth of Kuapa Kokoo Membership

- Sustained investment in village level education and skills with trainers, called society development officers, financed by the farmers' own company with some development assistance from time to time.

- Strong differentiation in management systems from previous state-owned buying companies, including a code of conduct and a requirement for respectful attitudes by employees towards farmers.

- A role for women at all levels (society, regional and national): this has been guaranteed and defended assiduously and publicly, leading more and more women to come forward.

- Devolution of responsibility: for example, formerly the buying clerks were not from the village and were only accountable to government HQ; now all local recorders (the new name was to signify a new era) are selected by and accountable to the farmers they serve.

- Swift and final punishment for cheats at all levels (including jail).

- Independently monitored elections – giving farmers a chance to eject unpopular leaders and ensuring full participation of women.

- Visible accountability – financial accounts are distributed, read aloud for all to hear and discussed at AGMs each financial year.

- Profit sharing ('dividends' and 'bonuses') in a transparent and consistent manner (from profitable performance and fair trade premiums).

- Foundation of an accountable trust to manage donations and fair trade premiums and to implement projects of wider benefit to members and their communities.

- Participation by elected farmers in all decision-making bodies, including the management of the Day Chocolate Company in London.

Involvement of national government

Each year officials from the government and the Cocoa Marketing Board have attended the annual general meeting of Kuapa Kokoo to pay their respects, explain and answer for government policies and offer congratulations. Kuapa Kokoo has the best overall credit track record to date of all new buying companies, with zero debt to the Cocoa Board or banks.[6] In early 2002, the rise in the farmers' 'visibility' and status culminated in a visit to the farm of Comfort Kwasibea, a woman member of Kuapa Kokoo, by the British Prime Minister, Tony Blair, and the newly elected President Kufour. Because of the contrast between the behaviour and performance of Kuapa Kokoo and other new buying companies entering the market, unsurprisingly, Kuapa has also become attractive to many cocoa farmers. There is a 'queue' of village societies wanting to join. Not all new licensed companies have thrived. In fact, several have ceased trading or have gone bankrupt, with spectacular debts to Cocobod, the government and the banking system. Profit sharing and paying above the government's minimum recommended 'producer price' – which are characteristic of Kuapa Kokoo – are not common elsewhere.

In the past, dedicated parastatal bodies ran all aspects of the cocoa sector. The importance of cocoa to the economy even meant that there was a Minister for Cocoa in the 1970s. In the 1980s and early 1990s, supervision was under the Office of the President. Supervision currently falls under the Ministry of Finance. There was no programmatic support in terms of seminars on business, marketing training, corporate governance or other technical assistance for any of the new companies entering the market from 1993 onwards, and farmers were certainly not envisaged as potential new licensees. The language of the regulations always refers to 'cocoa buying', while it was commonly believed that farmers effectively need only to 'sell' not 'buy' their cocoa. That said, there were a number of figures in key positions within the Cocoa Marketing Board who showed interest when they were canvassed in 1993 on the proposal to set up a farmer-owned buying company. They saw the process as an interesting pilot.

The cocoa marketing structure in Ghana has been defended strongly by the government. Even its vision of full liberalization is different from that of other countries (Table 2), based on lessons learned from neighbouring countries. The current structure (partially liberalized) has sustained international demand for Ghanaian cocoa which, with its high quality and sound export reputation, receives a price premium in the international market over cocoa from other sources. One important dimension of this structure is the role of a single exporter. All cocoa must pass through the Cocoa Marketing Company. This gives the CMC a strong negotiating position with the handful

Table 2: Ghana Cocoa Board Functions Before, During and After Full Liberalization

Function	Before Liberalization	After Partial Liberalization	Ghana: Full Liberalization*	Typical Full Liberalization
Agronomic assistance	Intensive, large number of workers	Limited, pest control emphasis	Limited, pest control emphasis	Rare, usually none
Cocoa research	Prestigious institution, significant research and field trials	Cut backs, reduced staff	Reduced activities, requiring donor support	Requires donor support
Buying	Monopoly parastatal acting as buyer of all cocoa produced	Local private companies emerge; role of parastatal declines	Local private companies	No parastatal, only private sector, usually international companies
Quality control	Comprehensive system	Comprehensive system still in place	System remains in place	None; or regulations and standards seldom enforced; quality problems
Input supply	State-owned companies source and provide all inputs	Private sector enters market; some state intervention in purchase and free distribution of critical inputs	Private sector role	Only private sector import and resell
Financing	Operated through Central Bank and state companies	Government borrowing and on-lending through local commercial banks	Private borrowing; discontinuation of seed fund lending by government	No 'central' source of credit, only local commercial banks
Export	All exports through state company	All exports through state company	Bona fide local buying companies permitted to export 30% directly	Exports by licensed companies permitted

* At proposal stage only, not yet implemented in Ghana

of major multinational corporations which buy cocoa on the open market. The market for cocoa and chocolate outside Ghana is a dominated market, i.e. one with relatively few large players.[7] This makes value adding harder, disadvantages smaller players and makes the market prone to speculative behaviour.[8] After discussion, and despite the importance of this system, the CMC agreed an exceptional 'set aside' mechanism for a small proportion of Kuapa Kokoo's cocoa to be sold in a transparent way (that is, not 'bulked up' with other cocoa in Ghana), for use in fair trade certified products. The rationale was that the Kuapa Kokoo operation is small overall, and the new (fair trade) export markets would not erode the CMC's bargaining power with the large companies. Moreover, the cooperative could provide tangible economic benefits directly to farmers and benefit Ghana's reputation, goals shared by the CMC.

'Fair Trade helps to boost the morale of farmers and helps us financially. We are very proud of the coca that we grow; it is the bridge that brings people together.'[9]

Involvement of international players

Twin Trading, a UK based fair trade organization, concluded by 1990 that small-scale farmers were not being supported appropriately during structural adjustment programmes, but were being left to fend for themselves against new private companies entering the market.[10] It used its own funds to offer working capital and bank guarantees to Kuapa Kokoo and obtained an *ad hoc* grant from the Small Enterprise Department of the UK Department for International Development (DfID) (then called the Ministry of Overseas Development) to enable farmers to take advantage of liberalization. Twin Trading began work in Ghana (cocoa) and Tanzania (coffee) in 1992–93. Comic Relief, a UK development agency, and the Netherlands Max Havelaar Foundation also contributed to the technical assistance work of Twin Trading during the first three years. In Europe, fair trade certification of cocoa and chocolate products was launched in 1993–94 by the Max Havelaar Foundation, following the successful entry of fair trade certified coffee into the Dutch market in 1989. There was demand for Ghana cocoa to make the Fair Trade Certification system attractive to chocolate companies, with West African cocoa needed to be added to Latin American sources to meet the taste profile of European palates. In Europe most chocolate is made with African cocoa which has a different flavour. To introduce fair trade cocoa to mainstream chocolate companies, Ghana cocoa was needed for taste and quality as only Latin American farmers had been registered up to that point.

The Dutch development agency SNV was primed by the Max Havelaar Foundation in The Netherlands to explore cocoa from Ghana for fair trade markets. In 1993 SNV had only just set up offices in Ghana and it joined with Twin Trading in supporting the foundation of Kuapa Kokoo with finance for personnel and local staff and training for farmers during the first three to four years. Later, other donors and public and private sector organizations (see Box 3) worked with and through the emerging Kuapa Kokoo structures to enable a variety of other projects to proceed. These include better conservation of the environment, organic production and pest management pilots, women's diversification and income-generating projects, new schools, scholarships and training courses, a healthcare service, credit union and savings/loan systems and preparation for full liberalization and export capacity building.

Box 3: Partners and Donors to Kuapa Kokoo	
The Body Shop International	USAID (via STCP)
Conservation International	DfID (formerly ODM)
Women's Vision	FLO International
International Cocoa Organisation	SNV
Cadbury	Comic Relief
The Max Havelaar Foundation	Twin Trading

3 The Cocoa Commodity Chain

Who does and gets what?

Cocoa beans are an international exchange traded commodity produced in tropical countries. The main producing countries are Côte d'Ivoire, Ghana, Nigeria, Indonesia, Malaysia, Cameroon and, until recently, Brazil. Africa produces about half of all world cocoa consumed, followed by Latin America and then Asia. Processing, called 'grinding', is almost all done in OECD countries except for countries where there is domestic consumption or manufacturing such as Brazil and Peru. Chocolate is the main end product – although the cosmetics industry also uses some cocoa butter. Chocolate is a mature market; it is large, with diverse uses, and well-established, with many familiar and strong branded names. With globalization and internationalization of branding strategies, many of these chocolate products, such as Mars Bars or Kit Kats, are well on the way to becoming universally sold.

The international cocoa market is now unregulated and subject to price fluctuations based on the usual factors: stocks, projected harvests, disease afflicting cocoa production, and demand and supply problems (for example civil unrest).[11] The volatility of the prices gained for Ghana's key export commodities (gold and cocoa) affects absolutely the income of the growers and the country as a whole.[12] In Ghana, cocoa farmers have seen the share of the FOB price they receive rise since liberalization (Figure 3) but the rises over the last decade have frequently been offset by devaluation internally and significant fluctuations in world market prices internationally. Prices fell to historic lows, for example, in 2002.

At the same time, the share of overall value going to raw materials producers like Ghanaian cocoa farmers has contracted compared with that going to 'brand owners'. Value adding, the concept where investment in processing and supplier performance is assumed to bring greater financial rewards in the marketing chain of traditional crops like coffee and cocoa, is less certain to deliver rewards now than, ultimately, ownership and promotion of a recognized and valued end product, a brand.[13] The processing of 'beans-to-bar' is a highly competitive business, with a few very large-scale operations operating on wafer thin margins occupying a commanding position in the market.

Figure 3: Cocoa Price Fluctuations, 1994–2003

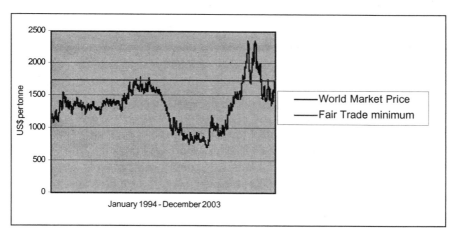

The processing of beans to ingredients and then ingredients to a vast range of processed food products makes the marketing chain long and complex (Figure 4). Chocolate is made from two of the three by-products produced from a processed cocoa bean, namely cocoa butter and cocoa liquor. The third by-product, cocoa powder, is used for industrial flavourings, drinks and baking. In a finished product containing cocoa the value of the beans in the final price is generally negligible.

Figure 4: From Bean to Bar – The Cocoa Marketing Chain

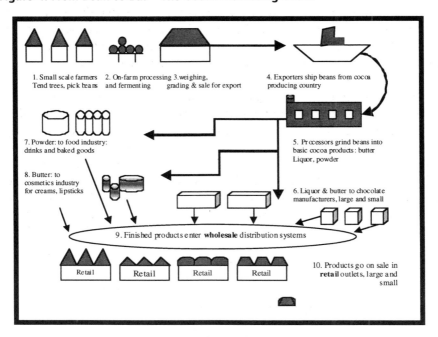

Chocolate manufacture in Europe often had humanitarian beginnings, being the preserve of Quaker-owned companies such as Fry's and Rowntrees. Product development has typically followed technology, for example the ability to mix milk with cocoa (Nestlé) or the first chocolate 'bar' (Fry's). Many products invented in the early 1930s are still with us; Mars Bars and Kit Kats have become household names, part of the landscape of consumption. While on an average shop shelf a customer may find as many as 600 bars to choose from, behind the colourful and prolific offering there is a simple story of market concentration. Over the last decade, smaller companies have been purchased one by one and absorbed by the major chocolate multinationals – Nestlé, Mars, Cadbury, Hershey and Philip Morris/Kraft. As a result, in key markets such as the US (worth $13 billion) and the UK (worth £4 billion), just three companies have more than 75 per cent market share. Beyond the brand owners are, similarly, a handful of major agribusinesses. Perhaps as many as 60 per cent of trading houses have been forced out of the market in the last decade, leaving giants such as Callebaut, Cargill, ADM and E.D. & F. Man to buy and process the raw materials for the manufacturers. Small and medium-sized 'grinders' and chocolate manufacturers have almost disappeared, except at the niche and gourmet end of the market.

Fair trade

In the non-multinational owned chocolate sector – sometimes called the independent chocolate sector – a few smaller, niche or specialist brands survive on their credentials and unique qualities. Fair trade and organic certification of commodities like coffee, tea and cocoa have given some of the independents new life. Trading directly with farmers can be labour intensive and may require active developmental assistance or, at least, relationship building. This has not traditionally been the preserve of – or even of interest to – the larger multinationals. In fact, unlike coffees, teas, wines and other major commodities sold to end consumers in packaged and processed form, cocoa-based products are rarely identified by their origin – their country, region, estate or farm. So the specialist companies, which are building a 'new' market where producers are identified and origins transparently identified, frequently become targets for take-over once they are successful. An example of this is the pioneering UK organic chocolate company Green and Blacks, which now counts global giant Cadbury among its investors and owners.

These trends informed the thinking behind the new Kuapa Kokoo chocolate company in the UK, formed in 1997. Characteristics of the company include:

- **A fair cocoa bean price:** The company, the Day Chocolate Company,[14] respects the needs of farmers for a remunerative cocoa bean price and uses cocoa purchased from Kuapa Kokoo under terms established by the international fair trade certification movement for cocoa trading (see Box 1).

- **Profit-sharing and equity:** The company recognizes in its structure a number of the market phenomena described above, including the 'devaluation' of the raw material and 'invisibility' of cocoa farmers. Kuapa Kokoo in Ghana owns equity in the UK company (one-third), holds two seats on the Board of Directors and its representatives are active in all decision making. As owners and shareholders, Kuapa Kokoo farmers share in the profits from all chocolate sold.

- **Social investment:** A small levy on each of the products – Divine and Dubble bars – sold by Day is returned to Kuapa Kokoo for it to continue its work of awareness raising, support for projects and training in the villages.

- **Visibility:** Central to the public marketing of Divine and Dubble chocolate products is the cultural identity of the cocoa farmers in Kuapa Kokoo villages. Via their chocolate company they actively join in promotions and materials, links and educational resources; the public relations work of the company is focused on representing and communicating positively farmers' interests, way of life and aspirations.

'*We want them* [Divine Customers] *to know that we work hard to produce cocoa beans and that they are produced under good conditions, with great care and pride!*'[15]

Since 1999, other consumer messages and approaches to cocoa marketing have also been developed. Two in particular stand out. They do not incorporate the fair trade emphasis on democratic farmer organization, relationships and a fair price, but they are designed to address two other serious systemic problems in cocoa production: environmental damage to primary and virgin forest, and child slavery.

Environment

In West Africa, the Sustainable Tree Crops Programme has been launched – an initiative of the Federation of Cocoa Commerce and a number of international development agencies such as USAID. The programme covers cocoa, cashew and coffee, and has active pilots in several countries. These include supporting research, technology transfer, capacity building, including Kuapa Kokoo, learning about integrated pest management methods, developing sustainable tree crop systems and improving productivity while conserving biodiversity.

Child Labour

In 2000, allegations were broadcast of widespread slave labour, including child trafficking, in the cocoa sector in Côte d'Ivoire. Journalists and human rights campaigners have followed this up with research and are publicizing the hardship, including slave-labour conditions, of workers on cocoa plantations in Côte d'Ivoire and putting pressure on the large companies to address the problems promptly. A report which has been part sponsored by the chocolate industry indicates that 200,000 children were involved in 'hazardous' work on cocoa farms in 2002. A US Congressional committee has committed US chocolate market leaders to work through a six-point action plan, called the Global Protocol, to eradicate all slave labour from the cocoa chain by 2005. In the light of this, and fearing adverse publicity, many large companies have started to review their buying systems to assess whether they can guarantee to a concerned public that there is no such malpractice behind their products. Since most buy in bulk, through local agents or middlemen, without documented connections to smallholders, this is proving difficult. Informally, industry representatives point to the fact that formalizing and making accountable commercial relations with millions of individuals will depress further the prices received by cocoa farmers because of the high transaction costs which will have to be covered.[16]

How is local linked to global?

Cocoa is an imported cash crop that is not indigenous to the African region, which has become the primary supplier. Planting was often imposed on farmers in francophone colonies. There are no real local uses for cocoa and Ghanaian farmers do not consume it. There is a small urban market for by-products like cocoa powder drink and some rural use of cocoa soap made from the husks of the pods, but the ultimate use – in chocolate, cosmetics and food – takes place in distant markets and beyond the knowledge and daily experience of the estimated 11 million farmers in the region.

Prices for cocoa are set in international commodity markets and there is little information and experience about this at the village level. In this respect, the role of the Cocoa Board in Ghana has been a double-edged weapon: it has shielded farmers from the unpredictability of the marketplace by offering guaranteed prices, but has deprived them of insights and contact. The value of the end markets has, as noted above, attracted the largest and most sophisticated multinationals in the world. The millions of farmers and their families are lined up on the other side of the bargaining table to these giants.

As a product with no meaningful local market, cocoa and the farmers who grow it must be linked to the international marketplace to turn their crop into a commodity and income provider. There is pressure on the government of Ghana to take the final step in liberalizing the cocoa sector and allow free export of cocoa; but the date is not set. Some of the modalities have been developed. For example, *bona fide* local licensed buying companies with good operational track records, like Kuapa Kokoo, would be permitted to export up to one-third of their cocoa directly into the market. However, even if plans for full liberalization are implemented, many doubt whether Kuapa and other local companies could reap big rewards. At present, an efficient, though state-owned, company, the CMC, tenders and negotiates sales of all Ghana's cocoa with the multinationals. All buyers must pre-qualify by joining the Ghana Cocoa Buyers' Association of London and bid competitively for Ghana's premium quality production against each other. In other countries, availability of capital and willingness to invest in local trading infrastructure would be the main determinant of acquisition of cocoa. Local companies, if they are able to get finance for operations at all, pay significantly higher interest rates than the subsidiaries of multinationals. This disadvantages local players and has left most liberalized commodity markets in sub-Saharan Africa in the hands of a few international companies. This is the trend even when, post-liberalization, large numbers of companies initially enter the market and start up in business.[17]

'Everything at the AGM [2003] was very well organized and I am very much overwhelmed by Kuapa Kokoo's accountability to farmers. We will report to the farmers what happened and how transparent it is. None of the other buying agencies are like this. The bonus is also very welcome by farmers.' [18]

In this initiative, farmers in Ghana have gained access to the global market through a joint venture company, buying shares and earning their place in the market in a dignified and sustainable manner. Kuapa's fair trade cocoa passes through, but is tagged and separated from, the system handling the vast tonnages of national production. So the access-to-market was not achieved at the expense of this vital 'bargaining mechanism' for the rest of Ghana's cocoa. Further, the linkage both respects the important role of the CMC in mediating between the millions of farmers and their families and the major buyers, and ensures an accountable counterpart for farmers – too often cheated by the canny, literate representatives of large companies and middlemen in free markets. The CMC remains a promptly paying buyer for all the farmers' quality cocoa that is not sold to fair trade partners. This type of controlled access does not exist in other cocoa producing countries. Most Kuapa Kokoo cocoa beans enter the conventional international market through the CMC and are sold as generic 'Ghana cocoa'. Clearly it would be advantageous to Kuapa Kokoo members to sell more under fair trade terms, but the market, although growing, is still small. The purpose and role of Kuapa Kokoo's chocolate subsidiary (the Day Chocolate Company) is to galvanize customers and gain market share for a range of fine fair trade chocolate products.

'The scales are very honest. We are paid accurately. The amount due will be paid without question.' [19]

Kuapa Kokoo's contribution to poverty alleviation

There has been a gradual regular decline in cocoa prices since the 1970s. In the last decade this fall has accelerated but there have also been some price 'spikes' (1997 and 2003) – i.e. short cycles of high prices. Shortages of cocoa affect prices considerably as, unlike some other commodities, the cocoa industry requires relatively long lead times for processing and production of finished goods.[20] The volatility and decline of prices have provided the backdrop for the rise of alternative trading initiatives like Kuapa Kokoo and the Day Chocolate Company and, more generally, of fair trade product certification.[21] The rise is being underpinned by a growth in the Western World of more 'conscious consumption' and the growing 'visibility' and awareness of cause-and-effect relationships between poverty, economic stability, terrorism, economic migration and civil unrest in commodity-dependent countries and local communities.

In Ghana, where as much as 10 per cent of the population is dependent on cocoa income in some form, the impact of radical business-oriented projects like Divine chocolate from Kuapa Kokoo beans has been both economic and psychological.

As recent thinking on development assistance and poverty reduction has shown, many intangibles are also critical to the processes by which people can improve their conditions. Morale, self-help, confidence and the growth of civil society organizations are part of the process of essential change. In this sense Kuapa Kokoo is making an impact, giving men and women farmers a mediating mechanism for their voice to be heard nationally and internationally. Kuapa Kokoo has embraced both large and small farmers – the small far outnumbering the large (70 per cent). Women farmers make up almost one-third of its membership of more than 40,000 cocoa growers.

The recent impact evaluation work of independent researchers such as Ronchi (2002) quantifies many of the facts and figures of the outcomes of Kuapa Kokoo – especially the premiums earned and the extra income generated from an effective organization in the form of profit and fair trade bonuses. Within the fair trade purchasing terms for cocoa beans there is a social premium of US$150 per tonne. This, plus the difference between the prevailing market price and the fair trade 'floor' or minimum price, contributed US$1 million additional income to Kuapa Kokoo farmers in the period 1993–2001. This additional income has been put to use in ways that effectively contribute to reaching the same poverty targets as are aimed at by the Millennium Development Goals: drinking water, education, women's income generation and healthcare (Table 3).

Table 3: Kuapa Kokoo Farmers' Trust Investments in Community Development

Potable Water Hand-dug Wells	Corn Mills	Schools	Public Places of Convenience	Small Bridges
174	27	4	2	1

Adapted from Kuapa Kokoo Annual Report, 2003

Kuapa has invested in improving the livelihoods of individual members and their communities across all the five cocoa growing areas where it operates. For example 100,000 people, both members and non-members, have received free medical attention under Kuapa Kokoo's healthcare programme.

Cocoa farmers are rated among the poorest people in Ghanaian society, often living in villages with minimal social services. Kuapa, through the

Kuapa Kokoo Farmers' Trust, has made a significant impact on the improvement of village infrastructure and social services. Significantly, through the provision of hand-dug wells in some communities, Kuapa has improved access to potable water which not only contributes to health improvement but also reduces the physical burden on women and children. Schools projects have targeted the various levels: nurseries that relieve women so that they can attend to their economic activities and provide a safe environment for children when their parents are away, and an improved learning environment at primary level enabling more children to have access to quality basic education. Opportunities have been created for thousands of people in communities where Kuapa operates.

Interestingly, farmers' own perceptions of a positive impact include the ability to diversify so as to reduce their dependence on cocoa income by starting some other economic activity and their 'ability to donate and help others', indicating raised self-esteem and sense of a proactive role in their society. This is indeed a far step from the 'tree-minders' of the monopoly marketing board era. Kuapa is now incubating a 'sister' organization, Sompa, to extend the reach of the Kuapa approach and benefits to more farmers in Ghana.

In a 'local is global' setting, Kuapa's farmers have also learned to defend their reputation and to represent themselves, their industry and their country in many forums. The goal of women's participation at village level is for there to be at least two female representatives on every committee. To date, approximately 60 per cent of all societies have met this goal, demonstrating both progress and the hurdles to women's participation in the cocoa business. Nevertheless, women hold all positions – members of boards of directors, society presidents, society recorders and employees of trading companies – and they travel at least as frequently as men when overseas representation is required (Box 4).

4 The Future

Replicability of Kuapa Kokoo within Ghana

The Kuapa Kokoo story can provide a model and inspiration to organize based on efficiency and business ethics, particularly where there has been perceived mismanagement in the past. Further, it represents a genuine attempt to ensure that women play important roles, and to promote and insist on these until they become closer to being a 'norm'. It shows that farmers can raise and manage finance, negotiate better market terms and gain direct recognition and reward for quality production. In a period when state-owned service companies have all but disappeared, the responsibility for purchasing and distributing inputs, or equipment such as reliable scales, can be

Box 4: UK and US Tours, 2002 and 2003

Comfort Kwasibea, aged 43, hails from Akropong in the Eastern Region of Ghana and is married with two children. She farms at Nankese where she has a large acreage of cocoa farm. She is an active member of Kuapa Kokoo Farmers' Union and a Director of Kuapa Kokoo Limited. The President of Ghana and Tony Blair visited her farm in March 2002. She came to the UK in March 2003 for Fair Trade Fortnight, travelling around the north of England and Scotland. She said that she was the first woman recorder in Kuapa and that she has helped other women in her area to also become recorders by working with them and showing them that they can do it. She recently spent more than a week with a newly elected female recorder to give her confidence. She also runs an active women's society which has initiated activities such as palm oil production and baking bread.

Comfort Kumeah and Mary Antwi Nyamekye did the tour in 2002. They tasted chocolate cake at a Women's Institute stall in Bristol; it was the first chocolate cake they had tasted and they thought it was great – they were keen to take some back to Ghana. Comfort, who is a teacher with five children and in her early 50s, said that fair trade was a lifeline for her family. 'We would like more cocoa to be sold fair trade because it means we get a better price for the producers. Before Kuapa Kokoo we farmers were cheated. People adjusted the scales. We got little money from the purchasing clerks and no bonuses. The farmer's welfare was neglected.'

Mary, aged 53, a widow with seven children, stated: 'Life before the farmer co-operative was set up was extremely difficult – even buying bread was a problem. There were lots of worries on my shoulders. Now, people look at me and they can't believe that I have money. I can now afford for my children to come home and I can feed them. Before I joined Kuapa I never had a voice. Now I am treasurer of my society and I can speak.' She is also on the board of KKFT.

Source: The Day Chocolate Company

devolved to farmers as long as there is an institution to mediate, define and implement these activities.

As rural finance mechanisms have increasingly dwindled or become heavily indebted and discredited, Kuapa Kokoo has reinvigorated and sustained financial flows through credit to farmers. It keeps records and has developed savings and creditworthiness for more than 40,000 farmers, as well as providing timely support to economic activities and for social needs. Kuapa Kokoo's self-financing (i.e. commercially viable) operations show that in the absence of heavily staffed and costly parastatals, the high unit cost of the outreach needed to reach many thousands of smallholders producing commodities can be covered.[22]

Further, as seen above, Kuapa Kokoo is setting up a sister organization, called Sompa, to extend the reach of the Kuapa approach in Ghana.

Relevance to other sectors in Ghana

The experience of Kuapa Kokoo has relevance for a number of other key cash crops in Ghana: shea nuts, cotton, rice, coffee, fresh fruit (bananas and pineapples), which are export crops, and palm oil for local and regional markets. Fair trade initiatives have already started with banana plantation workers in the Volta Region, one of the poorest and least developed areas of central Ghana, and there is also a direct link-up between the Swiss Migros supermarket chain and oil palm producers which is still at a pilot stage.

Given the stark poverty profile of northern Ghana, comparable initiatives in the shea butter and cotton sectors could have considerable impact. Leading the way, The Body Shop International has set up a linkage within its community trade programme with women producing shea nut butter since 1993. Replication of support for producer organizations and international linkages for this valuable crop could benefit producers with few alternatives in a semi-arid region who currently sell their crop into a market dominated by large multinational trading houses.

Financing crises in rural and commodities sectors have worsened since liberalization and there is a lack of effective and 'reliable' counterparts: traders, cooperatives, processors and input providers. Recent commodity price falls have often manifested themselves in producing countries as financial crises, with producers unable to repay credit and governments having to refinance debt through the banking system for the sector to survive at all. Cotton in Ghana is a case in point with accumulated debt levels of producers, input suppliers and banks significantly higher than revenues. In this case, US and EU subsidies to cotton production mean that depressed prices are likely to prevail for some time. A grouping of West African producing countries are currently pressing a claim for compensation through the World Trade Organization (WTO) for this vital income that is being lost to US and other subsidized farmers.

Robust market-linked farmers' organizations can gain momentum, become responsive to market signals and generate a strong motive to succeed because of improved returns and credibility. This, in turn, can translate into better credit track records in quality production and loan repayment.

Replicability in other countries

There are at least two dimensions to outreach and replication of this initiative in other countries, in the North and the South. In the North, the UK is Ghana's main export partner, followed by the US. Kuapa Kokoo's chocolate bar, Divine, has followed these traditional routes into the UK and US markets, which are chocolate markets of considerable scale. New linkages for Ghana in a range of different product categories (similar to those produced by the Day Chocolate Company) may be feasible with US companies, in particular, because of:

- the growing trade and export volume between the US and Ghana;

- the periodic initiatives being launched by the US to promote growth and opportunity in sub-Saharan Africa, giving 'windows' of opportunity and access to Ghanaian companies, for example the African Growth and Opportunity Act (AGOA);

- a growing awareness among US consumers of the connection between trade and national security, and a considerable interest in environmental protection and conservation.

Smaller individual markets in Europe may also be ripe for new initiatives, given the higher overall visibility of 'ethical' or 'conscious consumerism' there. There is a widespread realization by large and small private companies sourcing goods from overseas that good supply chain management requires investment and long-term vision about the local impact of their purchases. This trend stands to benefit new initiatives if partnerships between the private sector, development assistance organizations in Ghana and farmers can be forged with market-makers in OECD markets generally.

In the South, there is a potential for South–South exchanges and learning. Initial efforts have been made by Kuapa Kokoo to connect with other producing organizations in the region; South–South linkages could be fostered to the considerable benefit of neighbouring countries. For instance, the Cameroon has suffered significant problems in the coffee and cocoa sectors since liberalization, with many organizations weakened or simply collapsing. There has also been a rise in ruthlessness and exploitative practices by the middlemen and traders. Countries such as Sierra Leone, for which cocoa has been important in the past, could also benefit from learning about start-ups. Significant exploitation has taken place during the deterioration of the sector and its marketing systems. Such efforts will not be easy, given language barriers and other cultural and historic differences – cooperatives, for example, have had a troubled past in many francophone countries, frequently being co-opted by governments.

5 Lessons Learned

The lessons learned from this initiative are far reaching and diverse, covering trade and policy, brand equity and reputation, and farmers as 'businessmen and business women'.

Overview

Liberalization

Official opinions on marketing boards during the the period of liberalization in West Africa do not acknowledge the potential value of a 'gradual' liberalization, instead of outright full abolition of marketing boards, especially for local companies. The partial liberalization in Ghana gave Kuapa Kokoo a chance to develop internally without having to pit itself immediately against larger, better-financed and well-connected global players in its early years. Retention of the Quality Control Division under Cocobod in the public service has sustained attention to quality production and Ghana's negotiating edge in the market. Moreover, a single export company operating a tender system among the large multinationals offers an opportunity to negotiate strongly for terms and for syndicated finance.

Producer prices

Even as the share of the FOB value of cocoa rises, it is worth noting that a free market system does not guarantee that this extra share will be passed back to farmers. No new licensed buyers other than Kuapa Kokoo have offered significant incentives to farmers. It is inimical to private traders to share profit with growers. Thus this indicator, while often used to show the beneficial impacts of adjustment, is somewhat deceptive. Similarly, 70 per cent of a depressed, low market price, such as the price in 2002, may from a producers' perspective represent less than the costs of production, and the benefits of a new trade regime may not be directly felt, only the volatility of the market. The government of Ghana, through the Cocoa Marketing Board, still attempts to absorb some of the negative effects at the interface between the farmer and free market though setting a minimum producer price. This enables farmers to know at what level to invest in their farms (time, inputs) in advance each year. This is a significant difference from fully freed-up markets.

Commodity finance

The poor practices and corrupt histories of cooperatives mean that many key players in the sector – banks, government and farmers – view them with suspicion. Kuapa Kokoo started as a farmer-owned (shareholding) company and not as a cooperative. There has been a failure of imagination, however, about helping farmers to find other ways to aggregate purchases (inputs) and outputs (crops to market) since the generalized collapse of cooperatives in the region. The challenge is made all the greater by a continuing difficulty in pressing claims and obtaining clear and legal title for goods, land and inheritance in Ghana. This prevents people coming forward to offer collateral – as did a number of farmers at the outset of the initiative – and effectively excludes them from the formal economy.

Trade policy

In the trade policy area, sugar tariffs and labelling legislation have a direct bearing on the end market for cocoa – chocolate. Being able to label as chocolate a bar made with cheaper cocoa butter substitutes has become a contentious issue within the European Union, and low-

A woman cocoa farmer. PICTURE: BRIAN MOODY

priced, subsidized European beet sugar and oils have become important factors for large firms in controlling product pricing. This implies that non-European based manufacturers will not be able to compete and, in another form, African growers of tropical crops are being displaced by subsidized Western – and soon Eastern – European farmers producing 'alternatives', i.e. beet sugar.

Credible farmers' organizations

Over time, Kuapa Kokoo has gained momentum through developing – at every stage and in each marketplace – its track record, including repayment of loans and delivery of consistent high quality products (beans and bars). Reputation and brand equity provide significant ballast for initiatives at firm level, adding value and creating support and loyalty from users and service providers. Thus, successful farmer-oriented business promotion can produce impacts beyond agricultural production. There are few resources for, and many hurdles in the way of, investment in farmer-owned businesses. Often farmers are not seen as potential 'players' at all; they are considered to be ignorant of the market and illiterate. While this is often true – they have little if any access to market information and erratic schooling beyond primary level – it is surprising that so few inroads into enabling farmers to emerge as businessmen and women have been made. Financing rural economies – and many thousands of small-scale farmers – is becoming a major development challenge, one that is not met by the micro-finance revolution which, in West Africa at least, is predominantly an urban phenomenon. In this sense the initiative could serve as an example of how to support farmers to become proactive players in the marketplace.

Lessons for local organizations

The project has shown the importance of democratic organization and structures to ensure participation. Making women's place in the organization a *sine qua non* has required sustained effort and encouragement. Given the 'bad' experiences of many farmers working in cooperatives or in organizations run by professionals and literate urban staff, a good governance system with a role for independents and the presence of external local and expatriate resource persons was of key importance. The cocoa marketing system in Ghana kept farmers insulated from the external market. Kuapa Kokoo has enabled farmers and their representatives to open up to the international marketplace and deal effectively with international institutions. The farmers in Kuapa Kokoo have learned to represent themselves in a variety of fora – the International Cocoa Organisation, the Ghana government, aid agencies and the press – and to collaborate with researchers. Farmers need reliable and trustworthy professionals to help them run a complex business. To do this they need to be able to attract and retain high calibre professionals with integrity. Undoubtedly, the presence of international NGOs at the start-up phase meant that good candidates were interested. However, Kuapa Kokoo has trained its own staff, relies on them to comply with the code of conduct (including respect for farmers) and offers rewards. (The staff also have a shareholding and profit goes into a staff fund as well as farmers' pockets.) Finally, farmers' leaders have had to learn how to evaluate projects, and how to gain a mandate for and invest in new market opportunities. This has included expansion into regional operational centres and purchase of infrastructure, as the cooperative has grown, and also, given the nature of cocoa as a commodity, working overseas, it has involved developing their own company, the Day Chocolate Company and building a loyal consumer base.

Lessons for national governments

The government of Ghana entered the liberalization process without seeing farmers as needing help in the transition. The conventional wisdom implied that a new private sector would emerge – and indeed a dozen companies have tried to set up buying operations since 1993 although only a few have attained sustained growth. Farmers were not 'visible' as businessmen and women. A lack of any mediating institutions for rural sector business development in cocoa meant that farmers were on their own. They seized the opportunity that partial liberalization represented, but without official support. New institutions are needed which are cost effective and businesslike, but able to deal with many thousands of atomized individual farmers. This is a very significant challenge for which there are few corporate models. Co-operatives are one of the few, but much discredited, institutional models available. Traditional outreach to farmers has been through agricultural extension workers, but these employees do not work with reference to the market or market trends (for example interest in organic or low pesticide input production) and seldom have the objective or capacity to help build solid commercial grassroots producer organizations despite their access to farmers *in situ*. Reforms in the banking sector are needed to support the private sector, especially perceived high-risk groups such as farmers' organizations.

In the UK, the initial support of DfID was *ad hoc* and based on a desire to find out, through the project's work, if and how the outcomes of abolishing state marketing boards could be beneficial for small farmers. Later, in requesting a loan guarantee from DfID to support banking facilities in the UK for the new joint venture enterprise (the Day Chocolate Company), significant internal learning took place: the project called for a number of departments to come together (private sector, agriculture, country, ethical trade and environment) for support to be obtained. This was an unprecedented 'co-operation' of departments in a 'joined up' and holistic project, with sign-off also coming from Ghana's Ministry of Finance. However, although there is now interest elsewhere in the model (for example in US ethical and social investment circles), it is not being replicated by DfID and was therefore a one-off effort.

Lessons for international agencies

While there are an increasing number of NGOs entering the marketing and business development assistance track, dangers are involved. Frequently, production and local organization are supported without reference to the international market at all. The result is a lack of markets or false assumptions about market outlets. Many NGOs do not see the marketing chain as a whole. Thus, they underestimate the need to pressure multinational companies for 'space' and market share to ensure that positive negotiations are feasible. And NGOs can come under criticism (including, sometimes, from multinationals) for supporting 'commerce' with public funds. Sometimes developmental indicators are pushed for at the expense of commercial success and farmers' interest wanes.

NGOs do not always appreciate long-term commercial viability of their development interventions as a process for poverty reduction. Individual relief-type benefits tend to be the goal together with short-term impact. Bad experiences with cooperatives have scared many NGOs away from such ventures. Further pitfalls for NGOs include the 'funding cycle' – where support becomes untenable beyond the precise period of a project or where professional expertise is not available to provide what farmers really need. Traders, for example, do not often work for 'non-profit' salaries. The Kuapa Kokoo development process involved a sustained but flexible technical assistance effort for a number of years. What many NGOs and campaign groups have realized is the importance of ensuring that farmers' voices are heard in international fora: at the invitation of an NGO, Kuapa Kokoo representatives have been at Cancún, the ICCO and many international meetings. Cocoa farmers in Ghana have now accessed a global network and have a gained a platform for their product and their voices.

Notes

1   PAMSCAD – Programme of Action to Mitigate the Social Cost of Adjustment; ENOWID – Enhanced Opportunities for Women in Development.

2   Processing of cocoa is more widespread in countries that have become net importers due to a decline in production and rise in domestic consumption, for example Brazil and Peru. Most Ghanaians have never tasted chocolate.

3   Under these arrangements, the income to the worker from the – often absentee or aged – owner may be half (*abunu*) or one-third (*abusa*) of the revenue gained from the farm.

4   Anthony Bempong, President of the Ohaho Society, Kuapa Kokoo Ltd.

5   To this day, ensuring that the scale weighs cocoa accurately is a primary goal of Kuapa and the societies; many officers carry 'weight stones' in their trucks and vehicles and members are encouraged to 'know your own weight' and step on the scales themselves.

6   As well as repayment of loans and 'seed funds', the criteria for judging the performance of licensed buying companies used by the CMB include delivery of all cocoa purchased, consistent and high grade quality, fast turnaround of capital employed and payment of the producer price in full to farmers.

7   Just four companies – Mars, Nestlé, Cadbury and Hershey – account for most chocolate sold globally.

8   One company, Amanjaro, recently cornered the market, sending prices artificially high for a short period.

9   Helena Bempong, Ohaho Society, Kuapa Kokoo Ltd.

10   Twin Trading had worked since 1986 with farmers in Latin America (Mexico and Peru) where liberalization was also taking place; the organization specifically studied and published work on sub-Saharan export-led development prospects (*Short Changed – Africa and World Trade*, Pluto Press, 1990).

11   An international 'quota' and stock management system was in place in the 1970s and 1980s and was mediated between producing and consuming countries under the auspices of the ICCO.

12   In 1992, for example, 220,000 tonnes generated US$272 million. One year later, earnings were 10 per cent less, despite export volumes being greater (253,000 tonnes).

13   Of course, a brand is an abstract concept and accountants have struggled to value appropriately established brands; on balance sheets these become the 'intangibles', evidenced in valuations of, or the prices paid for, companies on sale. Hershey was recently valued at US$10 billion before being withdrawn from sale under pressure from workers and stakeholders

14   The Day Chocolate Company was named after one of Kuapa Kokoo's early UK advisers, Richard Day, who died suddenly in 1996. Day trades products under two brand names of its own, 'Divine' and 'Dubble', and also makes products for other companies which are prepared to respect the work of the organization, including the UK's Co-op with 2,400 shops and Starbucks, UK.

15 Helena Bempong, Ohaho Society, Kuapa Kokoo Ltd.
16 Some reports on child labour in Côte d'Ivoire have revealed that there may have been some confusion on this matter and have suggested that most of the children in the cocoa fields were the children of plantation owners or knew the intermediaries or brokers who hired them. The exact situation remains unclear.
17 For example, in Uganda more than 100 companies started out in coffee trading at liberalization; almost ten years later five multinationals dominate (more than 70 per cent) with many of the start-ups, mainly local companies, bankrupt and no longer in business.
18 Paul and Helena Bempong, Ohaho Society, Kuapa Kokoo Ltd.
19 Anthony Bempong, President, Ohaho Society, Kuapa Kokoo Ltd.
20 In the 2002–2003 season some of the reasons included civil unrest in Côte d'Ivoire, the world's biggest producer; falling production of cocoa in Brazil because of disease, to the extent that it became a net importer for domestic consumption; and falling production generally spurred by historically low prices.
21 In the last six years growth in fairly traded cocoa beans from Ghana and other countries has risen from 708 tonnes to more than 1,600 tonnes (FLO International).
22 One struggling cooperative reported in the 1990s that in the absence of any formal credit middlemen were offering to trade one sack of rice – provided during the 'hungry period', when no or little food production was possible – for one sack of cocoa beans at harvest time.

References

Accra Mail (2002). 'War and Cocoa', 7 November.
Amoah, J.E.K. *Marketing of Ghana Cocoa 1885–1992*, Cocoa Outline Series 2, Jemre Enterprises Ltd, Ghana.
The Big Issue Scotland (2003). 'Fair Deal: Farmers Benefit from Trade', November.
Commodity Risk Management Group (2002). *Ghana: Cocoa Price Risk Management, Phase II Report*, CRMG, World Bank, Washington DC, February.
Ghana Cocoa Board (2000). *Regulations and Guidelines for External Marketing of Cocoa*, Cocobod, Ghana.
Gilbert, Christopher (1997). *Cocoa Market Liberalisation – Its Effects on Quality, Futures Trading and Prices*, The Cocoa Association of London.
Government of Ghana (1998). *Ghana Cocoa Sector Development Strategy Task Force Report*, Ministry of Finance, Ghana.
Government of Ghana (1999). *Ghana Cocoa Sector Development Strategy*, Ministry of Finance, Ghana.
Kuapa Kokoo (2000, 2001, 2002, 2003). *Annual Reports*, Ghana.
Kuapa Kokoo (2002). *New Cocoa Districts*, Internal Operations Report, Ghana.
LMC International (1996). *The External Marketing of Ghana's Cocoa*, LMC International, Oxford.

New Internationalist (1998). 'The Chocolate Chain', August.

The Observer Food Monthly (2003). 'The Tribe that Survives on Chocolate', November.

Oxfam (2002). *Cocoa Best of the Best: The Story of the Kuapa Kokoo Farmers' Cooperative, Ghana*, Market Access Parables, Oxfam, Oxford, December.

Ould, David, Jordan, Claire, Reynolds, Rebecca and Loftin, Lacey (2004). *The Cocoa Industry in West Africa: A History of Exploitation*, Anti-Slavery International, London.

Petchers, Seth (2003). *Fair Trade Certified Cocoa Ingredients from Ghana*, October.

Ronchi, Loraine (2002). *Monitoring Impact of Fairtrade Initiatives: A Case Study of Kuapa Kokoo and the Day Chocolate Company*, Third World Information Network, UK.

Save the Children Fund (2003). *Children Still in the Chocolate Trade – The Buying, Selling and Toiling of West African Child Workers in a Multi-billion Dollar Industry*, Working Paper, Save the Children Fund, Canada.

Tiffen, Pauline (2003). *Development in Practice Reader, A chocolate coated case for alternative international business models*, Oxfam GB.

Tiffen, Pauline and Sarpong, Kofi (2000). *Making the Most of Liberalisation. The Story of Kuapa Kokoo*, unpublished monograph.

TWIN (2000). *Cocoa: Market Overview*, Third World International Network, UK.

World Bank (2002). *Reinvesting in African Small-holder Agriculture: the Role of Tree Crops in Sustainable Farming Systems*, World Bank, Washington DC.

Websites

http://www.divinechocolate.com/ImpactAssessmentLeaflet.pdf
http://www.newint.org/issue304/images/f_fish.gif
http://www.icco.org/
http://www.Fair trade.net/
http://www.divinechocolate.com/
www.dubble.co.uk/story/story_kuapa.htm
http://www.kuapakokoo.com/

Tradition, Trade and Technology: Virgin Coconut Oil in Samoa

John Cretney and Adimaimalaga Tafuna'i

1 Background

Country context

Samoa has a population of around 170,000 people mostly located on the two major islands, Upolu and Savaii. The Samoan economy, based on a narrow range of activities linked to agriculture, tourism, small-scale manufacturing and fisheries, has achieved significant growth recently compared with most Pacific countries (Government of Samoa, 2001a). Its GDP per capita of US$1,420 in 2002 compares with an average of US$950 for the East Asia Pacific region World Bank, 2003).

Within this overall picture, however, the rural economy has fared less well, with the share of GDP derived from agriculture and fishing declining from 21 per cent in 1997 to 14 per cent in 2001 (Government of Samoa, 2001a). While fishing has remained static over the period at around 8 per cent of GDP, agriculture as a percentage of GDP has fallen significantly.

Major factors in this decline have been the long-term damage to coconut and cocoa plantations from the 1990–91 cyclones, which destroyed 20 per cent of the trees, the fall in international copra and coconut oil prices (prices more than halved between 1998 and 2001) and the taro leaf blight which devastated a staple Samoan food supply in 1993. The Samoan economy is therefore highly vulnerable to external factors such as changes in commodity prices, crop disease and the weather – especially cyclones.

Around two-thirds of Samoan households rely on a mixture of subsistence agriculture and cash income, with subsistence agriculture contributing about half Samoa's total agricultural output.

Opposite: *Pressing dried coconut to extract the oil on the island of Upolu, Samoa.*   PICTURE: JOHN CRETNEY

Most of the land (82 per cent) is held under customary title in the collective ownership of the Samoan people and cannot be used as collateral to access financing (Japan International Cooperation Agency, 2003).

Rural communities in Samoa have always experienced difficulty in finding opportunities to generate cash income. Many rural Samoan families rely solely on remittances from family overseas (especially from New Zealand or the US) for all their cash needs. Over recent years this income has amounted to around 18 per cent of GDP and therefore has a significant positive financial impact on the economy (Government of Samoa, 2001a).

Approximately 50 per cent of households were found to be living below the food poverty line in a 1997 survey, with poverty focused in rural areas, especially on Savaii but also on Upolu outside the Apia urban area (Government of Samoa, 2001a). However, as there were some methodological flaws in this survey, it was proposed that a new government survey should be carried out in 2001–2002 but this has yet to be undertaken.

Around 55 per cent of the Samoan population is in the 15–60 age group (1998 figures) and in that year it was estimated that only around 23 per cent of this group were formally employed. The rest were involved on an informal basis in various forms of subsistence or semi-commercial agriculture, fisheries or self-employment (Government of Samoa, 2002a).

Census figures for 2001 indicated a significant imbalance between male and female employment with 36,722 males (22 per cent of the population) and 16,226 females (10 per cent of the population) over 15 years of age being economically active (Government of Samoa, 2000; 2001b).

Employment opportunities at village level for both women and men are very limited, and because of the lack of income-earning activities many village dwellers have migrated to the urban areas of Samoa's capital Apia or overseas to find work. This migration trend has increased the burden on relatives who live in town, leaving families in the village with few workers for even daily subsistence tasks. Many of those who have moved to Apia have not been able to find employment, placing further stress on families.

A UNDP *Pacific Human Development Report* (UNDP, 1999) observed that the 'encompassing image of poverty in the Pacific is poverty of opportunity'. People's talents, skills and aspirations are frustrated and wasted, denying them the opportunity to lead productive and satisfying lives. 'Poverty of income is often the result, poverty of opportunity is often the cause.'

This lack of opportunity is due, in part, to problems inherent in the situation in Samoa: dependence on ill-defined foreign markets; the high cost of public utilities and infrastructure; and vulnerability to natural disaster. There is a heavy dependence on remittances and donor assistance, leading to an economy vulnerable to internal and external market fluctuations.

The government of Samoa has set out nine key strategic outcomes in its long-term strategy. These include enhancing agricultural opportunities and strengthening the social structure. This strategy is relevant to the theme of this chapter; it refers to the need to diversify commercial agriculture, to revitalize village agriculture and to encourage the active participation of women in economic and social development (Government of Samoa, 2002b).

The commodity context

Throughout the Pacific, coconut is a long-established crop providing a wide variety of products which help sustain the village way of life. The following are some of these products.

Copra: Copra is the dried kernel (meat) of the coconut and is produced mostly by sun-drying the coconut meat which often introduces insects or moulds. However, it can also be produced by kiln or smoke-drying. Its main use is as a source of coconut oil (see below); the residue left after the extraction of oil is often used as grain feed.

Coconut oil (or copra oil): Coconut oil is extracted from copra by heating or by solvent extraction processes. Unrefined oil is not usually suitable for human consumption because of the way in which copra is produced. The oil is therefore generally refined, bleached and deodorized to produce refined, bleached and deodorized (RDB) coconut oil. The oil retains some coconut taste but often has an unpleasant flavour. It can also be hydrogenated to form a more saturated and higher melting product.

Virgin coconut oil: Virgin coconut oil is extracted directly from fresh coconut meat without the use of high heating or chemicals. Either minimal heating is used to dry the meat before the oil is extracted by pressing, or the undried meat is pressed first and the mixture of oil and water which is obtained is allowed to separate to produce the virgin oil. This oil retains the characteristic scent and taste of coconut and is suitable for human consumption without any further processing.

Copra and coconut oil are the traditional products based on the coconut. Their production has generally required large-scale facilities with prices highly vulnerable to international supply and demand dictated by the output from countries such as the Philippines which produce a high proportion of world supply. As the following table indicates, coconut has been the dominant commodity crop for Samoa, although other countries have a higher output.

Table 1: Commodity Outputs, 2001 ('000 metric tonnes)

	Cocoa	Taro	Coffee	Coconut	Bananas	Mangos
Fiji	0.1	38	0.1	215	6.5	0.3
Papua New Guinea	42.5	172	84	1,032	710	0
Tonga	0	4	0	58	0.7	0
Samoa	0.4	15	0	140	20	2.5
Vanuatu	1.6	0	0.1	248	13	0
Cook Islands	0	0	0	5	0.2	2.7
Solomon Islands	3.0	34	0	330	0.3	0
Philippines	6.6	97	130	13,200	5,060	884
Indonesia	340	0	377	14,300	3,600	950
Malaysia	100	0	12.5	713	560	19

Table 1 provides an indication of the relative output (expressed in 1000 metric tonne units for 2001) of conventional produce for Pacific island and nearby Pacific rim countries (FAO, 2002). As these figures illustrate, the output from Pacific countries of most commodities is dwarfed by the output of Indonesia and the Philippines.

The overall output of coconut oil in terms of production and export of the top ten countries is set out in Table 2 (US Department of Agriculture).

Table 2: Production and Export of Coconut Oil, 2002–2003

Production ('000 metric tonnes)		Export ('000 metric tonnes)	
Country	Production	Country	Export
Philippines	1,295	Philippines	1,060
Indonesia	852	Indonesia	552
India	440	Malaysia	166
Vietnam	149	Papua New Guinea	35
Mexico	106	European Union	32
Sri Lanka	58	Côte d'Ivoire	15
Thailand	46	Singapore	11
Papua New Guinea	35	Western Samoa	8
European Union	30	Vietnam	6
Côte d'Ivoire	28	United States	5
Japan	25	India	4
Others	121	Others	3
Total	3,185	Total	1,897

The Philippines is the major world producer of coconut oil. Production doubled from 1999 to reach a peak of 1.7 million tonnes in 2000, mostly exported to Europe and the US. Since then production has fallen as shown above, but as the source of the majority of the world's global supply of coconut oil, the Philippines industry is a powerful lobby in world terms with significant political clout. In contrast, small producers like the Pacific countries have little leverage. On 2002/2003 figures, Papua New Guinea and Samoa are the major producers in the Pacific region. Even so, Samoa accounted for just 0.4 per cent of world exports in 2002/2003 and since then production has fallen because of problems related to the large-scale mill responsible for oil production.

Coconut oil extracted from copra requires large-scale, high pressure, expensive, energy-intensive equipment; unhygienic copra produces oil of low quality which then requires refining, bleaching and deodorizing to create a commercially acceptable product. The refining process uses acid, solvents and steam to strip out the contamination, with some residual solvents remaining in the oil. The process also removes the natural volatiles and anti-oxidants that give pure coconut oil its unique flavour and aroma. In addition, the total process from farm to refined oil can take many months.

The coconut industry in Samoa and other Pacific island countries has nevertheless been a major earner of foreign exchange, contributing towards the livelihoods of many people. Given the processes described above, mechanized coconut oil production and sales have mostly benefited larger enterprises. The benefits of copra production have been more widespread, and when prices have been good, the income earned by villagers has made the effort worthwhile.

More recently, however, fluctuating world market prices for copra, combined with the labour-intensive nature of copra production, have dissuaded Samoan villagers from considering either copra or coconut oil production as viable activities at the village level. Prices are so low that many families have abandoned their plantations except to harvest coconuts for their own consumption.

Devastating cyclones in the past few decades have further damaged the coconut oil industry, forcing many copra producers to close down. As a result, many villagers now have a surplus of unused coconuts, and this abundant and available resource is often wasted.

In 2000, for example, coconut-based products (oil, cream, copra, dessicated coconut) provided exports valued at US$7 million – 15 per cent of Samoa's total commodity exports of US$45 million. In 2002 these products provided only US$4.7 million of revenue out of a total of $US47 million – 10 per cent of commodity revenue. In contrast, revenue from fishing rose from $US24.7 million (55 per cent of commodity exports) to US$29 million (62 per cent of exports) (Government of Samoa, 2003).

The trade policy context

Global integration has intensified the trade links between high-income and developing countries – over the past ten years, trade between these two group-ings has increased by 11 per cent because of lower transport costs, lowered trade barriers, faster communications and greater mobility of both people and capital. Trade has increased, particularly with East Asia, the Pacific, Latin America, the Caribbean and sub-Saharan Africa. However, the volatil-ity of the commodity products involved has had a significant impact on developing countries, and generally commodity and agricultural exports have been subject to higher tariffs than other products as high-income coun-tries protect their own farmers and producers.

The average tariff level globally across all agricultural products is 62 per cent, but this varies considerably between regions and between products (US Department of Agriculture).

Vegetable oils such as coconut oil attract an average tariff internationally of 62 per cent compared with a high for tobacco of 90 per cent and a low for horticultural products of 50 per cent. For vegetable oils, regional rates vary from 134 per cent in South Asia to 17 per cent for North America and 13 per cent for EU countries. For vegetable oils and for agricultural products gener-ally, the highest tariffs apply for countries outside North America and the EU. However, these two regions also deal with the highest volumes of prod-ucts because of the size of their markets. Tariffs were reduced by one-third as a result of the GATT Uruguay Round in 1996, and the lowering of tariffs which especially disadvantage developing countries remains a key objective of future multilateral trade negotiations.

2 The Virgin Coconut Oil Project

History

The initiative to develop the organic virgin coconut oil industry in Samoa was undertaken by Women in Business Development Incorporated, a Samoan NGO established in 1991 with the objective of assisting Samoan women and youth to develop sustainable livelihoods. Until 2002 WIBDI was the only major NGO in Samoa involved in micro-financing activities directly linking a micro-finance facility to micro-enterprise development. It was also the only one focusing on the mobilization of savings.

WIBDI was established by a group of women who faced difficulties in securing loans for their economic activities. From modest beginnings, WIBDI has grown significantly and is now active in around 90 villages across Samoa supporting a range of income-generating activities including organic farming, coconut oil production, beekeeping, fine mat production and handicrafts.

The organization has an office in Apia and employs an Executive Director and ten staff (in 2003) involved in training and in monitoring projects.

WIBDI has been involved in developing community-based projects at the village level aimed at alleviating poverty and creating sustainable local village economies. It has attracted funding support for this from a number of agencies, including NZAID, AUSAID, Oxfam New Zealand, the Food and Agriculture Organization (FAO), UNDP and the Canada Fund.

The move to produce organic virgin coconut oil in Samoa was prompted by the decline in the price for copra, the traditional major product from coconut. Farmers were getting little income from this established resource, with many villages having no sustainable income. Many villages, therefore, had a surplus of unused coconuts, and WIBDI felt that something needed to be done to help villagers utilize and profit from this abundant and available resource.

Investigations revealed that as far back as the 1800s, coconut oil production for export had traditionally been the economic activity of village women. Penelope Schoeffel states: 'Until Theodore Weber introduced the innovation of exporting dried copra in the 1870s, a prime source of income for the Samoans was the manufacture of coconut oil for export. This was traditionally a woman's economic activity, though men took part in it when it became a major commercial product' (Carr, 2001). This revelation encouraged WIBDI to look for ways of reviving the practice of coconut oil production by women as a source of income through exports.

Finding an appropriate technology

After many frustrating months of searching for viable income-generating ideas, including the revival of coconut oil production by village women and youth, WIBDI learnt by chance about the direct micro expelling (DME) technology for the production of coconut oil. It was the subject of the monthly satellite meeting run by the University of the South Pacific regional satellite network for ECOWOMAN) in April 1995. ECOWOMAN is a NGO network of Pacific women promoting women's involvement in science and technology, and WIBDI is the Samoan focal point.

While the copra process yields a low quality oil product, investigations indicated that with the new DME technology, coconut could yield high quality virgin oil with potential uses in cooking, cosmetics and health products.

Direct micro expelling is a new small-scale technology developed by Dr Dan Etherington at the Australian National University which enables rural families on tropical coasts to produce virgin cold-pressed coconut oil within an hour of opening their coconuts.

The technology has its roots in Tuvalu, where oil is extracted from dried grated coconut. A freshly grated coconut is mixed with each batch of dried

---

Box 1: The Direct Micro Expelling Process

The DME system involves four basic steps:

- collecting and husking the coconuts;

- finely grating the fresh mature coconut kernel with small motorized (usually electric) graters. It is important to note that diesel powered generators to run these graters can be fuelled by the virgin oil produced by the DME process;

- drying the grated coconut to a specific moisture content in about one hour on an innovative, all-weather, solar-thermal dryer fuelled by the discarded coconut husks and shells;

- pressing out the oil with a specially designed robust hand-operated press, known as a SAM press, that uses interchangeable cylinders.

---

coconut immediately before pressing using the press. This 'moisture-assisted' expelling principle has been adapted and developed in DME.

At the family farm level, using one DME press, the DME system is generally able to process 300 to 500 coconuts per day, producing 25–45 litres of oil with an extraction efficiency (OEE) of over 85 per cent of the available oil. The DME technology is simple and easy to use, and bypasses the arduous process of making copra. The technology enables village families to enhance traditional Pacific oil-making practice without having to take coconuts to a mill elsewhere for pressing. The DME process is an appropriately small-scale technology which enables poor rural families to use existing village coconut resources to produce pure virgin coconut oil, at the same time recycling materials in a sustainable process.

WIBDI saw the DME technology as being perfect for use in rural villages. It was simple and required very little training in its use. Copra production had always been seen as a man's job, and DME technology was seen as providing a pathway to involve women and youth in the viable production of coconut oil. The DME technology seemed ideal in that the final product – the coconut oil – would be produced in the rural areas and the technology could encourage rural people to remain in the villages where they lived because it provided them with much-needed work. It would be as if the process of village oil production in Samoa could come full circle, to again be produced by women in the village setting and exported to earn them an income.

In 1995 WIBDI contacted Dr Etherington in Australia and sought his permission to use the technology for a rural village project. The WIBDI Executive Director, Adimaimalaga Tafuna'i, then travelled to Fiji and

Figure 1: Direct Micro Expelling of Coconut Oil

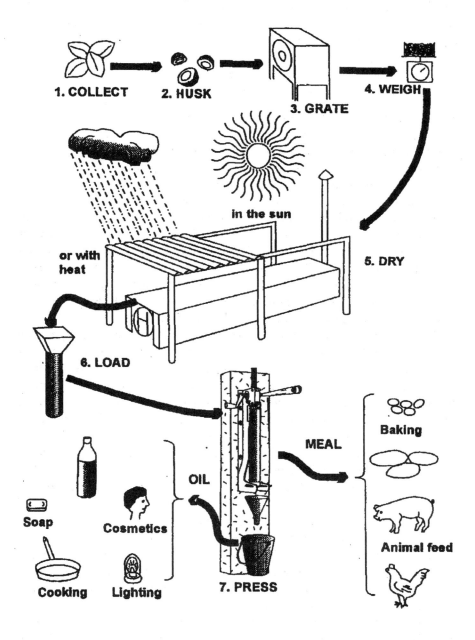

participated in a United Nations Industrial Development Organisation (UNIDO) training programme on the use of the technology which had already been introduced into a few villages in Fiji where the projects were being managed by village communities.

The Fijian projects were not seen to be successful, because of reluctance by village leaders to take responsibility for the activities at community level – especially the financial aspect of the operations.

Finding an appropriate organizational structure

From this experience, the WIBDI Executive Director envisioned an opportunity for Samoan family groups to benefit from the DME technology, given that many rural families have access to the coconut plantations of traditionally owned lands, with acres of coconut trees not fully utilized.

A sub-sector analysis of the coconut industry in Samoa was then conducted to see if producing virgin coconut oil would be viable. The results of the study were made even more encouraging by the fact that copra prices at the time were very much in decline. The analysis indicated that a ton of copra from approximately 5,000 nuts, would bring in about ST$1135 (US$454). If the 5,000 nuts were instead processed with the DME technology into coconut oil, the returns would be approximately ST$4400 (US$1,760), using the price of the locally produced coconut oil as the price base.

Based on the Fiji experience, and from their own early project experience in Samoa, WIBDI decided that rather than work with whole village communities, they would offer the coconut oil project to village extended families. Extended families in Samoa comprise a community in themselves, with families having anything from a few members to very large groups of a hundred or more people in very large families. An average extended family living in one village could be made up of around 40 people.

Previous projects had proved to be most successful when there was a strong leader to take responsibility. Working with families would allow WIBDI to work through one head of family, rather than the many village elders in a communally based project. In a village or community setting, WIBDI had found that people were always willing to take part, but were reluctant to take responsibility when payment was needed for maintenance bills. After the beginning of the project, at the first sign of a problem, they would lose interest. By contrast, when a family was earning cash for themselves from a project, they tended to stick to it longer and to put money back into the project because of the direct benefits gained.

WIBDI based selection for the project on a number of key criteria. Families needed to have access to a substantial supply of coconuts, the villages chosen needed to be geographically representative and the families needed to have the number of people needed to work on the project. Many families have since shown an interest in the technology and the project, but have been turned down because of lack of sufficient family members to make the project viable.

Finding appropriate markets

WIBDI provided the families selected with a DME press and assisted in providing technical plans to model a dryer and oven for the production of pure virgin coconut oil. The project produces organic, virgin, cold-pressed coconut oil – an extremely high grade product that is exportable to a growing niche market overseas. The families concerned are able to produce value-added products for local and overseas markets.

Husking coconut. PICTURE: JOHN CRETNEY

When the idea of producing virgin coconut oil for export was first mooted, there were two main problems to overcome in marketing the oil overseas as a desirable alternative to other cooking oils.

Firstly, the oil would have to compete on overseas markets with cooking oils produced in other areas from vegetable extracts – soy, peanuts, etc. These oils are familiar to the consumer, are produced in great volumes and can be sold quite cheaply. WIBF realized they would be unable to compete on volume or price, so it was important that the product be marketed in a 'value-added' manner to attract buyers and organic certification which would provide an avenue for greater value.

The second problem was that coconut oil has been considered unhealthy because of its saturated fat content. However, it is now known that the unique form of saturated fat in coconut oil actually helps to prevent heart disease and hardening of the arteries.

It is identical to a special group of fats found in human breast milk, and it has now been clinically proven that these fats improve digestion, strengthen the immune system and protect against bacterial, viral and fungal infections. The fats derived from coconut oil are now routinely used in hospital IV formulations and commercial baby formulas. They are also used in sports drinks to boost energy and enhance athletic performance.

The virgin coconut oil project began in 1996. With funding from the Canada Fund, five sets of equipment were purchased and projects were started on family farms in five villages on Upolu and Savaii. Canada Fund funded a further four sets of equipment in 1998. The project has introduced 13 sets of equipment to family farms around Samoa, with all the production sites being organically certified or in conversion status.

Feasibility studies on costs and likely virgin coconut oil prices indicated that virgin oil production offered an opportunity for a profitable farm-based production process. Armed with this information, WIBDI staff visited farmers on Upolu and Savaii to assess interest by farmers in seeking certified organic status for their farms and supplying oil to WIBDI to be marketed.

Obtaining organic certification

A key factor in the project has been obtaining organic certification for organic virgin coconut oil. This access has been managed by WIBDI on behalf of the grower group.

To provide the training necessary for farmers, WIBDI first contracted a certified BIO-GRO trainer and a local consultant to train their own staff in the requirements related to certification such as farm mapping and records. Assistance with training was also provided by a local organic farmer who provided access to his property.

Having assessed the different certification processes available, WIBDI opted for the National Association for Sustainable Agriculture Australia (NASAA) certification system. The trained WIBDI staff then trained farmers about both organic farming practices and the certification requirements, such as mapping the farms in preparation for the annual inspection visits of the NASAA certifying officers.

When families were ready to produce coconut oil, WIBDI staff assisted with building the dryers, installing equipment and training the production staff. A monitoring process involving weekly visits by WIBDI staff was also set up to ensure that certification requirements would be met.

The Pure Coconut Oil Company (PCOC) was then set up as the vehicle to market the virgin oil product and families were encouraged to sell 70 per cent of their oil to the PCOC for export and retain 30 per cent for local sale.

Full certification for five family farms was achieved through NASAA in 2001 and NASAA undertakes annual audit inspections as part of the process of maintaining accreditation. In 2001, following certification, exports to Australia rose significantly from one to three tons per month and further markets opened in Germany and New Zealand.

Involvement of local community, national government and international agencies

This project has been driven primarily by a community-based Samoan NGO, WIBDI, which is now working with the Samoan Organic Farmers Association, an organization set up by WIBDI and Malaefono Organic Plantation in 2001.

At a national level within Samoa, little support was initially received for the project. However, more recently support for organic farming initiatives has been forthcoming from the Ministry of Agriculture which is currently developing a strategy for the development of organic farming in Samoa.

At an international level, support has come from several sources. The Canada Fund has provided funding for capital purchases – initially for the purchase of equipment for farmers and subsequently for the purchase of three vehicles over a five-year period. These vehicles are used by WIBDI staff to visit growers regularly to monitor that organic certification requirements are being met and to advise on production and financial aspects of the project.

Volunteer support has been secured through the US Peace Corps and the United Nations UNV programme for two people to assist with helping farmers to meet their certification requirements. NZAID, the PIIDS (Pacific Islands Industrial Development Scheme) and the South Pacific Project Facility have provided funding support for improving marketing, and AUSAID has provided funding support for the organic certification process.

Oxfam New Zealand has also provided funding over the 1999–2003 period to WIBDI to support the expansion of the micro-finance project, which involves a range of rural initiatives; part of this funding has been used to support the costs of field visits and training.

Current status

The project combines three concepts at the heart of all Women in Business endeavours: tradition, trade and technology.

- *Tradition* is protected as family groups who remain within the village do the work. The product is a pure version of an ancient product.

- *Trade* is encouraged by the local and international sale of the oil and value-added products, such as scented oils and soaps. Furthermore, participants are given the opportunity to learn small business management and to partake in a micro-finance scheme which teaches them credit discipline and saving methods.

- *Technology* comes in the form of applying the DME technology.

Currently, family farms in 12 villages across Upolu and Savaii are involved in coconut farming operations which have secured organic certification under the umbrella of WIBDI. WIBDI manages the quality control, administrative and marketing aspects of the operation. Not all the farms produce regularly and some are involved in work to upgrade their facilities, for example for drying. At present six farms are able to produce when product is required

WIBF currently provides ongoing support to the families involved in the form of weekly visits by field staff to the sites to check on each farm. The quality of oil is monitored, a check is made that certification requirements such as record-keeping are being attended to and training is provided in small business management, production and packing of value-added products. Staff also introduce the families to a micro-finance programme which enables the them to be part of a banking system where they live.

The need for maintenance of the equipment is also identified on these weekly visits. This is done by the WIBF technical person who also gives training to family members on simple maintenance of the machines. Families are encouraged to save money to cover maintenance costs.

Once pressed, the extracted oil product is stored on each farm. The oil is then collected from the production sites and stored at the Pure Coconut Oil Company site. Some value-added products are also produced at this site, for example soap, insect repellent, scented oils and cooking oil. Bulk volumes are sold on to overseas buyers through contacts made directly or on the Internet

Families were initially encouraged to sell 70 per cent of their oil to the PCOC for export and to retain 30 per cent for local sale. However, the majority of current producers sell all the product to the PCOC with each producer also paying 5 litres of oil back to WIBDI per production week for process expenses.

The PCOC is responsible for exporting the virgin coconut oil, but it hires a customs agent to prepare documentation. The PCOC itself operates as cost effectively as possible. It commenced operations with two employees and the staffing remains at this level. Proposed expansion of oil production is likely to require an increase in staffing resources in the future.

At present, virgin coconut oil is produced primarily for export. The oil is used overseas mainly as edible oil, but also for soap making and other cosmetic purposes. Locally it is used as a skin and hair product. Some edible oils are also sold to small local cottage industries for production of biscuits and doughnuts.

Local markets have been secured by the PCOC for supplying local businesses with a gourmet cooking oil, moisturizing oils, insect repellent and coconut soap. However, these markets are small (for example 3–4 dozen of each item a month). Because of financing problems, a sun tan oil and skin balm have not yet been packaged or marketed. The residue of the DME process makes good food for human consumption as well as stock-feed.

Along with *nonu* juice and bananas, virgin coconut oil is currently the major organic product exported by Samoa. In 2001, 14 tonnes of virgin coconut oil was exported to Australia, New Zealand and Germany, but output has since dropped because of difficulties related to management and marketing arrangements. These difficulties are being addressed through greater resources which are now available to develop and market the product. This has arisen from expertise sought from Germany on technical aspects of processing and marketing, together with the sale of the Pure Coconut Oil Company, in late 2003, to a private New Zealand buyer with Samoan family connections.

3 The Virgin Coconut Oil Commodity Chain

Who does and gets what?

There are three major steps in the production of virgin coconut, commencing with the collection of raw material (coconuts) by families through to the marketing and distribution of the oil. These are set out below with details of the economic benefits which accrue at each stage.

Shredding coconut.   PICTURE: JOHN CRETNEY

Plantation owners

This step takes place at the family farm level. Coconuts collected from nearby land areas are sold to the family producer. The price per nut ranges between ST$0.06–0.10 and the truck transport costs ST$20 (US$8) per load. The collectors are members of the extended family and are paid by the site manager. A family can typically harvest around 500 nuts per day bringing an income of ST$30 (US$12) per day or ST$150 (US$60) per week.

The way in which families harvest nuts from their own plantations ensures that transportation is not a major problem. Family members who had no previous employment can now be gainfully employed picking up the nuts and transporting them to the production site if it is close enough. Problems are encountered on the larger plantations where appropriate transportation is not available. Some families do not have the workforce to gather the coconuts, as family members have moved away to find work.

At present, there is no competition for coconuts, as they are not normally being harvested except for family use for food. Copra prices are so low that small farmers are not interested in copra production.

Oil producers

This step takes place with families who have obtained the equipment required to undertake the oil extraction process.

Workers, including men, women and children, husk the coconuts, and grate and weigh the coconut meal. They are also involved in the drying and oil pressing process. They are paid ST$12 (US$4.80) per day or ST$60 (US$24) per week.

One problem encountered at the beginning of the project concerned the time spent on the production process. Families complained that once the dryer was lit, they had to produce continuously during the day and could not stop and start. They were not accustomed to spending a whole day working. Their frustrations receded as they became familiar with the process and saw how beneficial the cash earned was to their families.

Once the oil has been extracted at farm level, producers can either sell the oil locally or sell to the PCOC. Locally, the oil can fetch between ST$12–15 (US$4.80–6) per litre. Although this option is more lucrative, Samoan producers prefer to sell all the oil in bulk through the PCOC. Currently only two producers are taking regular advantage of the local market, which is encouraged by WIBDI.

Table 3 illustrates monthly production by oil producers in October 2001, and the volumes sold locally or to the PCOC.

Table 3: Oil Production and Sales, October 2001

Village	Oil Produced (litres)	Local Sales (litres)	Local Sales (ST$)	Sales to PCOC (litres)	Sales to PCOC (ST$)	Total Sales for Month (ST$)
Saoluafata	250	74	740	176	526	1,266
Siumu	450	50	280	400	1,200	1,480
Saleimoa	1,400	50	250	1,340	4,020	4,270
Patamea	1,200	200	1,000	1,000	3,000	4,000
Foailalo	120	120	1,200		1,200	1,200
Lano and Tafua tai	1,300	20*		1,280	3,840	3,840
Taga	200	100	1,000	100	300	1,300

*For personal use

There is a reluctance to produce other value-added products like scented oil and soaps, perhaps because of the time spent on the additional processing.

The PCOC initially set the wholesale price at ST$3 (US$1.20) per litre while markets were still being established. As the market has developed, the price has increased and the current price for organically certified oil is ST$4.65 (US$1.85) per litre or ST$5 (US$2) per kilo to the producer. Providing a market for the oil is available, a typical producer with an output of up to 200 kilos (215 litres) per week can earn up to ST$1,000 (US$400) per week selling through the PCOC. If they take advantage of the local market, this can be much higher.

As an example, one producer responsible for a family farm sells all her coconut oil on the local market and her family is totally dependent on the oil as well as the few pieces of handicraft that she produces from time to time. She has the capacity to produce up to 200 litres a week, but usually works only two or three days and production is around 60 litres or three buckets. By selling the oil in 500ml bottles for ST$5 a bottle, she earns ST$600 (US$240) per week.

Another family produces up to two and a half to three buckets of oil a day, and sells all the oil to the PCOC. It earns around ST$750 (US$300) a week, but can increase production if it needs money for a special occasion.

The Pure Coconut Oil Company – marketing and distribution

The PCOC either sells the virgin oil in bulk to overseas interests or produces value-added products for local or overseas distribution. A number of value-added products can be derived from the virgin oil or from other coconut material.

The PCOC takes responsibility for the sale of bulk virgin coconut oil to

Box 2: Production and Distribution of Value-added Products

The PCOC also undertakes limited production locally of value-added products. Current or potential products are outlined below.

Scented Oil

Scented oil was the first value-added product developed for the virgin oil in Samoa. It utilized the leaves of the *lau maile* plant and flowers from the *moso'oi*, frangipani and wild ginger. Although this process ensured a price of up to ST$15 (US$6) per litre, producers did not want to spend the extra time on the process. Local sales have been very promising, but families only produced enough when there was a great need for cash. There is much potential for this product at the village level.

Soap

Soap-making workshops were conducted for soap producers and other interested women, but this resulted in only two people taking this further with one exporting overseas. Soap is also produced by the PCOC, but the demand in the local market alone is high so that more women (including those not involved in oil production) could be involved in this activity. Originally local women produced the soap, but they could not be relied on for regular supplies and the PCOC needed to produce soap to ensure that the market was supplied. It remains difficult to attract women to produce soap, as often work ethics have not been established because of the traditional reliance on remittances for cash needs.

There is huge potential in the Pacific Islands for rural and urban women to produce soap, especially in countries where tourism is more established. In 2003, with the assistance of a German consultant funded by the Centre for Development of Enterprise (CDE) in the EU, the PCOC produced an organically certified soap. The soap will be produced for sale in New Zealand and Europe in the near future. Some virgin oil based soap is also being produced in both Fiji and Nuie.

Insect Repellent

A natural insect repellent was developed by the PCOC, when it needed to boost cash flow, while waiting for the export market to develop. The age-old practice of rubbing the body with coconut oil before going out in the evening was coupled with the benefits of citronella as an insect deterrent, to produce this pleasant smelling moisturizing insect repellent. Sales have been steady. In Fiji, there is the potential to combine the virgin oil with oil of the Neem tree for an effective insect repellent.

Box 2 (continued)

Edible Oil

It has always been the intention of the project to market the oil as an edible oil. This has been very difficult because of adverse publicity put out by the soybean oil industry since the 1980s. However, the dissemination of news of the benefits of coconut oil through books, video resources and the Internet is slowly changing attitudes. With appropriate advertising, the oil could also be sold in the villages for cooking, bringing health benefits for Samoan people.

Charcoal

A number of women produce charcoal from the coconut shell, which they sell either locally or at the produce market.

Coconut Meal

There is the potential to use the residue meal after oil pressing for baking and for animal feed. WIBDI has established youth groups to sell the meal for baking as a fund-raising project, and there are indications that meal as animal feed can improve milk yields – one dairy farmer noticed an increase of 10 per cent in the yield after feeding his cows on the meal for four days.

overseas purchasers and currently this has involved a single major purchaser, Kokonut Pacific, based in Australia. The oil sold is used primarily as edible oil and for soap and cosmetic production. Initially oil was purchased at a price of ST$6.50 (US$2.60) per litre or ST$7 (US$2.80) per kilo, which with organic certification has now risen to ST$11.50 (US$4.60) per litre or ST$12.50 (US$5) per kilo, a price still less than the price prevailing in larger countries such as the Philippines.

In contrast, recent prices for commodity coconut oil exported by countries like the Philippines has fluctuated from US$0.36 per litre in 2000 to a 15-year low of US$0.26 in 2001 – around a tenth of the price of virgin coconut oil.

4 Impact of the Project on Women and Men

The benefits of this project accrue at a number of levels.

Village level

At the village level, the project has provided a means of extracting a value-added niche product from a plentiful renewable resource which was previously either being wasted or which was providing a commodity product (copra) highly susceptible to international price fluctuations. The project provides a source of badly needed cash for families, as well as employment for family members in harvesting and processing the coconut. Typically, a family farm venture may involve up to 45–50 people if members of the extended family are included through their involvement in harvesting nuts. However, numbers fluctuate according to production needs or to family members' need for income.

Women's Economic Empowerment

Participation in this project is also injecting new skills into the community through the training needed both to manufacture the virgin oil and to manage the financial and budgeting aspects of each operation. Each village or family involved needs to manage the income, and the capital and operating costs of the operation. As can be seen in Table 4, women are playing an especially important role in this aspect of the project, with many of the ventures managed by women.

Through the project, many women have become responsible for bringing income earning opportunities to their families. As a result, they have achieved changes in their status in the family which would not have happened to such an extent in the past. Husbands, for example, may now seek advice from their partners and discuss more decisions with them, while other members of the extended family also seek advice on issues they would normally have discussed only with the father of the family.

This has been especially true of women who were not born in the village but are there because of marriage. Women manage all but three of the coconut oil production sites, and through these women the whole family has been empowered. In all its projects, WIBDI seeks to focus on benefiting the whole family, not only the women.

However, while women in rural areas are becoming increasingly acknowledged as sole income generators within the family unit in the villages, this change has not

Women drying coconut.   PICTURE: JOHN CRETNEY

automatically meant that they have gained an improvement in social status within the family or village community. Although women usually manage the finances within the family and their advice on some issues may be sought more often than in the past, their control of money distribution is limited as the male head of the family has the ultimate say as to how money is spent. However, this does not seem to have affected the way women feel about their traditional status.

Table 4: Virgin Oil-producing Villages from Inception

Village	No. of Youth Working	No. of Women Working	Year Installed	Year Ended	Status of Operation	No. of People Benefiting
Siumu	2	3	1996		Still in operation	20
Fasitootai		3	1996	1998	Equipment returned	12
Fagaloa	3	4	1996	1998	Equipment returned	15
Tuanai	1	2	1998	1998		8
Lefaga	4	2	1999	1999		12
Saoluafata	6	2	1998		Operating	47
Saleimoa	2	2	2000		Operating	50+
Foailalo	4	3	1996		Operating	16
Puapua	4	4	1997	1998		32
Tafuatai	3	2	1998	2001	Transferred to youth group	9
Lano	4	5	1998		On hold	36
Patamea A	4	3	1998	1998		
Patamea B	2	1	2000		Operating	50+
Taga	4	2	2001		Operating	18
Malua	6		2002		Operating	<100

It appears that Samoan women still mostly feel comfortable about their traditional status and their access to the decision-making processes in the village. Within the existing traditional system, as daughters and sisters, they can have access to the village council. As wives they have access to the village council through their husbands. As mothers they have access to their sons and daughters who make up the *nuu o alii* and *nuu o tamaitai*.

65

Nonetheless, the women involved in the coconut oil project and other WIBDI programmes have been empowered by the opportunity to be involved in an income-generating activity where they do not have to leave their villages. Their families have been collectively empowered by the opening up of alternative avenues for income generation and self reliance in the village itself. This has eased the pressure of total reliance on remittances for some families in the village and provided some welcome respite for the remitting family members to concentrate on their own livelihoods where they live.

Micro-finance and savings scheme

In addition, women on the project are empowered individually through their new ability, and the opportunity that WIBDI provides them with, to save money and to take out a loan, either collectively or individually. All project participants are required to commit to a micro-finance scheme by saving at least ST$5 (US$2) each time they are paid. The families have a savings account which is given the name that they give to their project operations.

Each family has access to this account for their family needs and for the maintenance of the DME equipment and drier. At least two families on the coconut oil project save up to ST$200 (US$80) at times through the scheme. Some women prefer to have a second savings account in their individual name for cash they earn themselves. This gives them a source of cash that they can spend without discussion with their husbands.

The micro-finance scheme enables women and their families to make savings and eventually to become eligible for a loan of up to 60 per cent of their savings. Analysis of loan applications shows that the three most common reasons to apply for a small loan are to pay for school fees, electricity bills and materials for cottage industries, such as pandanus leaves for weaving. Samoan women take it upon themselves to ensure that children are educated, clothed and stay healthy.

Women are considered by society to be responsible for the family's health and well-being. The self-esteem of our project women, and indeed of whole families, has improved greatly with the opportunity to earn cash in the villages. With the family now able to make cash donations themselves, rather than having to rely on other relatives, the social status of the family in the village has been elevated.

Village men involved in the coconut oil project are happy with the improved situation in their families and, although they are still 'in charge', they appreciate what the women have brought into the families through their extra efforts in our programmes. They show this through their cooperation with WIBDI field staff who visit. The husbands have been part of the training programme from the outset. They have gone through the processes of planning and budgeting and know how important it is that their partners are part of the decision-making process. They are also mindful that the projects were begun because of their partners and they give them credit for this by always conferring with them about spending the money.

Box 3: Examples of Change

Large amounts of cash are only used when there is a big family commitment, which the women understand as being made for cultural reasons and therefore must involve the whole family. For example, when the husband in one family was made mayor of his village, the family took out a loan of ST$2,000 (US$800) to pay for the presentations of fine mats and food to the village. Such presentations are accepted practice and without the coconut oil project, the family would have needed to ask their children living in Australia to provide this sum. It was a source of pride to them that the village knew that they could afford it, and that they were able to repay the total amount two weeks later when oil was sold. Income from the project has enabled the father of the family to care for his family financially and to make regular contributions to the village and the church.

Another family is a good example of the technology benefiting a whole extended family. Forty-seven people depend on the project for their livelihoods. This number includes two nuclear families living near the plantation who receive payment for nuts gathered; family members who help with production; and school children whose school fees are covered by money generated by the project. Furthermore, the family's church donations are made with proceeds from the project.

A family member sums up: 'The project has enabled members of our family who didn't have jobs to make meaningful contributions to the family, and not just sit back waiting for those working overseas to send money. Also, we save money, by using the oil for cooking our food, and the coconut meal is used for feeding our pigs.' She feels that her self-esteem has improved. However, there are some negative aspects. Some villagers think that they are now wealthy and are always asking for oil without offering payment. Nevertheless, her husband, who the head of their extended family, is very happy about being able to provide for his family financially.

National level

At a national level, the project has facilitated the development of new skills by WIBDI. The project has led to a skill base within the organization related to the management and monitoring of projects, about how to meet certification requirements and about how to develop and administer budgets. These skills are transferable both to other projects managed by WIBDI and to other organizations seeking to manage community-based projects.

5 Lessons Learned

Main findings

The virgin coconut oil project illustrates many of the issues faced by a developing country in identifying projects which can lead to a sustainable and marketable product through which people at different levels in the community can benefit. The key issues faced in developing this organic product based on a local resource are set out below.

Identifying suitable products

A first step is to obtain up-to-date market information about organic product demand and prices and target importing countries through trade organizations or government agencies. Possible organic products suited to local climatic conditions then need to be identified with the assistance of grower or farm advisory organizations.

Identified products then need to be assessed for sustainable sales and profitability based on factors such as:

- a combination of high value and low volume to offset distribution costs;

- a 'point of difference' compared with other competing countries;

- non- or low perishability;

- products based on crops which have high pest and disease resistance;

- ability to provide a sustained and reliable supply to export markets;

- availability of local markets to support exports;

- costings which demonstrate that production is profitable in the long term.

Advice on farming practices or growing techniques needs to be available through either grower associations or government advisory services, and product certification needs to readily achieved and sustained for export purposes.

The production of virgin oil meets many of these criteria for a suitable

Pacific-based organic product. It is based on a plentiful Pacific resource, the production process is cost effective and can be operated at a local level, the product has low perishability, low volume and potentially high value, and import regulations are not difficult to meet.

Training families to participate in the project

A factor in the success of the project is that each venture is family, rather than village, based. Earlier attempts to base projects at village level were not successful because it was more difficult to engender project responsibility with a wider group. At family level, it is possible to identify particular families with the aptitude and motivation to make the venture a success and to take responsibility for the financial planning and implications of being involved.

A key element has been the training provided through WIBDI to family members which has included budget and financial advice and training in administration and record-keeping, as well as in the skills required for oil production itself. These skills have particularly benefited women. One aspect which has proved to be an ongoing challenge has been the need to train farmers to meet ongoing certification requirements (especially record-keeping and quality control of the pressed oil) and the need for more effective marketing.

Achieving organic certification

Obtaining organic certification for virgin coconut oil as an organic product has assisted in overcoming buyers' comparison of it with copra oil; this was a key factor in the improved marketing which led to increased demand for the oil in 2001.

An intensive training and monitoring programme is required and mapping of farms takes up a considerable amount of time and energy. The annual costs of maintaining certification are also significant. These demands have imposed a heavy commitment on WIBDI, so that in 2001 it established the Samoa Organic Farmers Association to take over this role with the help of UN volunteers. The certification process is an intensive process that requires significant resourcing both initially and on an ongoing basis.

Marketing and exporting organic products

The export of organic products from the Pacific faces a number of barriers. These include identification of sustainable markets, handling and storage of export products, meeting quarantine and biosecurity requirements, transport costs, the lack of an organization devoted to product research or coordination and a lack of certified suppliers. Progress in Samoa includes the establishment of an organic farming association and an initiative by the Ministry of Agriculture and Fisheries to stimulate research on organic products and develop a strategic plan for organic production.

In the case of virgin coconut oil, a number of these barriers do not apply. Certified virgin coconut oil is a processed niche product with a relatively high cost-to-volume ratio, so that transport costs are manageable and quarantine issues are not significant.

However, distribution and marketing of the virgin oil has faced a number of problems.

Marketing the oil has been a very difficult process. Potential buyers tended to compare the product with copra oil and were concerned about the price sought despite the proven high quality of the oil (less than 0.1 per cent free fatty acids). The Pure Coconut Oil Company was then set up to manage the market aspects of the project and was able to negotiate arrangements with a major purchaser.

However, intermittent demand by this single purchaser for the product led to production back-up with both WIBDI and the producers experiencing cash flow problems and inability to meet costs incurred. Obtaining multiple outlets for the product to avoid this dependency is important.

Achieving fair returns for stakeholders

The families involved, when producing regularly, enjoy a better standard of living, as demonstrated by their ability to improve their material standard of living and to meet outside community and church commitments without resort to income from sources such as remittances. With the new partners in the PCOC, and vigorous marketing, production will step up and returns to the producers will be even better.

The PCOC is in the process of signing contracts with producers which are in line with fair trade practices. WIBDI is keen to see the final price of the product exported better reflected in the price to the producer. The long-standing problem with the traditional crop copra has been that the producer receives the least benefit while the greatest benefits have accrued to those milling the oil.

The Future

The Virgin Coconut Oil Project operating in Samoa has been successful primarily through its evolution as a grassroots-based operation based around the skills and commitment of women in Samoa.

It is an example of a programme in which a grassroots organization (WIBDI) has assisted families, and especially women, by coordinating their use of improved and appropriate technologies to produce a valuable product without resort to large enterprises which absorb profits, and which has also facilitated access to international markets. This model has been described elsewhere as a successful model.[16]

There is huge potential for the expansion of virgin coconut oil production in Samoa. Currently there is capacity to export just three tons of oil a month from the five farms in active production. A further five farms could be brought into production, in which case a total of ten family farms in active production could see output lifted to as much as six to ten tons a month. Emerging technology could see sites producing up to one ton of oil a week. There are vast areas of coconuts across the two larger islands of Samoa which have not been utilized for many years. Many more people in Samoa could be employed, not only in the production of virgin coconut oil, but also in the production of value-added products.

While the overall number of trees does not match that in larger countries such the Philippines, on a per capita basis Samoa has the second largest number of coconut trees in the world. Samoan coconuts are also larger than the coconuts of many other countries such as Fiji. For example, in Fiji it would take between 12 and 15 coconuts to produce one litre of virgin coconut oil, whereas in Samoa the number is between 8 and 12.

Refined coconut oil extracted from copra on an industrial scale has been plagued by exposure to price fluctuation and dependence on larger-scale operators able to undertake the processing involved. Such processing in Samoa has been especially prone to problems of stop-go mill operations, low prices and delayed payments to growers. As a result, many growers have ceased making copra and sell unprocessed coconuts instead.

Because virgin coconut oil is a newly emerging product, there are few statistics available on country or world output. However, compared with coconut oil extracted from copra, world output of virgin coconut oil is low and the product is in demand because of its health properties and its suitability for human consumption

Virgin coconut oil production provides a great way for Pacific Island countries to revive their coconut industries if they can work together to supply markets. While larger countries such as the Philippines, India and Sri Lanka can produce huge amounts of commodity refined coconut oil compared with smaller Pacific Island countries, the technology used for virgin coconut oil production relies on the production of small quantities at a time. This means that larger countries have less of an advantage.

The Pacific could also use marketing techniques focused on their clean green image, especially if they also made a commitment to organic certification. This market could be most effectively exploited by Pacific countries sharing information and markets.

An emerging potential market for virgin coconut oil is use as a substitute for diesel fuel. Companies are looking very seriously into this prospect, especially in Vanuatu and American Samoa.

This project has also assisted in strengthening organizational capacity at a national level. As WIBDI has evolved as an organization, it has built up its skill base through extensive networking with external agencies which have provided support at key stages to build capacity and to provide the capital required for project development. Government support has been a critical factor in this development.

The key challenges facing the project lie mainly in the ability of those managing the project to find and sustain multiple overseas outlets for virgin oil which will encourage increased production, and to ensure that income from the project meets the expectations of stakeholders and especially those operating at family and village level.

The project demonstrates the economic benefits which NGOs can bring to women and men in developing countries through working alongside their communities, governments and overseas agencies to supply a product sought in global markets. With government support, potential exists to develop products such as virgin coconut oil as a source of much-needed foreign exchange.

References

Carr, Marilyn and Chen, Martha (2002). 'Globalization and the Informal Economy: How Global Trade and Investment Impact on the Working Poor', Working Paper on the Informal Economy, No. 1, ILO, Geneva.
FAO (2002). *Selected Indicators of Food and Agricultural Development in the Asia Pacific Region, 1991–2001*, Food and Agriculture Organization, Rome.
Government of Samoa, Treasury Department (2000). *Statement of Economic Strategy*.
Government of Samoa, Treasury Department (2001a). *Annual Report*.
Government of Samoa (2001b). *Census*.
Government of Samoa, Department of Trade, Commerce and Industry (2002a). *Report on Coconut Sector*.
Government of Samoa, Treasury Department (2002b). *Strategy for Development of Samoa 2002–2004*.
Government of Samoa, Treasury Department (2003). *4th Quarter Report 2002*.
Japan International Cooperation Agency, *Country Profile Study on Poverty, Samoa 2003, www.jica.go.jp*
Schoeffel, P. (1977). 'The Origin and Development of Women's Associations in Western Samoa 1830–1977', *Journal of Pacific Studies* 111, p. 11.
UNDP (1999). *Pacific Human Development Report 1999: Creating Opportunities*, United Nations Development Programme, New York.
US Department of Agriculture, Economic Research Service, *Profiles of Tariffs in Global Agricultural Markets*, AER 796, Washington DC.
US Department of Agriculture, *www.fas.usda.gov/psd/complete_tables/OIL*
World Bank (2003). *Samoa at a Glance 2003, www.worldbank.org.data*

Currency ST$1 = US$0.40
Density of virgin coconut used for price conversion = 0.925kg per litre

Cashing in on Cashew Nuts: Women Producers and Factory Workers in Mozambique

Nazneen Kanji, Carin Vijfhuizen, Carla Braga
and Luis Artur

1 Executive Summary

Portuguese traders found the cashew tree highly valued by the Tupi of Brazil for its fruit, juice and nuts. Traders brought cashew to northern Mozambique and India in the sixteenth century, and it was locally adopted and spread in both countries. Mozambicans have therefore grown cashew trees on deep sandy coastal soils for hundreds of years. Nuts have been exported from Mozambique since the beginning of the twentieth century and when World War II closed shipping to India, a local processing industry was born (Penvenne, 1997). After the war, numerous factories were built for processing the nuts for export, with women providing the majority of the labour. Production peaked in 1972 when 216,000 tons were marketed and Mozambique was the world's leading exporter of shelled cashew (kernels). Since then, drought, war and displacement, and inconsistent policies towards the smallholder sector, as well as aging and diseased trees have affected production.

After ten years of armed struggle, Mozambique won independence in 1975 and the Frelimo government came to power. Frelimo articulated a non-racist policy and positioned itself against private property-based privilege. A post-colonial exodus occurred and many properties and industries were abandoned. In 1979 a state company, Caju de Moçambique, was created to operate the cashew processing factories. Post-independence policies also included the formation of communal villages, which had the effect of separating people's

Picking cashew nuts in Mozambique. PICTURE: STEFFEN CAMBON

homes from their trees and decreasing incentives for smallholders to invest in them.[1] From 1982, Mozambique was subject to a South African-backed war of destabilization which lasted until the signing of the peace agreement in 1992, when the one-party system was dismantled. During the war, up to half the rural population was forced to leave their homes, moving to towns or becoming refugees in neighbouring countries. Even peasants who were not displaced were often afraid to go to remote cashew trees to clean around them and harvest the crop (Hanlon, 1996; 2000).

The war had a devastating effect on the economy and the government increasingly turned to international agencies for aid. In keeping with the policies promoted by the IMF and the World Bank in other countries in the South, Mozambique implemented its first Structural Adjustment Programme in 1987. Since then, Mozambique has followed an increasingly neo-liberal approach to development, reducing state intervention and pursuing greater liberalization and privatization in the 1990s. Eighty per cent of the population live in rural areas and are mainly dependent on natural resources for their livelihoods. Smallholder agriculture employs 89 per cent of women and 63.2 per cent of men. Agricultural production contributed 20.1 per cent of GDP in 2001, a proportion which has declined from 27.2 per cent in 1998. (UNDP, 2001). It is estimated that Mozambique has 26 million cashew trees, but that these are reaching the end of their productive lives and dying at the rate of one million a year (Deloitte and Touche, 1997).

In the mid-1990s, the World Bank made it a condition that the government should liberalize the cashew sector if it wanted further loans (it was a necessary condition of the Bank's 1995 Country Assistance Strategy). It recommended that the government should drop the requirement that traders sell raw nuts to Mozambican industries and that it should reduce export tariffs on raw nuts. By 1997 most factories had closed and about 10,000 jobs were lost. Although intense national debate led to a raising of tariffs on raw nuts in 1999, most factories have not re-opened.

Since the end of the 1990s, the government has put in place a strategy to revive the sector, with the participation of the private sector, NGOs and communities. The revival of the sector includes aspects of production, processing and commercialization and has to address a complex set of factors at local, national and international levels. Despite the decline, cashew is still the third most important export for Mozambique. Smallholder farmers are responsible for about 95 per cent of total raw nut marketed production and in total about one million rural households (40 per cent of the rural population) have access to cashew trees (Wandschneider and Garrido-Mirapeix, 1999). It is also important to note that cashew is a high value 'luxury' nut with expanding markets in the EU, US and other parts of the world, with the potential to

---

Box 1: Characteristics of Cashew

Cashew is an extremely variable plant. In Mozambique, trees can produce 25 kilos of nuts one year and nothing the next. This is partly due to the impact of the powdery mildew (*oidium anacardium*), but rainfall, insect infestation, humidity and temperature all affect yields in a variety of ways. The raw cashew nut is attached to and hangs below a false fruit or cashew apple. The fruit is sweet, juicy, pungent in aroma and high in vitamin C.

The most significant difficulty in processing cashew nuts is that the hard outer shell, which contains the edible kernel, contains a caustic oil which can burn the skin and produces noxious fumes when heated. The oil, referred to commercially as cashew nut shell liquid (CNSL), contains 90 per cent anacardic acid and 10 per cent cardol. For household consumption, nuts are typically roasted in shell over an open flame until the oil burns away in a thick black smoke. Kernels from raw nuts roasted this way remain high in protein for consumption and are sold in local markets.

Cashew nuts are kidney shaped and brittle, which makes it difficult to remove the shell without breakage. Whole white kernels are the highest grade, and the industry standard is such that wholes at packing should constitute at least 60 per cent or more of the sample. The higher the percentage of white wholes, the higher the price.

---

enhance the income and livelihoods of smallholder producers and workers in the processing sub-sector.

The chapter begins by describing the current policy context in which the fieldwork has been carried out. It then maps typical export chains in Nampula province and examines key issues and constraints in production and processing activities, drawing out gendered aspects. A new initiative for decentralized processing around one factory is also discussed. Finally, we consider the effects for women producers and workers of broader processes of economic and social change and suggest ways in which their participation and benefits can be enhanced.

2 The Policy Environment

Liberalization of cashew nut exports

The liberalization of Mozambican raw cashew nut exports has become one of the most contentious policy reform issues in Mozambique (Wandschneider and Garrido-Mirapeix, 1999; Cramer, 1999; Hanlon, 2000). The World

Box 2: Characteristics of Cashew Processing Technology

Mechanized processing, using hot oil baths or drum roasting, followed by the use of automated cutting or impact-shelling machines to separate shell from kernel, were favoured in the colonial period. This required expensive capital inputs and factories typically employed several hundred people. The labour-intensive processes were peeling and grading; women were the majority of workers. More recently, smaller-scale factories use the steaming and cutting method. Raw nuts are steamed, then cooled and cut with a hand and foot pedal-operated machine. The shells are then burned in the furnaces to produce steam and heat for drying the kernels. Semi-mechanized shelling increases the contact of the worker with CNSL. Workers are given oil to cover their hands which provides limited protection. Gloves wear out quickly and in any case are not favoured by workers paid on a piece rate basis, since they affect dexterity and slow down the work.

The processing steps in the newer factories are:

• Steaming the raw nuts

• Cooling

• Cutting to separate the shell from the kernel

• Drying the kernel

• Peeling

• Sorting the kernels (separating broken pieces)

• Grading

• Packing

These small and medium-scale factories are much less capital intensive and employ more people per ton of processed cashew than the highly mechanized ones. Since people remain better than machines at separating the nut from the shell, kernel breakage rates are much lower in these factories. But, as Hilton (1998) argues, even small-scale processing plants are not suitable for small investors. One of the biggest costs is stock-piling sufficient cashew to keep the plant working for 200 days a year. The cashew harvesting season lasts for two to three months, so even the smallest plants require 100 tons of stock-piled raw cashew.

Bank's promotion of liberalization policies in the cashew sector,
which included price and trade
liberalization (and the lifting of
protectionist measures for industry), has to be understood within
the broader international mainstream arguments for 'free' trade
and market-led development. The
argument is that all countries
reap the benefits of freer trade,
whether they specialize in labour-
intensive primary commodities or capital-intensive manufactured products
because liberalization enhances the free movement of goods at international
market prices, as such increases outputs and thereby benefits all countries
according to their 'comparative advantage' and (the theory asserts) also
results in poverty reduction.[3] For Mozambique, this represented an enormous
change from post-independence, state-led, development.

Cashew nut tree.   PICTURE: LUIS ARTUR

The World Bank's rationale for liberalizing the trade in raw nuts is as
follows:

- The reduction in export tariffs on raw nuts would boost demand and spur
  competition among traders who export;

- Eliminating trader licences would increase the number of traders;

- Traders would compete for raw nuts and pay higher prices to smallholder
  producers;

- Higher prices to farmers would increase the incentive to market nuts and
  further increase farm income;

- The price incentive would encourage more farmers to enter cashew production and current farmers to improve tree management and plant new
  trees.

The policy's stated aim was to revive the smallholder cashew sector: '*As the
second* [now third] *largest export earner, and as a vital source of hundreds of
thousands of poor farmers, revival of the cashew sector is a key to economic
development and poverty reduction in Mozambique*' (World Bank, 2001:
51). The Bank's view was that export restrictions meant that peasants were,
in effect, subsidizing the factories. This approach embodies the neo-liberal
view that industries must be left to compete internationally and fail if they
cannot compete without government support. The loss of jobs in the pro-

cessing sector is offset against the gains which, it was asserted, would accrue to a much larger group of smallholder farmers (Cramer, 1999).

The World Bank (2001:51) concluded that real producer prices were, on average, 55 per cent higher in post-reform years and that the farmer's share of the export price has gone up significantly. These conclusions are contested by others. The first point is that prices of food and basic consumer goods need to be taken into account and increased (Wandschneider and Garrido-Mirapeix, 1999). Farmers' interests in selling cashew depends on its relative prices vis-à-vis other crops and consumer goods, as was also evidenced at the end of the 1980s when prices rose but there were few goods in the market. In our fieldwork, farmers often referred back to the time when the sale of cashew allowed the purchase of relatively expensive items such as bicycles, whereas now it bought them very little, even in terms of basic consumer goods. The Bank acknowledges that these terms of trade are low in comparison to what producers in countries such as India and Vietnam are able to buy with the proceeds of their cashew (World Bank, 2001:iii).

The second important point is that although prices increased, the main gains have been retained by the trading sector. The number of effective traders has remained restricted, due to their dependence on trader-based credit, and the major exporters are organized and coordinate prices. This has allowed continued control of farm gate prices, and therefore the greater share of additional profit from higher cashew prices has been retained by the trading sector (Hanlon, 2000; INCAJU, March 2002). The most recent economic study,

Woman smallholder pruning a cashew nut tree.   PICTURE: LUIS ARTUR

entitled 'When Economic Reform goes Wrong: Cashews in Mozambique' (McMillan *et al.*, 2002), echoes the findings of earlier studies and concludes that the net gains of farmers were disappointingly low and largely offset by the costs of unemployment caused by the collapse of the processing sector.

The final World Bank objective of liberalization, as stated above, was for expanded grower investment in trees. However, there has been limited evidence of increased planting (World Bank, 2001; Wandschneider and Garrido-Mirapeix, 1999: 61). The World Bank also identifies greater tree care and use of fungicide sprays as potential means of improving productivity. The irony is that these technologies – which may increase nut production – may in fact *not* be economically advantageous. The farmers who put in the extra labour and pay for the spray will always assess marginal and potentially negative returns more closely than researchers and advisors. Mole (2000:245) shows that employing technology is related to the price of nuts, but with prevailing input and cashew prices the different technology packages, including chemical control, *were not profitable* under sole cashew cropping conditions. He argues that price incentives must be combined with improved technology and marketing infrastructure for production to increase (Mole, 2000: 248). There is an additional point here. Unprotected market integration also exposes farmers to price fluctuations. The collapse of raw nut prices in the 2000–2001 season (World Bank, 2001: iii) should be expected to have as much negative impact on the incentive to invest as the occasional high price has positive effect. This is one reason why farm subsidies began in currently developed countries.

What then, is our assessment of the liberalization policies promoted by the World Bank? Promoting trade liberalization is unlikely to increase benefits to producers in Mozambique without a range of supporting policies ensuring marketing infrastructure, availability of goods and fair prices, appropriate technology for growing and storing the nuts, and extension services. It is increasingly recognized, even by some parts of the international financial institutions, that a much broader range of factors, including institutions at local level and a range of policies and resources, material and social, affect the outcomes of trade liberalization (Kanji and Barrientos, 2002). This wider contextual analysis was lacking in the World Bank's policy advice.

Revival of the cashew nut sector

The current government strategy for the cashew sector recognizes the need for a broader approach and calls for active participation of government, private sector, communities and NGOs to revive the cashew sector. The government's Institute for the Promotion of Cashew (INCAJU) has developed an integrated strategy which tries to stimulate activities in the three interlinked areas of production, processing and commercialization (INCAJU, 1998).

New initiatives in the last few years have been undertaken to revive the sector, including:

- **Production:** Subsidies, implementation and coordination of treatment of trees against powdery mildew disease by spraying trees; new plantations; nurseries with new varieties training; extension work including, cultivation techniques and pruning and research (INCAJU, 1998);

- **Processing:** Stimulation of the construction of small-scale factories through loans to the private sector because, according to INCAJU, small-scale factories using semi-mechanical cutting technology give a better quality output, have less management problems and have fewer problems in acquiring raw material (INCAJU, 2001);

- **Commercialization:** Setting the export tax on raw cashew between 18–22 per cent; grading the quality of nuts (INCAJU, 2001).

At present, marketed production is only about 50,000 tonnes as against over four times that amount in the 1970s. Processing initiatives provide only about 2,000 jobs compared with 10,000 before liberalization, although this does not include many small unregistered processing initiatives for domestic and regional markets, which need further study. Factories only purchased 6,000 tons of raw nuts in 2002 as compared with 25,000 tons in 1995–96.

So far, we have discussed the liberalization process and the government's strategies to revive the sector. In this wider current context, we will now analyse from a gender perspective the cashew export chains, production and processing in Nampula province.

3 Cashew Nut Commodity Chains

Who does and gets what in Nampula Province?

The government no longer buys or sets the prices for raw cashew nuts. Prices are now based on the level of supply and demand in international markets. A few major exporters (eight or ten) control the trade in Mozambique and they tend to roughly fix the purchase price at the beginning of the year (Matule, cited in McMillan *et al.*, 2002: 15). In order to have price indications, a Cashew Committee (Comite do Caju) was established, in which various stakeholders such as Customs, INCAJU, private producers and association representatives of smallholders are represented. In fact, since India is the main buyer of Mozambican raw nuts, the price level is mediated by the situation of supply and demand (of Indian processors), which in turn is linked to international market prices for kernels (Matule, 2003). We will return to the international ends of the chain at the end of this chapter. However, it is important to note that smallholders are used to the government setting prices and that the indicative price, which some district administrations provide at the beginning of the marketing season, is often interpreted as a set minimum price.

In Nampula, at the time of the research, there were only two functioning medium-scale factories which bought raw nuts. Almost all the rest are exported to India through Nacala, the main port serving the northern provinces. A small number of large traders/exporters have an extensive network of small intermediaries who buy the raw cashew for them. This is bought directly from farmers in rural areas or from retail shopkeepers usually based in small urban centres, who buy from the farmers. Two such companies in Nampula with which we had contact and which export raw cashew are Joao Ferreira dos Santos (JFS) and Gani Comercial. Both have strong contacts in India and as Leite (1999: 5) points out, liberalization has involved the renewal and strengthening of old merchant networks between Mozambique and India. These large companies deal in many different commodities and also own cashew plantations.

The number of mobile (and unlicensed) traders has increased as a result of liberalization and they have motor vehicles to travel to areas of production. However, the situation is variable depending on several factors, including road access. In the two sites where we looked into marketing, key informants reported that there had been an increase in the number of itinerant traders in one of the sites, the Namige area, but this was not the case in the other, Itoculo, which is further from a main road.

At the local level, there is some flexibility and prices are also shaped by supply and demand. If farmers are able to store and wait to sell their raw nuts, prices are higher at the end of the season than at the beginning (the season runs from October to January in the north of Mozambique). Prices can double, for example 7,000 meticais (US$0.35) per kilo as against 3,500 meticais (US$0.17) per kilo.[4] An NGO, Assistance to Development for the People by the People (ADPP), working to support the cashew sector in Itoculo, advises farmers to hold on to their nuts in order to obtain a better price. However, when cash is desperately needed and/or the harvest of other crops is low, farmers will sell early or consume them instead. The quality of the nut is also assessed by the buyer and is increasingly judged to be an important factor on the international market. Larger, well-dried nuts command a better price.

Prices are also influenced by the turn-around period required by Indian importers. When containers for a ship in Nacala port needs to be filled quickly, we were told that prices could go as high as 10,000 meticais (US$0.5) per kilo, which exporters had instructed their intermediaries to pay.

At least one local buyer, who owns a local processing factory, stops acquiring nuts until the ship is filled and prices fall again, but the farmers who can market their nuts at this time do much better than others. Prices therefore vary greatly depending on the quality of the nuts, the location of sale, the number of intermediaries, proximity to ports and the time of the sale in relation to the marketing season.

In this study we found that women are actively involved in the marketing of raw cashew nuts. Our findings contradict those of some previous studies in Nampula (including CASCA, 2002:19), that most income-generating activities, including the marketing of cashew nuts, is dominated by men. For example, 87 per cent of our sample households in Namige did sell raw nuts (39 out of 45). Seventy-four per cent of women (in the sub-sample of households which sell nuts) are directly involved in marketing the nuts. However, the study also shows that cashew remains an important crop for household consumption and as such contributes to household nutrition and food security. Ninety-three per cent of the women interviewed said that they processed nuts themselves (at home) for consumption, with only one woman reporting that her husband did this work. Sixty-four per cent of the women process the fruit in some way, making juice and alcohol which may be consumed, sold or given as gifts or payment in kind, for example, for help in their fields. Women are therefore highly involved in both the processing of fruit and nuts at the household level and in the marketing of raw nuts. Although production for the market is important, due importance should be given to the production of cashew for consumption and for sale in local, as opposed to international, markets. The use of cashew at the local level has a role in household food security, provides income and strengthens social relations (in today's terms, it builds social capital). A typical cashew chain in Nampula is summarized in Figure 1.

The chain illustrates the vertical links between different actors in the chain. Although women smallholder producers do market cashew, the higher and more lucrative ends of the private sector chains in Nampula do not directly involve women.

Initial research on the international trade in cashew kernels suggests that considerable value is captured at the northern end of the chain and that the market is buyer driven (Eapen *et al.*, 2004). Cashew imports into the UK, for example, are dominated by a small number of big buyers, with a series of economic and non-economic barriers to entry. Large profits are concentrated in the final stages of processing at the northern end, that is, roasting and salting the shelled nuts, and by retailers, particularly the large supermarkets who do their own packing and sell to the final consumers. For these reasons, Mozambique should also pay attention to potential domestic and regional

Figure 1: Typical Cashew Export Chains in Nampula Province

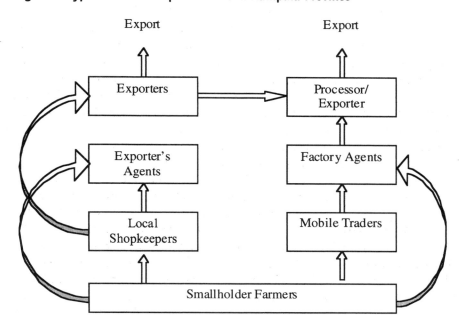

markets for cashew nuts), as well as to the quest to capture a share of the international market. Local markets can also make a valuable contribution to livelihoods, particularly of women producers, and the consumption of nuts at household level is also important. Much depends on the location of production and processing in relation to existing markets. In the north of the country, exports through Nacala are likely to dominate for some time, particularly for producers who are close to the main roads. Cashew produced in the southern provinces may find an important outlet in markets such as that of South Africa, which does not produce cashew, provided cashew processing in Mozambique can be increased.

The next sections will focus on women smallholder producers and workers (men and women) in the processing sub-sector, and discuss the gender and institutional issues which affect production and processing,

Smallholder producers

All land in Mozambique belongs to the state. Citizens are legally permitted to use the land they occupy under customary tenure systems. Communities in large areas of northern Mozambique, including Nampula province, follow a tradition of matrilineal succession and inheritance (Braga, 2001; Waterhouse and Vijfhuizen, 2001). While land tenure patterns are diverse and the relationship between land and tree tenure is complex, our study found that women have considerable security of tenure in relation to both land and trees.

Previous studies have tended to interview men and have asserted that most land and trees are owned by men. The World Bank financed a gender study in the cashew sector in Mozambique between 1996–98 (Ministry of Agriculture/World Bank, 1998; Hirvonen, 1998). The study generated a wealth of data on numbers of trees, local processing and commercialization, but the information was only gathered from 'heads of households', predominantly males. The concept of headship and its use in surveys is contested by feminist researchers. The designation of men as 'heads' fails to recognize the many spaces in households where women participate in and have control over resources and resource use; it ignores the complementarities that may characterize the division of labour in households with couples, and it marginalizes the majority of women by referring to women in so-called 'female-headed households' at the expense of other women (Pitcher, 1998). As Vijfhuizen (2002:97) puts it, '... women and men are heads of specific domains from which they derive their gender identity and authority and are able to wield power' and it makes more sense to speak of multiple headship, which often goes beyond husband and wife, to include sisters, brothers and other members of extended families. In the World Bank study, of the 1,400 households in the sample, 77 per cent was considered to be headed by a male and 23 per cent by a female. The study found an average of 68 trees per household and allocated them to 'heads'. Hence, in 77 per cent of the households, the women (as wives) were not interviewed about their role in the cashew sector, let alone daughters and sisters who may also have had cashew trees.

A study carried out in the Namige area (CASCA, 2002:8) states that most of the trees (an average of 80 per family) are owned by men (60 per cent), while the other 40 per cent are divided among women (10 per cent), the family as a whole (15 per cent) and grandparents (15 per cent). Once again, men were interviewed and women's views were not represented. We carried out our study of women producers in the same area, Namige, and found that most women inherit land which they cultivate. This practice of land allocation to women provides them with considerable security of tenure, although this is stronger when a marriage is uxorilocal (the husband moves to his wife's place), rather than virilocal (the wife moves to her husband's place). Hence the patterns regarding the planting of trees also vary. The answer to the question of who 'owns' the trees goes back to who planted them, usually grandparents; the present 'owners' are the ones who inherited them. 'Ownership', particularly in an African setting is enormously complex and it is preferable to refer to tenure. Lastarria-Cornhiel (1997:2) defines land tenure as the social relations established around land that determine who can use what land and how. Similarly, social relations influence who can use which trees, who takes care of them and who decides about their produce. We found that women in Nampula tend to have use rights to cashew trees, both where they are born and where they are married, if this is different (though in the latter case of virilocal marriage, we did find cases in which women did not have use rights). We also found that there is no distinct gender division of labour in cashew, apart from pruning, which in most cases is only done by men. In activities such as weeding, clearing, planting and sowing, both women and men participate, albeit in different proportions.

As has been mentioned, value is added to the cashew apple as well as to the nuts. Women tend to decide how much of the harvested cashew nuts and other cashew products should be allocated to consumption. Both women and men are involved in marketing the nuts. However, in discussions with farmers (both women and men) about the value of cashew in their livelihoods, it became clear how little the trees were producing compared to the past and how much more they felt they could pay for in the past with cash from selling cashew nuts and alcohol – school fees, hospital visits, clothes and agricultural inputs were all paid for by the sale of cashew.

Despite efforts by INCAJU to promote production, our study found that very little information on the *causes* of low production have been disseminated to smallholder farmers, both women and men. The various strategies and interventions, from preventing bush fires to effective pruning, chemical treatment and replanting have not been adequately discussed with farmers, nor have their views and constraints been solicited. So far attempts to promote fungicide spraying on smallholder farmer trees, sometimes through farmers' associations, have not been effective. The intervention is technically complex and small farmers have often been unable to pay the required contributions to the costs of spraying, although spraying has been more successful with the few larger producers. New improved strains of cashew have not been bought from the nurseries. Farmers are reluctant to travel long distances and to use their limited cash for buying strains that have not been *shown* to be beneficial in their context.

INCAJU, with limited staff and resources, has been trying to learn from experience. Thus, spraying programmes in Nampula have now begun to work with private operators with their own groups of farmers who are able to pay for this service. However, as some NGOs have argued, it is difficult for poorer and smaller farmers to implement a regular fungicide spraying programme. Alternative low-input cultivation improvements again rely on good information and extension, which is lacking, although NGOs could at least provide support to promote pruning, weeding at the base of the tree (which also creates a fire break) and the identification of superior trees for grafting of new shoot material to young seedlings. These methods would also avoid the use of chemicals which are potentially hazardous, particularly if they are not used correctly.

Women farmers are even less likely then men to have access to information and inputs. They are less likely to belong to farmer associations, which are male-dominated, or to attend village meetings. Spraying contracts through associations are signed by men and the operators of the spraying machines are always men. Extension workers are usually male and tend to contact and pass on information to men. Despite the fact that women are important actors in cashew production, interventions to promote production have so far largely excluded women. If women are to really benefit from cashew income, and if they are to contribute effectively to the revival of the sector, then organizations have to actively recognize them as primary actors in cashew production.

Cashew processing workers

Our study in Nampula province included interviews with women and men who used to work in large factories in the coastal town of Angoche, which are now closed, as well as interviews with workers in the two functioning factories, Cageba and Namige. This section discusses working conditions for women and men in the old and new factories.

Angoche

In Angoche, cashew processing in three large factories was a major source of employment. Former workers from two of these factories were included in our study, namely Angocaju and the Companhia do Caju de Nacala (CCN), Angoche division, with a sample of 25 women and 25 men from each plant. Both factories were privatized in the first half of the 1990s and were closed by 1999.

In Angocaju, for which we have full data, privatization increased the percentage of male workers. In both factories, men secured more jobs than women, not only by doing the shelling (100 per cent men), but also by entering into all the other areas of work in the factory. Although women remained dominant in the peeling and selection sections, 14 per cent of the workers in these sections were men, doing work that was stereotypically seen as women's work, requiring patience and dexterity. Women and men sometimes worked on different tasks but women worked more hours than men in the Angoche factories, yet received the same wages.

In our sample of 50 women, 38 per cent were widows or divorced women and had families larger than the average five members. Paid work was critical for them. Some married women also pointed out how factory income was a valuable source of independence from their husbands. Women have been particularly affected by the loss of jobs because they have fewer sources of income and are less mobile.

Cageba

The factory in Geba was established in 1995 by Joao Ferreiro dos Santos (JFS), a large company which is involved in other commodities. It is located in the district of Memba which is close to the port of Nacala. The factory was set up in buildings that were previously used for cotton and sisal processing by the same company. It uses steam heating and pedal-operated cutting technology, using equipment that was purchased in India. It is important to note that this company has the purchasing power to stock large quantities of nuts and the factory has a capacity of 2,000 tons a year. The company subcontracts traders to buy raw nuts. It employs large 'brigadas de comercializacao', groups of people who are contracted to buy nuts between November and January, when farmers harvest them. Nuts which are processed in Cageba are exported by JFS, almost all to the United States.

In 2002 there was a total of 642 workers (538 men and 104 women, 84 and 16 per cent, respectively). Men work in all the sections, shelling (100 per cent), peeling (more men than women) and they are also involved in selection. Women do not work in shelling. Peeling, often perceived to be 'women's work', is being done mainly by men. This illustrates clearly that when paid employment is scarce and there is huge competition over jobs, men will readily move into areas that were dominated by women. Factory owners do not show any resistance to this and furthermore, women are not encouraged to learn to use the cutting machines, which are used to shell raw cashew. Both women (98 or 41 per cent) and men (140 or 59 per cent) work in the peeling section and both women and men (about two-thirds of the workers) are very young. Hence both women and men seem to be perceived as having 'nimble fingers' in youth.

Sixty workers were interviewed in this factory (30 women and 30 men). Many workers expressed enormous fear of the 'chefes' (heads) and there seemed to considerable lack of information about rights and obligations on both sides, which caused great insecurity for the workers and arbitrary decisions by those who were heads of sections or in other management positions. Access to healthcare also seemed arbitrary, since it appeared to depend on the type of relationship the worker had with his or her superiors. From the point of view of the workers, the union was more of a tool of the employers to control the workers, rather than an organization which would defend their interests. There is no crèche.

This factory, viewed as particularly efficient and competitive (Abt, 1999) is not viewed positively by the workers, and provides far fewer job opportunities for women than for men.

Namige

The factory in Namige opened in April 2002. It was set up by a private entrepreneur with a one-year low-interest (18 per cent) bank loan, guaranteed by the government cashew institute, INCAJU.[5] The factory was designed with the help of TechnoServe, a US NGO which aims to promote entrepreneurial women and men in poor rural areas. It uses the steaming method (see Box 2) and semi-mechanical cutting machines, but a key difference from the Geba factory is that all the equipment, including the ovens, was manufactured locally. The owner reconstructed a ruined building and the factory has a maximum capacity of 1,000 tons of raw cashew per year. In 2002, the factory began by processing 120 tons. The owner of the factory has two cashew plantations in the area with a total production volume of approximately 50 tons per year (CASCA, 2002:16). The kernels produced are graded and vacuum packed for export. The Dutch NGO, SNV, has assisted the owner to contact a Dutch buyer who operates from Rotterdam and exports to various parts of the world.

At the time of this study, the factory employed 92 workers (56 men and 36 women, 61 and 39 per cent, respectively). When the factory opened, about 1,000 people turned up to apply for jobs, illustrating the need for cash income in the area. Male workers in the factory are mainly married, whereas almost half the women workers (47 per cent) are divorced and/or widowed. This percentage is high because it was used as a selection criterion, based on the view of the management that 'female heads' are most in need of cash and are therefore more likely to work hard. Again, the women workers in the factory look after larger families than the men.

Workers receive a free meal at work and according to their contracts they have access to health assistance, paid annual holidays and severance pay in case of illness caused by the job or work accidents. There are plans to set up a trade union and a crèche is also under construction – that is, a clean, sheltered area where mothers can arrange for someone to look after their babies, but with no provision of food and trained child carers as in the old government-owned factories.

Men are found in all the leadership roles in the factory. Only men (43) work in shelling. Peeling and selecting is mainly done by women (peeling 32, selecting 4), but men have also managed to get work in these sections – there are six men in the peeling section and one man in the selection process. The owner of the factory says that the door of the shelling section is open to women, but that they prefer to work separately. One thing is clear: the men started work a few days before the women did and were trained to use the machines. According to one manager, before the factory opened he called a few women to try and use the machines, 'but the women said they could not handle the machine'. However, when the authors tried to use the machines, it was obvious that while it is a skill that may require some time to acquire, no issue of strength is involved. Women are often excluded when it comes to the use of machines, but this case is complicated by the fact that shelling involves contact with CNSL, which burns the workers' hands. What were the reactions of women themselves to their exclusion from shelling? Some explained they do not want to burn their hands, adding that it would affect their farming work, but other women said they want the jobs in the shelling section because 'it is also work through which money can be earned'. Interestingly, there are now plans to import castor oil to protect workers' hands since this is more effective than coconut oil, which is currently used (Pal, 2003).

Both women and men work long hours, but more women worked the longest hours per day. At the time of this study, in our sample of 34 workers (17 men and 17 women), ten women worked more than ten hours a day as compared to five men. Women tended to earn less than their male counterparts, that is, more women than men reported earning the lowest wages: four women and only one man earned between 100,000–300,000 meticais (US$5–15); only men earned the highest wages – six men earned 600,000–700,000 meticais (US$30–35). Wages are not fixed, but are paid on a piece-rate basis. Piece rates are worked out using the minimum monthly wage for industrial work and then dividing this by expected kilogram outputs. The outputs set at the time of the study were 35kg per day for shellers, 12.5kg per day for peelers and 60kg per day for those who work on selection (Pal, 2003). These benchmarks were set using the productivity levels of workers in another factory in Mozambique, Cageba, but set at lower targets for new workers. At the higher end, part of the difference between women and men is explained by two men in supervisory posts. The fact that more women than men earned the lowest wages may be based on productivity (as some factory managers argued) but may also be because women took more days off work because of illness or domestic responsibilities.

There is currently no minimum wage for workers in rural industries. The industrial wage, which tends to relate to urban areas, was about 800,000 meticais (US$40) per month at the time of the study (2002), so in fact none of the workers in the sample earned this minimum. The rural agricultural minimum wage was about 560,000 meticais (US$28) per month, but many workers did not earn this amount either. One of the recommendations of this study is the setting of a minimum wage for rural industries such as cashew processing units.

4 A New Intervention: Decentralized 'Satellite' Processing

Within the national strategy to promote the cashew sector, SNV, with support
from TechnoServe, has developed the CASCA programme (Support Programme
for the Cashew Sector). The programme involves ADPP-Mozambique and the
Mozambican Association for Rural Development (AMODER). It entails support for cashew production and small-scale cashew processing. It has a training component for production and processing which will be implemented by
ADPP. A micro-finance component for processing will be implemented by
AMODER. SNV will provide advisory and facilitation services. Namige has
been chosen as the first intervention zone because of the new factory we have
just discussed: the CASCA programme intends to develop small-scale processing units (so-called satellites) around that factory; the owner is willing to buy
produce from the small units.

It is planned to establish 12 units over the period 2002–2005, each with
the capacity to process 24 tons of raw cashew. A Brazilian expert has helped
develop the selected model for the processing units (Medeiros, 2002). The
units will buy the raw cashew, steam, crack, dry and peel it, and pack it for
transport to the factory. In the factory, the nuts will be sorted, graded and
packed for export. The owner of the factory is responsible for finding the
buyers, although in the case of Namige, he already has a good relationship
with a Dutch buyer who can absorb high volumes of processed nuts for
export to various parts of the world.

To minimize risks of management failure and to test technical and economic viability, the first three units in the first year will be run by individuals
who have an entrepreneurial background and experience in buying and marketing cashew. The idea is that if the units show viability, they can be owned
by less experienced individuals or run by interest groups, associations or
family groups.

During our second round of interviews in September 2002, we learned
that three individuals had been chosen for the first three experimental units,
one being a woman. The latest information we have (Pal, August 2003) is
that all three units have started operating, two of them owned by men and
one by a woman. The owners have received support from TechnoServe with
the machinery and its installation. AMODER has provided loans for initial
working capital at 2 per cent interest payable over one year. ADPP is providing training and the units each employ 12 people. However, so far only men
have been employed to work the cutting machines. One view is that it will
only be possible to recruit women when there is better protection from CNSL
through the import of castor oil (Pal, 2003).

The Namige factory provides an interesting example of a 'partnership' approach between government, NGOs, communities and the private sector, with potential to increase the quantity of nuts which are processed as well as the employment generated for local people. In these cases, the chain becomes much shorter (Figure 2), minimizing the number of intermediaries between producer and exporter and adding value locally. This is a positive initiative, which should provide greater benefits to rural communities than the more typical chains (Figure 1). However, it remains to be seen whether the satellite units will benefit women directly through employment. It also remains to be seen if the satellite units are economically viable. At present, the owner of the Namige factory and TechnoServe have some reservations about the financial viability and sustainability of the satellite units, because quality and productivity has been low (the appearance of the nuts and the proportion of 'whole' nuts produced), costs are high and prices of kernels on the international market have remained low (Pal, 2003).

Figure 2: Namige Factory and Satellite Processing Export Chain

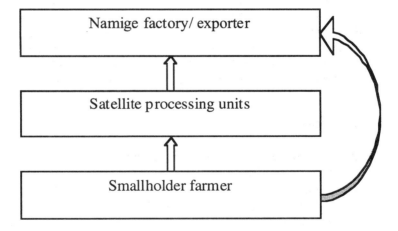

Efforts to shorten the marketing chain at the provincial level may be important in providing greater returns to smallholder producers and processing workers. However, the constraints posed by extremely powerful northern actors in the chain should be recognized.

5 Lessons Learned

Main findings

Rural livelihoods in countries like Mozambique are becoming ever more dependent on a variety of sources: small-scale farming, agricultural labouring,

Peeled cashews. PICTURE: LUIS ARTUR

petty trading and service provision, migration and remittances (Bryceson, 2002; Francis, 2000). Diversification into several income sources is seen as a major strategy to decrease vulnerability, because it allows households to spread the risks they face. Weak and poorly developed local markets can represent one further source of uncertainty rather than an additional means for managing risk (Whitehead and Kabeer, 2001) and this is certainly the case in most parts of Mozambique. We found that access to raw cashew markets was very variable and that prices were largely controlled by a few large traders.

Although the government has made efforts to promote cashew production, our study found that the various interventions, from preventing bush fires to effective pruning, chemical treatment and replanting, have had limited success. The strategies have not been adequately discussed with farmers, and their views and concerns have not been solicited. Women in Nampula's predominantly matrilineal culture have considerable access to and control over land and trees, but they have had even less access to information and inputs.

The closure of three cashew processing factories in Angoche in Nampula province resulted in the loss of critical sources of regular income for both women and men. Almost no ex-workers have found other employment. Women have been particularly affected by the job losses because they have fewer sources of income and are less mobile than men. There is enormous competition over jobs in the two new, smaller and semi-mechanized factories that we studied in other parts of the province. The wages and working conditions in the liberalized environment have deteriorated in relation to the earlier government-run factories and CNSL is much more of a problem with semi-mechanized technologies than it was with mechanized impact shelling, although initiatives are underway to ameliorate the situation through better protective oil for workers' hands. Men have entered into sections of the factory, such as peeling, which were previously seen as the domain of women, while women do not work in the sections which use semi-mechanical shelling machines.

Our study shows that although women are key actors in the cashew sector, interventions to promote production have usually excluded women, and they have lost jobs to men in the processing sector. A gendered approach is important not only from an equal rights perspective, but also in order to improve the effectiveness of interventions, since women have considerable knowledge of cashew production and processing. A gender perspective is also important in reducing income poverty more effectively, since women tend to be over-represented in poor groups, and because women have greater domestic responsibilities than men and tend to direct their earnings towards improving household welfare.

In Mozambique, post-independence state policies were not particularly favourable to smallholder farmers and neither was liberalization, in the way that it was initially pursued. Social and institutional factors, in Mozambique's historical context, have been critically important. As Pijnenburg and Nhantumbo (2002:199) put it: 'Decades of (often brutal) colonial rule, top-down socialist policies, civil strife and now political strife do affect trust and confidence within communities and between them and external agencies'. This history takes time and political will to address.

A wide range of studies have already shown the ways in which liberalization, and particularly agricultural liberalization in sub-Saharan Africa, tends to benefit those with greater power, information, access to land, financial assets and markets (Whitehead, 2001; Grown *et al.*, 2000; Oxfam, 2000; Mehra and Gammaye, 1999; United Nations, 1999; Kanji, 1995; Afshar and Dennis, 1992). Liberalization tends to widen the gaps between socio-economic groups and between women and men, unless disadvantaged groups become organized to defend their interests and/or specific policies and interventions are put in place. Some of this research has also pointed to an intensification of women's work as the state withdraws from the provision of basic services, and health and education fees rise. Women, in particular, struggle to balance a multitude of activities: domestic work, childcare, caring for the sick, farming and income-generating activities.

At the macro-level, competition between countries in the South for shares of the international cashew market has increased. Some Indian states are working hard to increase production to meet their huge in-country processing capacity needs, which would reduce their imports of raw nuts from Mozambique. The market in kernels also faces competition from new entrants, such as Vietnam, where the government protects the sector and is now investing heavily in research and development. All this makes it even more difficult to maintain decent returns for smallholder producers in Mozambique and to ensure decent wages and working conditions for cashew processing workers, both women and men.

Recommendations for the future

The comprehensive strategy which the government has recently put in place recognizes that much more needs to be done if Mozambique is to revive the cashew sector. Agricultural extension, credit, roads for market access, prices and local processing are all important factors which can stimulate the small-holder sector. However, the political will to really implement this strategy, the *way* in which programmes are implemented and the *ideas and values* of those with considerable power will influence how different groups in rural areas, particularly women, respond to new opportunities.

In the predominantly matrilineal setting of northern Mozambique, women have considerable control over land and trees and there is no doubt that women are important actors in cashew production. Without recognition of these facts, the effectiveness of interventions will inevitably be undermined. Communication between researchers, extension workers and small-scale producers, particularly women, has to be improved. It is essential that interventions such as the CASCA programme, which provides training for cashew production and processing through the 'satellites', take a gender-aware approach.

A more differentiated approach is needed to implement the government cashew strategy effectively. In terms of cashew production, policy needs to distinguish between the few larger-scale producers and the vast majority of small-scale producers. A production strategy which is centred on the use of fungicides and pesticides, which are difficult to apply correctly and relatively costly, may be inappropriate for the majority of producers. Good agricultural extension services (currently lacking), which emphasize what can be done without significant outlays of cash (or free provision of inputs) are critical if smaller, poorer farmers are to benefit. There are limitations to the proposed 'privatized' solutions to such problems, which may favour large producers. For example, a new strategy in the liberalized context is to devolve extension work to private companies and NGOs which are interested in cashew production, but it is questionable whether they will opt for time- and communication-intensive paths to increasing production for small farmers. The role of the government in funding and regulating extension services is therefore essential. Improved marketing is another key priority. Ironically, much of Mozambican cashew production is organic and could benefit from growing niche markets for organic products at a global level. However, the institutional capacity to organize such marketing and 'branding' is lacking and the transaction costs of acquiring certification are high.

Turning now to processing, as we have discussed, minimum wage levels for rural industries in Mozambique have not been set. Workers and unions are currently in a weak position, and the government should be an important arbitrator in defending the rights of workers to decent wages and living conditions and the right to negotiate with employers for reasonable wages in a competitive liberalized environment. Women are losing much-needed income-earning opportunities to men in the processing sector. This trend can only be reversed if policies are put in place to encourage women to work in any section of factories and other processing units. The social construction of what constitutes 'appropriate work' for women is very clear in cashew processing; in India, women comprise 95 per cent of the entire processing sector, using the very same machines as those used in Mozambique. However, in that context, too, men hold the leadership positions and the wages in this sector are even lower than in other 'traditional' processing sectors such as coir (prepared fibre from the husks of coconuts).

The promotion of local grassroots organizations can bring women together as producers and workers to defend their interests, and to begin to participate actively in other parts of the cashew chain, although this is usually a slow process. Producer associations are increasing in Nampula province and a key challenge is to enable women to be well represented or to form their own organizations to promote their access to market-based livelihoods.

It remains to be seen whether Mozambique can increase its share of the international market in both raw nuts and cashew kernels. It is essential that in-country processing is supported in Mozambique, both for the economy as a whole and because it provides an important source of employment. The volatility of the international market and the difficulties in gaining access to kernel markets mean that strengthening local and regional markets may have an important role to play in enhancing livelihoods.

Notes

1   Sherilyn Young provides a historical overview of the way in which contextual and policy shifts in Mozambique relate to the cashew sector (see Kanji *et al.*, 2002).

2   The research included interviews in four sites in Nampula province: Namige (Mogincual district) to examine production and marketing by smallholder women farmers, the functioning of a new, small scale semi-mechanized factory and its workers' livelihoods; Itoculo (Monapo district) to assess government and NGO interventions to increase production, improve marketing and provide training and extension; Geba (Memba district) focuses on the functioning of a medium-scale factory, wages, working conditions and livelihoods; and finally Angoche (Angoche district) to follow-up ex-workers from two closed factories and examine the changes in their livelihood strategies. The authors would like to thank all those numerous individuals and organizations who made the research possible, the farmers and workers who gave us their time, our research assistants and the Irish and Netherlands Embassies in Maputo for funding the research. Finally, thanks to Joe Hanlon for useful comments on an earlier draft of this chapter.

3   However, this does not mean that the US and EU have 'freed' their markets and there are still huge subsidies to farmers and selected industries in the North.

4   US$1 was equivalent to approximately 20,000 meticais at the time of the research. The exchange rate in May 2003 was 24,100 meticais to US$1.

5   Since this study, three more factories have opened in Nampula province: the owner of the factory in Namige has opened a second factory in Angoche and other entrepreneurs have opened factories in Namialo and Murrupula. Incaju and TechnoServe have provided support for these ventures. The physical conditions of the Namige factory have been improved and workers now have overalls (Pal, August 2003).

References

Abt (1999). *Assessment of the Status of Competitiveness and Employment in the Cashew Processing Industry in Mozambique*, Abt Associates Inc., prepared for the National Directorate of Industry, Ministry of Industry and Tourism, Republic of Mozambique.

Afshar, H. and Dennis, C. (eds) (1992). *Women and Adjustment Policies in the Third World*, Macmillan, Basingstoke.

Braga, C. (2001). '"They're Squeezing Us": Matrilineal kinship, power and agricultural policies: case study of Issa Malanga, Niassa Province', in R. Waterhouse and C. Vijfhuizen (eds), *Strategic Women, Gainful Men: Gender, Land and Natural Resources in different rural contexts in Mozambique*, UEM/Action Aid, Mozambique.

Bryceson, D. F. (2002). 'The Scramble in Africa: Reorienting Rural Livelihoods', *World Development* 30:5:725–739.

CASCA (2002). *Programme Proposal. Support to the cashew sector in Nampula Province, Mozambique*, ADPP, AMODER and SNV, July 2002.

Cramer, C. (1999). 'Can Africa industrialize by processing primary commodities? The case of the Mozambican cashew nuts', *World Development* 27: 7: 1247–66.

Deloitte & Touche ILA (Africa) (1997). *Cashew Marketing Liberalization Impact Study Mozambique*, Deloitte & Touche ILA, October, final report, Maputo, Mozambique.

Eapen, M., Jeyaranjan, J., Harilal, K. N., Swaminathan, P. and Kanji, N. (2004). 'Revisiting the Cashew Industry in India. Liberalisation, Gender and Livelihoods: the Cashew Nut Case', IIED Working Paper 3, International Institute for Environment and Development, London

Francis, E. (2000). *Making a Living: Changing Livelihoods in Rural Africa*, DESTIN, LSE, London; Routledge.

Grown, C., Elson, D. and Cagatay, N. (2000). 'Introduction to Special Issue on Gender, Macroeconomics, Trade and Finance', *World Development* 28:7, pp. 1145–56.

Hanlon, J. (1996). *Beggar Your Neighbours – Apartheid Power in Southern Africa*, James Curry, London.

Hanlon, J. (2000). 'Power without responsibility: the World Bank and Mozambican cashew nuts', *Review of African Political Economy* 83.

Hilton, B.R. (1998). 'Our Experience with Cashew', *Echo Development Notes* 62: 4–5.

Hirvonen, S. (1998). *Inquérito sobre caju ao sector familiar, Sintese dos rel, Matórios das entrevistas colectivas.* Ministerio da Agricultura e Pescas, Departmento de Estatística, Maputo, Mozambique.

INCAJU (1998). *Componente produção, Plano director do caju*, Instituto de fomento do caju, Ministério da agricultura e desenvolvimento rural, Maputo, Mozambique.

INCAJU (2001). *Componente comercialização e industrialicação (parte 1, texto)*, Ministério da agricultura e desenvolvimento rural, Maputo, Mozambique.

INCAJU (2002). *Boletim e estatisticas da campanha 2000/2001*, Maputo, Mozambique, March.

Kanji, N. (1995). 'Gender, Poverty and Economic Adjustment in Harare, Zimbabwe', *Environment and Urbanization* 7:1.

Kanji, N., Vijfhuizen, C. and Young, S. (2002). 'Cashing in on cashews. Policies, production and gender in Mozambique', paper presented at the 8th International Interdisciplinary Congress on Women, 21–26 July 2002, Kampala, Uganda.

Kanji, N. and Barrientos, S. (2002). 'Trade Liberalisation, Poverty and Livelihoods: Understanding the Linkages', IIED/IDS (International Institute for Environment and Development/Institute of Development Studies), Working Paper 159, July, IDS, University of Sussex, Brighton, UK.

Lastarria-Cornhiel, S. (1997). 'Impact of privatization on gender and property rights in Africa', *World Development* 25(8): 1317–33.

Leite, J.P. (1999). 'A Guerra do Caju e as Relacoes Mocambique-India na epoca pos-colonial', mimeo, Universidade Tecnica de Lisboa, Portugal.

Matule, R. (2003). Deputy Director, INCAJU, personal communication, February.

McMillan, M., Rodrik, D. and Welch, H. W. (2002). 'When Economic Reform Goes Wrong: Cashews in Mozambique', Faculty Research Working Paper Series, Harvard University, US.

Medeiros, de J. I. (2002). *Processamento descentralizado de castanha de caju. Nampula, Moçambique,* Programa CASCA, SNV Organizacao Holandesa de desenvolvimento.

Mehra, R. and Gammaye, S. (1999). 'Trends, Countertrends and Gaps in Women's Employment', *World Development* 27:3, Special Section: Women Workers in a Globalizing World.

Ministry of Agriculture Mozambique and World Bank (1998). *Cashew production and marketing among smallholders in Mozambique: a gender differentiated analysis based on household survey data,* preliminary report of the gender/cashew pilot study, Discussion Paper 1, Maputo, Mozambique.

Mole, P. N. (2000). 'An Economic Analysis of Smallholder Cashew Development Opportunities and Linkages to Food Security in Mozambique's Northern Province of Nampula', PhD thesis, Michigan State University, Ministry of Agriculture and Rural Development, Directorate of Economics, Mozambique.

Oxfam (2000). *Agricultural Trade and the Livelihoods of Small Farmers,* 1–11, Oxfam, Oxford.

Pal, S. (2003). Personal communication, August.

Penvenne J. (1997). 'Seeking the factory for women: Mozambican urbanization in the later colonial era', *Journal of Urban History* 23:3.

Pitcher, M. A (1998). 'Disruption without transformation: Agrarian Relations and Livelihoods in Nampula Province, Mozambique 1975–1995', *Journal of Southern African Studies* 24:1, March.

Pijnenburg, B. and Nhantumbo, I. (2002). 'Participatory Development Interventions in Mozambique', *Development in Practice* 12:2, May.

United Nations (1999). *World Survey on the Role of Women in Development: Gobalization, Gender and Work,* United Nations DESA, New York.

UNDP (2001). *Gender, Women and Human Development: An agenda for the future,* United Nations Development Programme, Maputo, Mozambique.

Vijfhuizen, C. (2002). *The People You Live With: Gender Identities and Social Practices, Beliefs and Power in the livelihoods of Ndau women and men in a village with an irrigation scheme in Zimbabwe,* Weaver Press, Harare, Zimbabwe.

Wandschneider T. S. and Garrido-Mirapeix, G. (1999). 'Cash Cropping in Mozambique: evolution and prospects', Technical Paper No. 2, Food Security Unit Mozambique, European Commission, Brussels.

Waterhouse, R. and Vijfhuizen, C. (eds) (2001). *Strategic Women, Gainful Men: Gender, Land and Natural Resources in different rural contexts in Mozambique,* UEM/Action Aid, Mozambique.

Whitehead, A. (2001). 'Trade, Trade Liberalisation, and Rural Poverty in Low-Income Africa: A Gendered Account', Background Paper for the UNCTAD 2001 LDC Report.

Whitehead, A. and Kabeer, N. (2001). *Living with Uncertainty: gender, livelihoods and pro-poor growth in sub-Saharan Africa*, Institute of Development Studies Working Paper 134. November.

World Bank (2001). *Cashew production and marketing in the smallholder sector in Mozambique*, World Bank, Washington DC.

National Labour Legislation in an Informal Context: Women Workers in Export Horticulture in South Africa

Stephanie Barrientos, Andrienetta Kritzinger
and Hester Rossouw

1 Executive Summary

South Africa has undergone an important process of transformation and integration into global markets since the end of apartheid in 1994. This has involved social, economic and political change internally, as well as the expansion of its export industries. Deciduous and citrus fruits are now a prominent agricultural export from South Africa, taking a significant share of the global fruit market for the first few months of each year.

South African exports go mainly to Europe (especially the UK) where supermarkets increasingly dominate food retailing. The larger supermarkets do not use traditional wholesale markets to purchase fruit; instead they use tightly integrated networks of producers and agents who are linked into their global value chains. These value chains are governed by supermarket buyers, who directly affect all aspects of production and distribution. This not only includes strict technical and quality specifications, but also, increasingly, the introduction of social codes determining minimum employment standards that suppliers must adhere to. The better codes cover core International Labour Organization (ILO) conventions on freedom of association, discrimination, forced and child labour, as well as other issues such as wages and health and safety.[1]

As part of its social transformation policies, the South African government has introduced a raft of legislation since the end of apartheid. This includes labour legislation aimed at enhancing the rights of agricultural

Opposite: *Women grape-pickers in the Cape, South Africa.*

workers, as well as addressing inequity based on gender and race. As part of its reintegration into the global community, the South African government has also ratified a number of important ILO Conventions. The combination of government regulation and supermarket codes of conduct represents a potential advance for women working in South Africa's horticultural export sector. They are now formally able to enjoy better conditions of employment and labour rights. These advances are an important part of South Africa's reintegration into the global community.

Women have long been employed on South African fruit farms. Traditionally, Coloured women workers lived on-farm and worked seasonally as required by the grower as a condition of their husbands' employment. Agricultural workers were not covered by government employment legislation. A system of paternalist employment relations prevailed in which the conditions of workers were at the behest of the grower. However, since the end of apartheid, employment relations in South African agriculture have undergone a process of transformation. The industry has been subject to a number of changes, including the rapid introduction of employment legislation and, more recently, social codes of conduct. Some of these changes have had negative and others positive effects on workers, creating both challenges and opportunities for women workers.

However, positive advances have been tempered by a restructuring of farm employment that has led to many workers (male and female) becoming unemployed or moved off-farm. Government legislation has contributed to increasing costs of labour and housing of farmworkers. In a competitive global economy, South African growers have faced volatile or falling real prices and have had to raise labour efficiency to survive. All these factors have contributed to the retrenchment of labour and an increasing use of off-farm labour. Those women workers remaining on-farm with their partners often experience an improvement in their security and conditions of employment. But many women are now employed as casual or contract seasonal workers living off-farm. These workers experience significant problems of low pay, insecure work and, depending on their family circumstances, can endure poverty. However, government legislation and supermarket codes of conduct have the potential to address the problems of casual and seasonal off-farm workers, if they are more effectively implemented.

This chapter examines the implications of the combined legislative and private sector codes that have been introduced for women working in South African export horticulture. The key question it will address is: in the context of labour market restructuring in the fruit export sector, what are the implications of different forms of labour protection through legislation and private sector social codes of conduct for women workers? The paper is divided into four sections. Section 2 examines female employment in fruit export production, exploring the effect of market, supermarket and government changes on employment. Section 3 looks at the changing policy environment which is facilitating improved protection for women workers, both through state legislation and through private sector codes. We will then consider their implications for women workers in the context of the gender hierarchy of work which still prevails in the South African fruit sector. An important issue is whether different forms of enforcement can reach more insecure seasonal and temporary employment, where women are often concentrated, and whether the combination of legislation and codes is able to ensure good employment practice for *all* workers, including women in insecure employment. The final section examines the implications and future prospects of these changes for the sector and beyond.

2 Creating a Favourable Policy Environment

The commodity context

South African exports of deciduous fruit come mainly from the Western and Northern Cape. They make up 20 per cent of the Western Cape's agricultural output and most of the country's deciduous fruit exports which are valued at close to R1 billion (US$1,612,903 million) a year (Greenberg, 2003). It is estimated that there are currently over 2,000 farms in the deciduous fruit sector. South Africa produces its fruit in a particular season from December to April each year; its main competitors in that period are Chile and New Zealand (with China beginning to enter the market as a major future exporter). With globalization, exports from all three countries have been increasing, especially from Chile, and there is increasing global competition. The repositioning of South Africa as an important fruit exporter post-apartheid came about partly as a result of the liberalization of the fruit industry in 1997, when the government-regulated single marketing channel for fruit exports was disbanded. This opened South African fruit producers up to the direct forces of global competition and international quality standards. The latter include employment standards for fruit workers; these, together with the effect of national labour regulation, are the focus of this chapter.

Europe is South Africa's main market, and especially the UK. Between 1998–2003 Europe took an annual average of 67 per cent of South Africa's total fruit exports, with 34 per cent of the total going to the UK (PPECB, 2004). Within the European Union, producers are protected from international competition through tariffs, even though imports contribute only a small proportion of total consumption in the EU. Bilateral trade agreements, such as the South African-European Union Trade Development and Cooperation Agreement (TDCA) do not really assist producers in market access and many products, including much deciduous fruit, have been excluded from the agreement (Greenberg, 2003 quoting Lee, 2002). All these pressures are leading South African producers to cut labour costs, and to raise productivity with a smaller, more efficient and more professional labour force.

An important external influence on employment is the changing nature of exports, which are increasingly channelled through global value chains dominated by large retailers rather than wholesale markets. This is particularly the case with South African fruit because of its exports to the UK. There, supermarkets are the main buyer, representing over 80 per cent of the retail market (with the big four accounting for 50 per cent). Supermarkets formally operate through the open market, but in reality have tightly integrated global value chains through which they source fruit. A global value chain 'describes the full range of activities that are required to bring a product from its conception, through its design, ... its marketing, its distribution and its support to the final consumer' (Kaplinsky, 1998:13). An overview of the value chain of South African fruit through to the UK is shown in Figure 1. Supermarkets have designated importers, exporters and growers with whom they pre-programme their orders on a week-by-week basis six months in advance. In coordination with these agents, supermarkets control detailed aspects of production (fruit variety and appearance), as well as its distribution through a highly sophisticated 'cool chain' into their final distribution centres (Barrientos and Kritzinger, 2003). Some supermarkets are increasingly outsourcing the management of their value chains to specific agents called 'category managers' who control all aspects of the chain for any particular category of products globally throughout the year.

Although supermarkets demand stringent quality and production conditions, payments are made on a consignment basis and prices are only agreed once fruit reaches the distribution centre. This allows supermarkets to take advantage of competitive global fruit prices, while controlling the flow of fruit through the value chain. Global competition has led to over-supply on the fruit markets, contributing to volatility, falling real prices and declining revenues for fruit growers. For example, the real net export realization in Rands per ton of apples fell from R2,130 (US$343.5) in 1993–94 to R935 (US$150.8) in 1998–99 and only climbed back to R1,352 (US$218) by 2001–2002, equivalent to 63 per cent of its value eight years previously (DFPT, 2003). This has allowed supermarkets to keep the prices they pay down. However, accessing supermarkets provides on average better prices for the best quality fruit, and gives growers a more stable market environment than the more volatile free market. Supermarket pressure for quality in production puts pressure on growers to develop a more productive and skilled workforce, but their payment of low market prices also puts growers under pressure to reduce labour costs by using more off-farm seasonal and contract workers (Barrientos and Kritzinger, 2004).

Figure 1: Overview of Global Value Chain and Employment – South African Deciduous Fruit

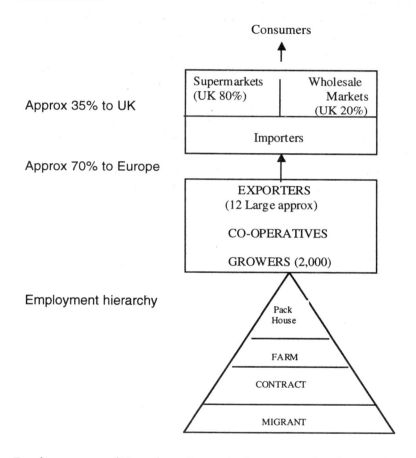

Employment conditions have increasingly come under the scrutiny of large supermarket buyers, especially in the UK. Many supermarkets have introduced codes of conduct that cover labour conditions within their value chains and require all suppliers to abide by relevant employment legislation, which in South Africa is now quite stringent. This has reinforced the need for producers supplying supermarkets which have labour codes to comply with legislation. The introduction of codes provides an international rationale for raising labour standards, which South Africa is well positioned to meet through its post-apartheid employment legislation. In the next section we will examine the changing forms of employment in the South African fruit sector, and following that we will examine the combination of changing state legislation and supermarket codes of conduct that now apply to fruit workers.

Traditional and changing patterns of employment

Traditionally, employment arrangements on South African fruit farms followed the historical pattern of Western Cape fruit and wine farming. This involved the employment by producers of relatively large numbers of workers who lived on the farm. Since the inception of the industry in the eighteenth and nineteenth centuries and due to historical developments, the farm labour force has been structured along race and gender lines. Women have been concentrated in seasonal and temporary jobs with men enjoying permanent employment status. Women not only earned less than men, but were excluded from employment benefits enjoyed by male permanent workers. Given that the worker family was the unit of employment, women had virtually no independent claim to either employment or on-farm housing. Women were employed as a condition of the employment of a male partner or relative, worked seasonally as and when required by the farmer and few had written contracts of employment. While this reinforced the subservient position of women in the farm hierarchy, women did have indirect access to some benefits through their male partner. Paternalist employment relations did provide a form of security for families living on farms (Kritzinger and Vorster, 1996).

Traditional paternalist relations have been disrupted and eroded by the extension of employment legislation to farmworkers (Hamman, 1996). This has led to the downsizing of the permanent labour force living on-farm, and to changing employment relations following the industry's reintegration into global markets in the 1990s. An important trigger for labour downsizing was the introduction of the Extension of Security of Tenure Act, which provided greater security for workers living on-farm to remain in their farm houses. As a consequence, many producers scaled down their on-farm labour force, resulting in the shedding of on-farm labour (Barrientos and Kritzinger, 2003). This has resulted in women and men workers who used to live on-farm losing many of the benefits and services that were provided by producers under more traditional paternalist arrangements.

An important influence on employment conditions and the strategies of producers has been the wide range of legislation affecting employment introduced by the government since 1993. South Africa has now ratified a number of ILO Conventions addressing workers' rights and has enacted these princi-

Women packing fruit.

ples in a comprehensive programme of employment legislation (see below). Growers have had to accept external regulation that previously did not exist. This is undermining traditional paternalist relations and establishing the independent rights of women and men farmworkers. Employment legislation has contributed to the increasing 'professionalisation' of the labour force and the improvement of working conditions, particularly for those remaining in permanent employment. But it has also contributed to the retrenchment of labour (especially a reduction in the number of permanent on-farm workers) and to the casualization of labour through increased use of seasonal and contract labour. The extent to which producers restructure and lay off workers depends in part on their own level of efficiency and on the competitive pressures they face. The market context provides an important influence on changing the employment trends within which South African fruit exporters operate (Barrientos and Kritzinger, 2003).

Involvement of national government

The extension of labour regulation has been reinforced by the introduction of codes of conduct covering employment by supermarkets. We will briefly examine the rationale for each of these separately and will then consider their content in more detail, and how they combine to provide new forms of labour protection for women workers in the deciduous fruit sector.

A wide raft of national legislation has been introduced in South Africa over the past decade. The main reason for this has been the transition to democracy, and the need to address many of the injustices, especially for black and Coloured workers, that existed during the apartheid era. An additional reason has been the need to improve South Africa's standing in the global community as a country with equitable laws and regulation. Much of the labour legislation that has been introduced is radical and comprehensive. The trend to regulate labour markets is very different to many other developing countries, where pressure under structural adjustment has often led to moves to deregulate labour markets. Regulation now applies to all sectors of the labour market, but it has had a large impact on agriculture which was previously exempted from most labour regulation that existed under apartheid. This has now changed. As we have seen, the expansion and extension of labour regulation to agriculture is one reason why farmers have moved labour off their farms, and developed more modern and professional labour practices.

Involvement of the private sector

Supermarket codes of conduct covering labour practices have come about for quite different reasons. The trend towards deregulation of labour markets and the mobility of global sourcing to countries with cheap labour have allowed poor employment practices in many developing countries. NGO and trade union campaigns have helped to highlight labour abuses by suppliers to some of the leading brand name and retail companies in the North. This has prompted them to introduce codes of conduct within their value chains in order to limit abuses and the damage to their reputation that these campaigns may cause. The codes set down minimum employment standards that a supplier should meet in order to maintain business with the global buyer or retailer. Company codes of conduct were initially drawn up by the companies alone, and varied in their content and forms of implementation. Some companies were accused of 'window dressing'. Continued pressures, and the recognition by some companies that improving employment conditions in their value chains can make good business sense, have led some companies to work with NGOs and trade unions in order to develop more comprehensive codes that are more widely accepted. One example of this is the UK Ethical Trade Initiative (ETI), a coalition of UK companies, trade unions and NGOs. It has a base code that incorporates core ILO conventions that must be applied by all member companies (ETI, 1998). All the main UK supermarkets are members of ETI, and apply its code to their fresh produce sectors. Given that UK supermarkets are a significant buyer of South African fruit, this has exposed farmworkers to the employment conditions set out in the ETI base code.[3]

ILO Conventions and national–international linkages

Although they formally arose through different means, there are important linkages between South African legislation and company codes of conduct. A factor which partly links national legislation and company codes are ILO Conventions covering employment. As a tripartite body, ILO Conventions are established through agreement by governments, employers and trade unions. The core ILO conventions set international labour standards that are now binding on all ILO member countries, whether or not they have ratified them.[2] But the ILO has also agreed Conventions covering a wide range of employment issues. South Africa has long been a member of the ILO, but has only signed up to the core ILO Conventions since the end of apartheid (see Table 1). The ILO itself has no formal powers of enforcement and it is up to member countries to implement Conventions they have ratified through national legislation. These conventions set important standards covering labour.

Table 1: Fundamental ILO Conventions

Number	Convention Title	Date Ratified by South Africa
C.87	Freedom of Association and Protection of the Right to Organize Convention	1996
C.98	Right to Organize and Collective Bargaining Convention	1996
C.29	Forced Labour Convention	1997
C.105	Abolition of Forced Labour Convention	1997
C.111	Discrimination (Employment and Occupation) Convention	1997
C.100	Equal Remuneration Convention	2000
C.138	Minimum Age Convention	2000
C182	Worst Forms of Child Labour Convention	2000

Private sector companies do not formally have any obligation to implement ILO Conventions through their codes of conduct covering suppliers. However, some companies do include core ILO Conventions in their codes, and they form a core part of multi-stakeholder initiatives on codes of conduct such as the ETI base code and the Social Accountability International Code, SA 8000. More companies are signing up to these codes, and ILO Conventions thus form one link between some company codes and national legislation. In addition, the ETI base code and SA 8000 (as well as some individual company codes) stipulate that legislation must be adhered to as part of the code, helping to reinforce national legislation.

Protection for workers: state and private

National legislation and company codes of conduct address a wide range of common employment issues. These are compared in Table 2 below, taking the ETI base code as the basis for a comprehensive company code of conduct (ETI, 1998) and comparing it with relevant South African legislation. Jointly these cover all core ILO Conventions, as well as a number of other employment issues as detailed in the table.

Table 2: Summary of Private and Public Provision for the Protection of Workers in South Africa

Private Sector Codes of Conduct (ETI Base Code)	State Regulation
Employment is Freely Chosen	
There is no forced, bonded or involuntary prison labour. Workers are not required to lodge 'deposits' or their identity papers with their employer and are free to leave their employer after reasonable notice.	Relevant Legislation: The Basic Conditions of Employment Act The Sectoral Determination The Extension of Tenure Security Act Constitution of the Republic of South Africa: all forced labour is prohibited.
Freedom of Association and Collective Bargaining	
Workers, without distinction, have the right to join or form trade unions of their own choosing and to bargain collectively. The employer adopts an open attitude towards the activities of trade unions and their organizational activities. Workers representatives are not discriminated against and have access to carry out their representative functions in the workplace. Where the right to freedom of association and collective bargaining is restricted under law, the employer facilitates, and does not hinder, the development of parallel means for independent and free association and bargaining.	Relevant Legislation: Labour Relations Act (No. 66 of 1995) The primary objectives of the Act are: • to give effect to and regulate the fundamental rights conferred by section 27 of the Constitution;[4] • to give effect to obligations incurred by the Republic as a member state of the International Labour Organization; • to provide a framework within which employees and their trade unions, employers and employers' organizations can collectively bargain to determine wages, terms and conditions of employment and other matters of mutual interest; and formulate industrial policy; and • to promote orderly collective bargaining; collective bargaining at sectoral level; employee participation in decision-making in the workplace; and the effective resolution of labour disputes.

Table 2 (continued)

Private Sector Codes of Conduct (ETI Base Code)	State Regulation

Working Conditions are Safe and Hygienic

A safe and hygienic working environment shall be provided, bearing in mind the prevailing knowledge of the industry and of any specific hazards. Adequate steps shall be taken to prevent accidents and injury to health arising out of, associated with, or occurring in the course of work, by minimizing, so far as is reasonably practicable, the causes of hazards inherent in the working environment.

Workers shall receive regular and recorded health and safety training, and such training shall be repeated for new or reassigned workers.

Access to clean toilet facilities and to potable water, and, if appropriate, sanitary facilities for food storage shall be provided. Accommodation, where provided, shall be clean, safe, and meet the basic needs of the workers.

The company observing the code shall assign responsibility for health and safety to a senior management representative.

Relevant Legislation:
Occupational Health and Safety Act
The Compensation for Occupational Injuries and Diseases Act

The purpose of the Compensation for Occupational Injuries and Diseases Act (No. 130 of 1993), as amended by the Compensation for Occupational Diseases Act 61 of 1997, is to provide for compensation for disablement caused by occupational injuries or diseases sustained or contracted by employees in the course of their employment, or for death resulting from such injuries or diseases; and to provide for matters connected therewith.

Child Labour Shall Not Be Used

There shall be no new recruitment of child labour.

Companies shall develop or participate in and contribute to policies and programmes which provide for the transition of any child found to be performing child labour to enable her or him to attend and remain in quality education until no longer a child; 'child' and 'child labour' being defined in the appendices.

Children and young persons under 18 shall not be employed at night or in hazardous conditions.

These policies and procedures shall conform to the provisions of the relevant ILO standards.

Relevant Legislation:
The South African Schools Act
The Basic Conditions of Employment Act
The Sectoral Determination for Farm Workers

Children under 15 or any child who is under the minimum school leaving age in terms of any law, if this is 15 or older, may not be employed in agricultural activities. No person may employ a child in an employment that is inappropriate for a child of that age and/or places the child's well-being, education, physical or mental health or spiritual, moral or social development at risk.

Table 2 (continued)

Private Sector Codes of Conduct (ETI Base Code)	State Regulation
Living Wages are Paid	
Wages and benefits paid for a standard working week meet, at a minimum, national legal standards or industry benchmark standards, whichever is higher. In any event wages should always be enough to meet basic needs and to provide some discretionary income.	Relevant Legislation: The Basic Conditions of Employment Act The Sectoral Determination for Farm Workers The Unemployment Insurance Legislation The Labour Relations Act
All workers shall be provided with written and understandable Information about their employment conditions in respect to wages before they enter employment and about the particulars of their wages for the pay period concerned each time that they are paid.	In December 2002 the Minister of Labour introduced a Sectoral Determination establishing conditions of employment and minimum wages for employers and employees in the farm worker sector.
Deductions from wages as a disciplinary measure shall not be permitted nor shall any deductions from wages not provided for by national law be permitted without the expressed permission of the worker concerned. All disciplinary measures should be recorded	
Working Hours are Not Excessive	
Working hours comply with national laws and benchmark industry standards, whichever affords greater protection. In any event, workers shall not on a regular basis be required to work in excess of 48 hours per week and shall be provided with at least one day off for every 7 day period on average. Overtime shall be voluntary, shall not exceed 12 hours per week, shall not be demanded on a regular basis and shall always be compensated at a premium rate.	Relevant Legislation: The Basic Conditions of Employment Act The Sectoral Determination for Farm Workers *Normal hours (excluding overtime)* A farm worker may not be made to work more than 45 hours a week; work more than nine hours per day for a five day work week; work more than eight hours a day for a six day work week. *Overtime* An employer may not require or permit a farm worker to work overtime except in accordance with an agreement concluded by the employer and the farm worker; to work more than 15 hours' overtime a week; or to work more than 12 hours, including overtime, on any day.

Table 2 (continued)

Private Sector Codes of Conduct (ETI Base Code)	State Regulation
	Extension of ordinary hours of work A worker and an employer may conclude a written agreement in terms of which the farm worker's ordinary hours of work are extended by not more than five hours per week for a period of not more than four months in any continuous period of 12 months; and are reduced by the same number of hours during a period of the same duration in the same twelve month period.[5] Such an agreement may not extend the farm worker's ordinary hours of work to more than ten hours on any day.
No Discrimination is Practiced There is no discrimination in hiring, compensation, access to training, promotion, termination or retirement based on race, caste, national origin, religion, age, disability, gender, marital status, sexual orientation, union membership or political affiliation	Relevant Legislation: The Employment Equity Act The Skills Development Act The purpose of the Employment Equity Act 55 of 1998 is to promote equal opportunity and fair treatment in employment through the elimination of unfair discrimination; and to implement affirmative action measures to redress the disadvantages in employment experienced by designated groups, in order to ensure their equitable representation in all occupational categories and levels in the workforce. It therefore aims to: • promote the constitutional right of equality and the exercise of true democracy; • eliminate unfair discrimination in employment; • ensure the implementation of employment equity to redress the effects of discrimination; • achieve a diverse workforce broadly representative of our people; • promote economic development and efficiency in the workforce; and • give effect to the obligations of the Republic as a member of the IIO.

3 The Fruit Export Commodity Chain

Changing employment patterns – who does and gets what?

The combination of state regulation and company codes of conduct represents a positive advance in the level of protection covering all workers, including women. They have arisen for different reasons, but they are also interrelated. Ultimately, the two reinforce each other, particularly in South Africa where there is progressive employment legislation which codes help to enforce. They comprise two tenets of labour protection[6] (public and private) that now cover fruit workers. But a key challenge from a gender perspective is whether they reach women in insecure forms of employment (where many are located), or whether they only really extend to the tip of the employment hierarchy. At a simple level, the employment hierarchy is composed of those workers at the top end who have good conditions of employment and labour protection, and those at the other end who do not. This is depicted in the form of the pyramid in Figure 1 where packhouse and some farmworkers are at the top of the hierarchy, while seasonal, contract and migrant farmworkers are at the bottom.

The downsizing of the on-farm labour force and its professionalization has led to a new form of labour hierarchy that has affected women. The employment of women who remain on farm is still implicitly linked to their male partner or relative, but they are more likely to be employed in their own right with an independent contract of employment and access to those benefits prescribed under legislation. Some growers have also moved to employing women working on-farm on a permanent basis (providing a house for two permanent workers is more economical than one), giving them improved access to employment benefits and security. Permanent women workers can be found in more skilled and supervisory roles, and more progressive growers are moving to multi-skilled teams of women and men as a means of raising labour productivity, breaking down traditional gender divisions.

Traditionally, women have always been concentrated in packing, which has become increasingly important with greater emphasis on quality and presentation under globalization. Women employed in packhouses – although usually only employed seasonally – are well-off relative to women farmworkers in other categories. They are more likely to be unionized and enjoy relatively good pay and employment conditions, and in this respect are among the better off at the top of the employment hierarchy (Barrientos and Kritzinger, 2003). In the middle of the hierarchy, permanent farm employment is primarily male, and these employees receive relatively good pay and conditions at farm level. More women are being given permanent employment on farm, but research suggests they are still a minority of the workforce at this level. At the other end of the hierarchy, employment conditions are not as good. The majority of workers who have been shifted to employment living off-farm are now employed as off-farm seasonal and, especially, contract labour. Official data are not available for these categories of employment, but case study evidence suggests that women workers are concentrated in this group. Recent studies into the restructuring of employment on fruit farms found that at least 50 per cent of producers are now employing off-farm contract labour (Du Toit and Ally, 2001; Barrientos and Kritzinger, 2003; Theron, 2000 and 2001). This use of contract labour enables producers to

meet flexible but tight production schedules set by large supermarkets while minimizing costs and contractual commitments of employment. Migrant labour, which has historically been used, is at the bottom end of the employment hierarchy in terms of pay and conditions.

Off-farm contract workers experience a range of employment, health and other risks. These include insecurity of employment, low wages and variability of earnings, absence of labour organization, poor knowledge of employment rights and usually no contract with their employer. While both men and women experience risk and insecurity, there is a gender dimension to this type of employment. There is an increase in the availability of day care facilities in the case of on-farm women which facilitates the management of paid employment and reproductive responsibilities, but many contract workers do not have access to such facilities and have to manage their domestic work in alternative ways. Gender relations also structure the wage levels and working days of contract workers. Women's weekly wages are lower than those of men and they work for shorter periods during the year. This relates to traditional practices whereby the allocation of tasks often excludes women, for example, from pruning during winter months. Given that women take responsibility for childcare, they lose a day's wage when they accompany their children to a day hospital or doctor.

While recent employment restructuring has tended to erode paternalist relations on fruit farms, paternalism has not entirely disappeared. It has reinvented itself within the contracting sector. Recent research (Barrientos and Kritzinger, 2003) has confirmed the development of a relationship of dependence between many women contract workers and their contractor which resembles the paternalist relationship existing between producers and their on-farm workforce in the past. The relationship is often very personalized and women are highly dependent on their contractor. Contractors not only provide assistance when workers experience financial and personal difficulties; they also assist women in generating income and accessing credit and transport.

Gender dimension of labour protection

The enactment of legislation and introduction of company codes of conduct mean that over the past decade labour rights and employment conditions have come to be addressed in the agricultural sector. These are potentially important for the large number of women workers employed in the sector, and represent a progressive move in relation to protecting their employment conditions. However, a key challenge from the standpoint of women is that much of their employment is temporary, seasonal or on a contract basis. Further, the fact that they are employed on this basis is a result of embedded gender discrimination within the labour market, which assigns women to insecure work on the grounds of their domestic and childcare responsibilities, and where provision for those responsibilities is not deemed to be the responsibility of the employer. To be effective for women workers, legislation and company codes need to extend beyond permanent employment and address the needs and rights of workers in insecure forms of work. To be gender sensitive, they also need to address specific gender issues, such as childcare and the safety of women. Here we examine selected issues covered by the code of conduct and national legislation through a gender lens.

Formally, the most relevant issue for women is covered by the principle on discrimination in the ETI base code and by the Employment Equity Act (EEA) in South Africa. The former provides basic coverage of all aspects of discrimination based on gender, ethnicity and religion. In its Purposes and Principles, the ETI (1998) cites ILO Conventions 100 and 111 and Recommendations 90 and 111 on equal remuneration for male and female workers for work of equal value, and discrimination in employment and occupation as the relevant international standards that apply. South Africa's Employment Equity Act is even more comprehensive, and is an important tool in addressing current discriminatory practices.

The purpose of the EEA is to achieve equity in the workplace by promoting equal opportunity and fair treatment in employment through the elimination of unfair discrimination and implementing affirmative action measures to redress the disadvantages in employment experienced by designated groups,[7] and to ensure their equitable representation in all occupational categories and levels in the workforce (Taylor, 2003). The Act stipulates that all farmers must review discriminatory practices on their farms, no matter how many workers they employ or what their annual turnover is. Farmers have to submit employment equity plans if they employ 50 workers or more. Many farmers employ more than 50 workers in any given year if workers hired to do seasonal work are included (Taylor, 1999). For this reason, the Act is likely to have a significant impact within the sector, although some farmers have indicated that they will not submit plans, even if they are penalized.

A number of other provisions are laid down in legislation and the code of conduct which formally apply to all workers. However, a more gendered analysis can highlight constraints on the extent of their provision for insecure women workers. One of the most relevant of these is the provision that all employment is freely chosen. This is important for women farmworkers in the South African context because of the tradition of employing women as a condition of their husband's or male partner's contract. The ETI base code as a generic code does not formally address this, but it could be interpreted to include such forms of employment where women have no choice but to work for a farmer on a seasonal basis or risk her partner losing his job. The legislation is aimed at ensuring that persons residing on a farm have the freedom not to work or to choose to work off farm if they wish. Those that choose to work on the farm should have their own contracts of employment (Taylor, 2003). Given that the base code also insists on the implementation of legislation, it therefore indirectly covers this issue via legislation. However, traditions of gender discrimination die hard, and the employment of many women is still implicitly linked to that of their partners. One means by which this happens is that when housing is allocated to a permanent male employee, his female partner has to pay rent if she works elsewhere, effectively penalizing the farmworker if his female partner does not work on the farm.

Living wages are covered by both the ETI base code and more recently through the Sectoral Determination added to the Basic Conditions of Employment Act in 2002. What constitutes a living wages is often hard to determine and is defined by the ETI as a wage that is enough to meet basic needs and provide some discretionary income. The Sectoral Determination for Agriculture was based on an extensive survey of wages and living standards in different regions of South Africa, and a minimum wage was set for different categories in each district. The ETI code refers to the ILO convention on equal remuneration, which sets out the right to equal pay for work of equal value. The Employment Equity Act cites remuneration as one area where unfair discrimination is prohibited, but does not expressly prohibit payment of unequal remuneration for work of equal value (Du Toit *et al.*, 2003). The gender division of labour in agriculture means that men and women often do different tasks. Women's tasks are often classified as having lower remuneration than men, reflecting in part women's lack of access to more skilled jobs and the embedded undervaluation of the types of task performed by women. One exception is women who work in packing, who are able to earn more than male general farmworkers. Neither national legislation nor the base code have been able to easily redress unequal pay, although the move to multi-skilled teams of men and women on some farms might begin to erode this gender inequality.

Another pertinent issue covers the provision of regular employment. This is particularly important to women workers who are temporary and seasonal, but who may often work for the same farm for years. The ETI base code states that this must be based on a recognized employment relationship established through national law and practice. The Labour Relations Act covers all workers, be they seasonal, temporary, casual or permanent, and these workers may not be subjected to unfair labour practices or unfair dismissal (Taylor, 2003). The ETI base code also stipulates that obligations to employees under labour or social security laws should not be avoided through the use of labour-only contracting or the repeated use of fixed term contracts. Formally, the Basic Conditions of Employment Act (BCEA) and the Unemployment Insurance Act, which makes provision for unemployment and maternity leave,[8] are extended to non-permanent workers who work more than 24 hours per month.[9] However, research has found that many female temporary and seasonal farmworkers do not receive Unemployment Insurance Fund (UIF) coverage, even though they are likely to become unemployed or have children (Barrientos and Kritzinger, 2003).

Under the Basic Conditions of Employment Act, even where an employee is employed by a labour contractor or broker, the labour contractor and the client are jointly and severally liable if the labour broker does not comply with the BCEA (Taylor, 2003). Formally, therefore, growers should not be able to circumvent their legal obligations in relation to employment conditions and standards through the use of outside contractors. However, contract workers can only be covered by the UIF if the contractor is registered at the Department of Labour. Again, research has indicated that very few contractors are registered, which means that their workers are excluded from access to the UIF (Barrientos and Kritzinger, 2003). Women contract workers often work for shorter periods than men, and again gender inequity in employment means that women contract workers, who are the most vulnerable, often have no cover. This indicates an important area where there is a failure of enforcement.

Freedom of association and collective bargaining also establish important labour rights for workers, and are laid down in both the base code and in legislation. Here, the two complement each other well, with the relevant core ILO Conventions 87 and 98 being a common element. There are currently 12 independent trade unions operating in the deciduous fruit sector. These tend to be weak and fragmented. There is also one union which is affiliated to the Congress of South African Trade Unions (COSATU). However, the level of unionization is relatively weak in South African agriculture, and informed estimates of unionization in the agricultural labour force vary between 2 and 8 per cent (Murphy, 1995). This is partly because of historical problems of organizing on remote farms. Unions do not have the capacity or resources to recruit among poor farmworkers. Farmworkers steeped in a long tradition of paternalism often do not understand the reasons for joining unions, which organize around workers rights and relate to a more formalized type of labour relations. But there are also gender constraints which prevent women from joining trade unions, which often ignore seasonal and casual workers in their recruitment and do not have the capacity to organize workers who move between different employers, undermining the ability of women to join unions. Further, women workers are sometimes discouraged from joining rural unions which are often dominated by a male bureaucracy that takes little account of women's problems in terms of childcare, domestic responsibilities and gender issues such as reproductive rights.

4 Lessons Learned

Enforcement of legislation and codes

However well formulated a code or piece of legislation, a key factor in whether it reaches down the gender hierarchy to women in more insecure forms of employment is the level of its enforcement. Without proper enforcement, legislation and codes will remain paper exercises, except among the most enlightened employers. Despite good legislation, legal enforcement remains an issue in South Africa. Growers continue to treat their workers in a paternalist way, and workers with low literacy levels are often unaware of their rights. The labour inspectorate is poorly resourced and lacks the capacity to ensure that legislation is adhered to across a wide area that is often comprised of isolated farms. Where an employee is employed on a fixed term or temporary contract, and that contract is not renewed, the employee may pursue this legally as an unfair dismissal dispute. However, she will have to

Women checking grapes.

prove that she had a reasonable expectation that the contract would be renewed. Many insecure workers lack the capability to pursue their case.

In relation to private sector codes, enforcement is meant to take place through monitoring and verification procedures. These can take the form of desk-based assessment as a minimum through to third party social auditing, where an independent auditor is appointed to audit the farm against a buyer's or the ETI base code. In reality monitoring and verification are still at a very early stage in South African agriculture. The main buyers applying codes are UK supermarkets who have suppliers across the world and they can only inspect a certain number at any one time. They tend to concentrate on countries where they think the 'risks' of non-compliance with their code are highest. These are, for example, countries with a high incidence of child labour or unsafe working conditions, which could damage the buyer's reputation if they came to light. South Africa does not rank as a high-risk country, partly because of its employment legislation. Hence, auditing is still fairly limited within South African agriculture.

Given that the ETI base code states that employers have to apply legislation or the code, whichever standard is higher, legislation will normally take precedence in the South African situation. Therefore, the base code's primary role becomes one of contributing to the enforcement of legislation, rather than setting the standard. Even without proper monitoring and verification of the code, it is likely that employers will increasingly abide by legislation if they want to supply large supermarkets. They know that failure to do so could lose them an important market, and that if they do not comply, a competitor will.

Overall, therefore, legislation tends to be more detailed than the ETI base code in addressing gender issues in employment. Essential to the base code is that labour legislation applies, and in that respect the two reinforce each other as a means of addressing and improving the position of women working in South African fruit export sector. This represents a significant advance for women workers, but as we have seen it is tempered by women's traditional subordination in a paternalist employment environment, by the poor conditions and insecurity faced by women at the bottom of the employment hierarchy and by women's double burden combining childcare and domestic responsibilities with paid work. While there have been rapid strides over the past decade at the formal level of enhancing labour protection for women, there is still a long way to go in embedding more equitable employment practice.

Formally, most legislation is meant to apply pro rata to all workers and to extend employment rights to them whether they are permanent or not. Codes are also meant to apply to all workers, including those in insecure employment, where the risks of non-compliance are more likely to be higher. But the reality is that non-permanent workers are often less aware of their rights, are more difficult to reach because of their mobility and insecurity, and are less likely to be organized in trade unions, which could be a means of accessing their rights. Women have the additional burden of reproductive responsibilities, which restricts their ability to voice concerns or access their rights.

It is unlikely in a competitive global environment, especially given the seasonal nature of fruit, that non-permanent work will decline. The key, therefore, is to ensure that the benefits of the progressive employment legislation and codes that have been introduced in South Africa extend to *all* workers, especially women. This requires a concerted effort by all relevant actors. Global buyers can help by ensuring that codes apply to and are monitored in relation to seasonal, contract and migrant workers, male and female. Trade unions can help by ensuring that they actively try to recruit such workers, not just those in permanent employment. Government can contribute by extending information and training on labour law to more vulnerable and insecure women workers, as well as by giving more resources to the labour inspectorate. NGOs can contribute by keeping up the pressure on global buyers, government and other relevant bodies to raise labour standards for women workers.[10]

The future

In some respects, the expansion of employment legislation in South Africa singles it out from other countries. Few other developing countries have the breadth of labour regulation and protection that now formally exists in South Africa. The pressures of global competition and economic liberalization have also led many countries to relax labour market regulation, for example through the expansion of export processing zones. Compared to other African horticultural exporters, such as Kenya and Zambia, South Africa therefore has good legislation. However the issues facing women workers are similar in other countries, independent of their legislative environment. Research in Zambia and Kenya found that many women workers in the vegetable and flower sectors were also concentrated in insecure forms of work and were lower down the employment hierarchy than male workers in terms of pay and conditions (Barrientos, Dolan and Tallontire, 2003; Smith *et al.*, 2003).

Codes of conduct operated by global buyers relate to all their suppliers in that sector, independent of the country from which they are sourcing supplies. In counties such as Kenya and Zambia, where legislation is weaker than South Africa, codes are beginning to address the position of some workers. For example, in the Kenyan flower sector there has been a move to give more workers who are currently on rolling insecure contracts permanent employment status. This is important in extending labour protection to these workers by recognizing that their work is permanent. Thus, while the main role of codes in South Africa is to enforce legislation, in other countries it can help to reinforce labour standards where legislation is weak.

At the same time, there is increasing recognition that voluntary sector codes cannot be a substitute for good employment legislation and legal enforcement. The weakness of voluntary codes is that they only apply to producers supplying specific global buyers and they do not apply outside the export sector, even within a given industry. Codes also vary between different global buyers and many individual company codes (apart from multi-stakeholder initiatives such as the ETI and Social Accountability International) fail to incorporate core ILO conventions. Codes are applied in a top-down fashion through global value chains and often lack sustainability (particularly where buyers move between different suppliers). Legislation, on the other hand, normally results from a democratic process, is comprehensive in that it covers all producers in all sectors within a given country, relates to both export and domestic sectors and is legally enforceable. Codes can thus complement legislation, but they can never provide a comprehensive substitute.

As codes have been introduced in a wide number of global value chains across different sectors and different countries, the complexity of the task of using a voluntary approach to improve labour standards is becoming more apparent. Individual global buyers can put resources into ethical trade, and large numbers of suppliers can be monitored by external auditors, but this can only touch the tip of the iceberg. The number of producers and subcontractors, across different sectors and countries globally, makes it impossible for an individual global buyer to be satisfied that compliance exists across the whole of their complex value chain. Emphasis is beginning to shift within ethical trade towards the need for a more locally based approach that involves all stakeholders including trade unions, NGOs and government. This could take the form of local multi-stakeholder initiatives that also include government.[11] But a local approach again raises the question of why this needs to be done through voluntary means and whether government is not best placed to undertake this function. However, in a global context, government needs to work in collaboration with other stakeholders and be sure that any action it takes does not preclude its country from being used as a source by global buyers. In this respect local multi-stakeholder initiatives involving government could form a link between public and private approaches to raising labour standards.[12]

Codes have arisen in a global environment in which buyers are under pressure from civil society organizations to address poor labour conditions in their value chains. The implementation of codes has indicated the ability of different civil society groups to lever change by global buyers within their value chains. However, those same global buyers themselves have leverage, both over the countries from which they source supplies, as well as their home governments and multilateral organizations. A greater coming together of global civil society organizations, global buyers, national governments and multilateral organizations (especially the ILO) would help to bring the issues of labour standards full circle. Potentially it could provide the impetus for improvement in labour standards as a competitive advantage of countries, in which governments could play a fuller part.

In this situation, it is crucial that the rights of women workers at the bottom of the employment pile are addressed. Labour protection will only be comprehensive if it includes the weakest. Insecure employment is a feature of global labour markets, and the rights of those workers, many of whom are women, must be included. South Africa has made a move in the right direction. For political reasons it has gone against the trend and introduced comprehensive employment legislation. This still needs much better enforcement, and codes are one means through which this can be encouraged. There is clearly a long way to go in ensuring that the employment rights and conditions of *all* workers, especially women in the most vulnerable and insecure positions, are addressed. The important thing is that progress is being made in the right direction.

Conclusion

This chapter set out to examine the combination of national legislation and private sector codes that now cover workers in South African export horticulture. It compared the different forms of labour protection introduced under legislation and private sector social codes of conduct, and considered their implications for women workers. Although the factors behind the introduction of each are different, ultimately they both relate to the positioning of South Africa in the post-apartheid era as a transformed and professional country operating within global markets. Traditionally, women workers lacked rights or independent employment in the context of paternalist employment relations. The advance of labour protection represents an important gain in terms of addressing the rights of women workers, and provides the basis for improving their conditions of employment.

However, these gains have taken place in the context of labour market restructuring in the fruit export sector. The combination of government legislation and increased global competition have spurred many growers to shed labour, and have contributed to changing employment relations. There is now a smaller permanent on-farm 'professional' labour force, and many women who are part of this have gained from the enhanced employment rights and benefits enshrined in legislation and reinforced by codes. But there is an increasing off-farm temporary and seasonal workforce, and many of these workers are women. Formally, legislation and codes offer protection to all workers, but in reality they often fail to reach those more insecure and vulnerable workers in temporary, seasonal and contract work.

We have seen that legislation introduced in South Africa is relatively progressive, including on gender issues, and is more advanced in its detail than the generic ETI base code. Given that women form an important part of the fruit workforce, this provides the potential for significant gains for women workers. Although there is formally an enhancement of gender equity, the biggest challenge is to ensure that this is translated into more gender equitable employment practices that benefit insecure seasonal and temporary workers as well as those in permanent employment. If this can be ensured, then the potential for women workers to gain could be greatly enhanced. In the case of South Africa, legislation sets a higher standard than codes, therefore the latter are another form of enforcement rather than a standard setter. However, insofar as both legislation and codes are failing to reach the more insecure workers, there is an important issue of enforcement. How to enhance labour inspection and social auditing in order to ensure that both legislation and codes of conduct reach all workers remains an important challenge.

There remains a risk that the benefits will disproportionately accrue to permanent workers, rather than to temporary and seasonal workers, and to men rather than women. This is partly because, despite recent refining of the legal recognition of temporary, seasonal and contract workers, legislation and codes are more easily applied to permanent workers. The mobility of temporary, seasonal and contract work makes enforcement much more arduous for these categories of worker. Gender inequality is deeply embedded in South African employment practice and change is bound to be slow. However, advances in labour protection represent a progressive move for women workers. They raise the potential for future changes to benefit women, and shift the gender environment from one in which the subordination of on-farm women workers was the norm to one which establishes the principles of greater equality in their rights. Labour protection has undergone a fundamental shift in a more equitable direction, but that progress still has a long way to go if it is to be consolidated for all women workers, including the most vulnerable.

Notes

1   A number of codes operate in the South African deciduous fruit sector that cover purely or primarily technical or environmental aspects of production, such as the EUREPGAP (European Retailers Representatives Good Agricultural Practice) code. This paper only covers social codes relating to labour standards and does not refer to other codes.

2   The 1998 ILO Declaration on Fundamental Principles and Rights at Work stipulates that all member states have an obligation to respect and promote the core ILO Conventions and Recommendations, whether or not they have been ratified.

3   Given that most UK supermarkets are members of the Ethical Trading Initiative, and that the UK is an important market for South African fruit, many producers are likely to have to implement the base code if they supply UK supermarkets.

4   Section 27, which is in the Chapter on Fundamental Rights in the Constitution, entrenches the following rights: (1) Every person shall have the right to fair labour practices; (2) Workers shall have the right to form and join trade unions and employers shall have the right to form and join employers' organizations; (3) Workers and employers shall have the right to organize and bargain collectively; (4) Workers shall have the right to strike for the purpose of collective bargaining; (5) Employers' recourse to the lock-out for the purpose of collective bargaining shall not be impaired, subject to section 33(1).

5   In Greenberg (2003) it is indicated that 'flexibility provisions' allow the arrangement of working time to be varied by agreement. This allows for intense work during peak periods in exchange for lighter work in slack periods.

6   We use the words 'labour protection' to include both legislation and private sector social codes of conduct. Labour protection is one aspect of social protection for insecure workers in a global economy (Barrientos and Ware Barrientos, 2002).

7   The designated group refers to women (of all races) and black people (a generic term used to describe all persons who are not white, including Coloured people and Indian people).

8   Under the UIF, employers and employees each pay 1 per cent of their pay towards the fund, which allows workers to make claims during unemployment and maternity leave.

9   The Basic Conditions of Employment Act provides that temporary workers have the right to written particulars of employment; pro rata annual leave (one day for every 17 days worked); pro rata sick leave (one day for every 26 days worked); payment for overtime work, etc.

10   This has recently been the focus of the 'Labour Wedge' campaign by Oxfam International, which included South African deciduous fruit and wine as one of its studies (Oxfam, 2004).

11   An example is the Wine Industry Ethical Trade Association in South Africa. This is a voluntary initiative involving wine producers, trade unions, NGOs and

government, set up in 2003 following the ETI wine pilot in South Africa (Smith *et al.*, 2004). See *www.wosa.co.za* for more information.

12 The issue of the relationship between voluntary initiatives and government has been raised in a World Bank report on corporate social responsibility (see World Bank, 2003); it plans to examine this further in a future report on the topic.

References

Barrientos, S. and Kritzinger, A. (2004). 'Squaring the Circle – Global Production and the Informalisation of Work in South African Fruit Exports', *Journal of International Development* 16, pp. 81–92.

Barrientos, S., Dolan, C. and Tallontire, A. (2003). 'A Gendered Value Chain Approach to Codes of Conduct in African Horticulture', *World Development* 31(9): 1511–26.

Barrientos, S. and Kritzinger, A. (2003). 'The poverty of work and social cohesion in global exports: The case of South African fruit', in Chidester, D., Dexter, P. and W. James (eds), *What holds us together. Social cohesion in South Africa*, HSRC Press, Cape Town.

Barrientos, A and Barrientos, S. Ware (2002). 'Extending Social Protection to Informal Workers in the Horticulture Global Value Chain', SP Discussion Paper, No. 0216, World Bank, Washington DC, June.

Barrientos, S., Dolan, C. and Tallontire, A. (2003). 'A Gendered Value Chain Approach to Codes of Conduct in African Horticulture', *World Development* 31(9): 1511–26.

DFPT (2003). *Key Deciduous Fruit Statistics*, Deciduous Fruit Producers Trust, Paarl.

Du Toit, A. and Ally, F. (2001). *The Externalisation and Casualisation of Farm Labour in Western Cape Horticulture*, Report compiled by the Programme for Land and Agrarian Studies, School of Government, University of the Western Cape for the Centre for Rural Legal Studies, Stellenbosch.

Du Toit, D., Bosch, D., Woolfrey, D., Godfrey, S., Rossouw, J., Christie, S., Cooper, C., Giles, G. and C. Bosch (2003). *Labour Relations Law: A Comprehensive Guide*, 4th edition, Lexis Nexis Butterworths, Johannesburg.

ETI (1998). *Purpose, Principles, Programme, Membership, Information, Ethical Trading Initiative*, London.

Greenberg, S. (2003). *Women Workers in Wine and Deciduous Fruit Global Value Chains*, Report for Women on Farms Project, mimeo, Stellenbosch.

Hamman, J. (1996). 'The Impact of Labour Policy on Rural Livelihoods in the Western Cape' in Lipton, M., de Klerk, M. and Lipton, M. (eds.), *Land Labour and Livelihoods: Understanding the Linkages*, IDS Working Paper 159, Institute of Development Studies, Brighton, UK.

Kaplinsky, R. (1998). 'Globalisation, industrialisation and sustainable growth: the pursuit of the Nth rent', IDS Working Paper No. 110, May.

Kritzinger, A. and Vorster, J. (1996). 'Women Farm workers on South African deciduous fruit farms: gender relations and the structuring of work', *Journal of Rural Studies* 12(4): 339–51.

Kritzinger, A and Vorster, J. (1999). *The Labour situation in the South African deciduous fruit export industry: The Producer: A follow-up study*, Department of Sociology, University of Stellenbosch, Stellenbosch.

Kritzinger, A. and Vorster, J. (2001). 'Food industry responses to global integration: fruit producers, state legislators and women farm workers in South Africa' in Tovy, H. and Blanc, M. (eds), *Nature and Society. Rural Life in Late Modernity*, Ashgate, Aldershot.

Murphy, M. (1995). 'South African farm workers: is trade organization possible?', *South African Labour Bulletin* 19 (3): 393–62.

Oxfam International (2004). *Trading Away Our Rights, Women Working in Global Supply Chains*. Oxfam, Oxford.

PPEBC (2004). *Exporters Handbook*, PPEBC, Cape Town.

Ray, M. (1997) Flexible production. Shaping up to globalisation. South African Labour Bulletin, 21 (5) pp. 24–29.

Rees, R. (1997). Flexible labour. Meeting the challenge. South African Labour Bulletin, 21 (5) pp. 30–36.

Samson, M. (1997). Globalisation. Women pay the price. South African Labour Bulletin, 21 (1) pp. 8–13.

Simbi, T. and Alibar, M. (2000.) The Agricultural Employment Crisis in South Africa. Paper presented for the TIPS conferences 2000 Annual Forum, Muldersdrift, 18–20 September.

Smith, S., Auret, D., Barrientos, S., Dolan, C., Kleinbooi, K., Njobvu, C., Opondo, M. and Tallontire, A. (2004). *Ethical Trade in African Horticulture, Gender Rights and Participation*, UK Workshop Report and IDS Working Paper, Institute of Development Studies, Brighton, UK (forthcoming).

Sunde, J. and Kleinbooi, K. (1999). *Promoting Equitable and Sustainable Development for women Farmworkers in the Western Cape*, Centre for Rural Legal Studies, Stellenbosch, Stellenbosch.

Taylor, N. (1999). Briefing Paper on the Employment Equity Act No. 55 of 1998 and its implications for agriculture, Centre for Rural Legal Studies, Stellenbosch.

Taylor, N. (2003). 'Briefing on Wine Industry Ethical Trading Initiative', mimeo, Cape Town.

Taylor, V. (2001). 'Globalisation, the disappearing state and poor women: a view from the South', *Agenda* 48: 51–60.

Theron, J. (2000). 'Responding to externalization: Part 1', *South African Labour Bulletin* 24 (6): 59–65.

Theron, J. (2001). 'Responding to externalization: Part 2', *South African Labour Bulletin* 25 (1): 63–68.

World Bank (2003). *Strengthening Implementation of Corporate Social Responsibility in Global Supply Chains*, World Bank, Washington DC, October.

Rags, Riches and Women Workers: Export-oriented Garment Manufacturing in Bangladesh

Naila Kabeer and Simeen Mahmud

1 Introduction

This chapter is concerned with women working in the export-oriented ready-made garment industry in Bangladesh. Although the majority of these women are located in what is officially classified as 'the formal economy', the nature of their contracts and their terms and conditions are more typical of work in the informal economy. Their situation illustrates the point made by a number of authors that the relationship between the 'formal' and 'informal' economy in much of the world, particularly the developing world, is a continuum rather than a dichotomy. What was traditionally described as 'formal sector' employment, characterized by written contracts, full-time work, permanent status and various forms of social benefits, accounts for an increasingly smaller share of total employment, while employment characterized by differing degrees of informality accounts for an increasing share (ILO, 2002; Lund and Srinivas, 2000; Standing, 1999).

Clothing is a highly labour-intensive, low-technology product, the manufacture of which, along with textiles, has provided many countries of the world, including today's advanced industrialized economies, with the first rung on their ladder to industrialization. While there has been diffusion of microelectronic equipment in the pre-assembly stages of grading, marking and cutting, the limpness of materials used in clothing has made mechanization in the labour-intensive assembly stage extremely difficult and, as long as there are plentiful supplies of cheap labour available, uneconomical. The global restructuring of the garment industry in recent decades is in part

Opposite: *Women garment workers demanding their rights.* PICTURE: ABDULLAH ZUBERI, *THE NEW AGE*

driven by the search for such labour which, for a variety of reasons that have been summarized as the 'comparative advantage of women's disadvantage' (Arizpe and Aranda, 1981) in the labour market, has been mainly female.

This chapter examines the global restructuring processes which led to the emergence of an export-oriented garment industry in Bangladesh in the late 1970s. While market forces have clearly played a role in these processes, the history of the industry in Bangladesh, its current conditions and its future prospects are all closely bound up with policies formulated at the national, and even more, at the international level. We analyze where the Bangladesh industry is located in terms of the global value chain for garments and what this location has implied for its structure, the profile of its labour force and the terms and conditions under which it works. Finally, we explore the implications of the industry for the broader developmental goals of economic growth, poverty reduction and gender equality. We start, however, with a brief history of the garment industry and the process of global restructuring it is currently undergoing.

2 The Global Restructuring of the Garment Industry: The International Story

Before the first industrial revolution in Europe, tailoring was a skilled craft occupation carried out by 'master tailors' who cut and made up cloth purchased by their customers or by themselves to the specifications of their customers. The mechanization of production, starting with the invention of the sewing machine and the band knife in the 1850s, increased the rate at which garments could be made up and led to the emergence of a market in ready-made garments. As the market expanded, it became possible to sub-divide the production process into a series of increasingly simpler tasks which could be carried out by less and less skilled, and hence cheaper, labour, mainly women and girls. However, in Britain the active role played by male-dominated trade unions, seeking to defend the interests of the skilled tailors who made up their membership, saw the enactment of various forms of protective legislation which served to keep married women out of the industry. This meant that till the early decades of the twentieth century, most of the female workforce in the garment industry was made up of young single women from the rural areas for whom the only alternative employment was domestic service (Kabeer, 2000).

The production of garments evolved historically along broadly dualistic lines. One sub-sector was made up of women's wear, which was characterized by considerable product differentiation, limiting the extent to which tasks could be subdivided for assembly line production, while seasonal fluctuations and changes in fashion served to limit the size of retail orders and hence the length of the production run. Men and boys outwear, on the other hand, has always been a more standardized product, particularly at the cheaper ready-made end, and lent itself quite early on to a greater subdivision of operations, particularly in the machining stage. This led to a form of production in which each machinist only made one section of a garment ('section work') instead of making the whole garment ('make through').

By the 1950s, growing concentration in the retail sector at this end of the market increased the length of runs and made production planning more possible. There was steady growth of larger manufacturing firms and of mass unionization across much of the industry during this period. However, it was also a period of full employment, the growing incorporation of women into the labour market and the successful claims of a highly organized trade union movement, all of which led to rising costs of labour in the industrialized countries. Because competition in the mass clothing end of the market revolved primarily around price, the search for profit began to lead to the relocation of sections of the clothing industry, initially out of expensive urban locations within these countries, and subsequently to the low-wage economies of Taiwan, South Korea and Hong Kong. The states in these newly-industrializing countries had opted for open, as opposed to protective, economic policies and boasted a highly disciplined and non-unionized labour force which could produce the same quality goods at a fraction of the price. As might be expected, the process of global restructuring has gone furthest in the production of standardised clothing such as men's shirts and, in recent years, casual outwear, items which lent themselves to assembly-line production.

However, anxieties about the levels of import penetration of developed country markets threatened by this restructuring process gave rise to the Multifibre Arrangement in 1974, which brought together various disparate attempts to regulate the rapid growth in developing country exports of clothing and textiles in the interests of 'orderly trade'. At a time when protective barriers were being dismantled in other areas of trade, the MFA ensured that trade in textiles and garments (along with agriculture) remained the most regulated in the world. The agreement set the acceptable rate of increase in exports from developing to developed countries at 6 per cent a year and allowed importing countries to impose 'quotas' or quantitative restrictions on the volume of exports from any particular country which grew at a rate higher than bilaterally agreed levels.

However, the imposition of quotas did not succeed in dissipating the flow of cheap imports. Instead, it gave rise to the enterprising practice of 'quota hopping' as producers and buyers, many from the Newly Industrializing Countries (NICS), went in search of fresh, low-wage sites which were still 'quota-free'. It was at this stage that Bangladesh came into the picture. It had a traditional custom-made garment industry working out of tailoring shops to service a very small domestic market, as well as a small ready-made garment industry catering primarily to urban markets: the most common clothing worn by Bangladeshis, lungis for men and sarees for women do not need stitching. In the late 1970, a number of entrepreneurs from quota-restricted countries set up subcontracting relationships with some of Bangladesh's ready-made garment factories with a view to taking advantage of the absence of quotas. However, the industry did not really take off until changes had been made in the domestic policy environment.

3 The Global Restructuring of the Garment Industry: The Bangladesh Story

The emergence of an export-oriented RMG industry in Bangladesh can be traced to a confluence of policy trends at global and national levels. At the global level, the imposition of quotas on clothing exports from some of the early industrializing countries in East Asia led them to search for quota-free locations to set up garment assembly plants. A significant example of this in the case of Bangladesh was Daewoo from South Korea. Daewoo met the 'quota hopping' requirement of having a product which was not a fully Korean operation by entering into an agreement with a local firm, Desh Garments. Following an agreement signed in 1978 for production and export of apparel for a five-year period, Daewoo gave virtually free training in production and marketing to 130 Desh supervisors and managers at its state-of-the-art garment plant in Korea, but then left production itself to Desh. The effectiveness of the technology transfer involved was demonstrated when, after the agreement with Daewoo was abandoned because of internal problems in Korea, production within Desh continued to grow. Of more interest is the fact that within one year, 115 of the 130 people trained in Korea had left Desh to set up their own garment export firms or to be hired at several times their salary by the many new factories being set up in the country (Easterly, 2000).

At the national level, investment in the RMG industry was made even more attractive by changes that occurred around this time in the domestic policy environment. Until this point, Bangladesh had retained its pre-independence commitment to an industrial policy of import substitution which entailed a complex set of protective measures intended to curtail imports and build an industrial base to cater to the domestic market. By the end of the decade, however, a succession of crises, including a major cyclone, war, famine and political turbulence, together with declining receipts from raw jute and jute manufactures, the country's main export, and an increasing import bill,

> **Box 1: Daewoo/Desh: A Story of Leaks, Unintended Consequences and Increasing Returns**
>
> Daewoo managers had created new knowledge about garment manufacturing and marketing when they first began producing garments in 1967. This was transmitted at a price to Desh workers and applied in the Desh factory in Bangladesh, where it continued to be adapted to local conditions to increase returns to investment. The benefits spread well beyond what Daewoo had intended. The Desh workers and managers took with them what they learnt about 'making shirts, selling shirts abroad, using special bonded warehouse systems and using back-to-back import letters of credit' and started their own factories. Using the knowledge 'leaked' from the Desh factory, they were able to benefit from vastly greater returns to investment and the numbers of plants rapidly multiplied. The majority of entrepreneurs were relatively young men with a fairly high level of education and able to communicate in English. The majority of firms were private limited companies with relatively low initial investment and mostly locally owned.

dominated by food imports, left the country with a precarious balance of payments situation. It also faced a growing deficit within the domestic budget due to virtually stagnant government revenue collection.

From the early 1980s, Bangladesh undertook a series of economic reforms to open up its economy under the aegis of the IMF and the World Bank. A new import policy in 1982 announced an export-led growth strategy to be spearheaded by the private sector (Rashid, 2000:30). A number of direct export incentive schemes were put in place[1] while foreign direct investment was encouraged through the establishment of export processing zones outside Dhaka and Chittagong. Further incentives for stimulating investment in RMG were instituted in the early 1990s (Bhattacharya and Rahman, 2000:8–9).[2] This incentive structure explains why 95 per cent of firms are locally owned private limited companies. Only about 5 per cent are joint ventures and these are mainly in the EPZs.

The incentive structure also led to a dramatic expansion of the export-oriented RMG sector from around 50 factories employing a few thousand workers in the early 1980s to over 3,000 factories employing around 1.8 million workers by 2000. Eighty per cent of this workforce are estimated to be women (Table 1). In addition about 0.2 million people are employed in other industries linked to garment manufacturing (Khundker, 2002). RMG employment growth has averaged about 8 per cent per year and accounts for about 40 per cent of total manufacturing employment.

Table 1: Employment in the Ready-made Garment Industry in the 1990s

Year	Male	Female	Female as % of Total	Total
1991–1992	8730	494700	85	582000
1992–1993	120600	683400	85	804000
1993–1994	124050	702950	85	827000
1994–1995	120000	1080000	90	1200000
1995–1996	129000	1165042	90	1294042
1996–1997	139756	1257808	90	1397564
1997–1998	150000	1350000	90	1500000
1998–1999	160000	1350000	90	1500000
1999–2000	160000	1440000	90	1600000
2000–2001	360000	1440000	80	1800000
2001–2002	360000	1440000	80	1800000

Source: BGMEA, cited in Khundker, 2002: 67

Quite apart from the employment it has generated, the implications of which we return to below, the RMG sector has made a significant contribution to the country's growth and foreign exchange earnings. The share of manufacturing in GDP growth increased from 9.8 per cent at the beginning of the 1990s to 11.4 per cent in 2000. That this growth was largely driven by the RMG sector – which grew at a compound rate of 15 per cent per year during the 1990s (Bhattacharya and Rahman, 2000: 2–3) – is evident from the fact that value added for total large-scale manufacturing grew at 7 per cent annually during the 1990s, but at 4 per cent when RMG was excluded (Mahmud, 2003: 5).

Relatively strong GDP growth was underpinned by even stronger export growth, which doubled in value from 5.6 per cent of GDP in the late 1980s to 12 per cent in 2000. Here too the RMG sector has played a leading role. Its share of the country's foreign exchange earnings has grown steadily from 4 per cent in the early 1980s to 41 per cent at the beginning of the 1990s to 77 per cent in 2001–2002 (Table 2). Within RMG the share of knitwear increased even more dramatically from a negligible proportion in 1989–90 to 25 per cent of total exports in 2002–2003, accounting for one-third of total RMG exports. Between 1978 and 1999 the RMG sector earned US$26 billion for the country, of which the value-added component was US$7.6 billion or 29 per cent. In addition, a host of ancillary industries producing accessories have also emerged and grown alongside the garment industry. One estimate suggests that 80 per cent of garment accessories were locally produced, valued at $0.5 billion a year (Bhattacharya and Rahman, 2000).

Despite this spectacular performance, however, there is considerable pessimism about the future of the industry, particularly given plans to phase

Table 2: Total and Ready-made Garment Exports, 1984–2002

Year	Total Exports (US$ million)	Export of RMG (US$ million)	Export of RMG (volume)	Knit as % of RMG Exports	RMG as % of Total Exports
1983–1984	811.00	31.57			3.89
1984–1985	934.43	116.2			12.44
1985–1986	819.21	131.48			16.05
1986–1987	1076.61	298.67			27.74
1987–1988	1231.2	433.92			35.24
1988–1989	1291.56	471.09			36.47
1989–1990	1923.70	624.16			32.45
1990–1991	1717.55	866.82			50.47
1991–1992	1993.9	1182.57			59.31
1992–1993	2382.89	1445.02			60.64
1993–1994	2533.9	1555.79			61.4
1994–1995	3472.56	2228.35			64.17
1995–1996	3882.42	2547.13	72.00	-	65.61
1996–1997	4441.28	3001.25	80.99	-	67.93
1997–1998	5161.2	3781.94	98.19	25.40	73.28
1998–1999	5312.86	4019.98	101.45	28.13	75.67
1999–2000	5752.19	4352.39	111.02	30.02	75.66
2000–2001	6467.50	4859.82	124.02	30.77	75.14
2001–2002	5986.09	4583.75	140.44	32.42	76.57

Sources: Kaniz Sidique, Deceleration in the Export Sector of Bangladesh and Women Workers: Assessing Impact and Identifying Coping Strategies, CPD Occasional Paper Series No. 26, p. 19; Export Promotion Bureau, Dhaka (September, 1999) and Bangladesh Garment Manufacturers and Exporters Association, cited in Khundker, 2002: 63.

out the MFA entirely by the end of 2004. The Bangladesh garment industry is a creature of the MFA quota system and the quota system has shaped its history, simultaneously protecting it and distorting its growth. It has protected it from potential competitors who face quotas in the items that Bangladesh exports, but it has also suppressed its incentive to diversify out of these items. One result of this is that its expansion has been largely horizontal (an expansion in volume of production) rather than vertical (an increase in value of production). The implications of this concentration in low-value clothing manufacturing are graphically illustrated in a report by the Asia Foundation which compares Bangladesh's performance in the US clothing market with that of 17 other major exporting countries (Asia Foundation, 2001).

The report points out that between 1997 and 1999, Bangladesh was sixth of the 18 largest importers into the US in terms of its share of the *volume* of imports. Although the volume of imports from Bangladesh grew during these years, its share of the US market declined from 5.9 per cent to 5.5 per cent. Turning to the *value* of imports into the US, here too the overall value of imports from Bangladesh grew, but its share in the overall value of imports into the US declined from 3.4 per cent to 3.3 per cent during this period. Its lower share of the value of imports compared to the volume of imports is indicative of the fact that the value received per unit item of clothing from Bangladesh was lower than worldwide averages. Finally, comparisons of value per square metre equivalent of fabric (total value of imports into US from different countries divided by total square metre equivalent of fabric from that country) show that the value of apparel exports by Bangladesh into the US was lower than that of all 17 other major importers included in the study. In other words, Bangladesh is the sixth of the 18 largest exporters of garments to the US measured by volume, but eighteenth in terms of value received per item of clothing.

The second major weakness of the Bangladesh RMG sector is the very low value addition that it represents. Value addition measures the contribution made to the total value of a product by each stage in its production. From the point of view of the individual RMG factory, the value added in making up a garment is the value of the garment received by the factory net of the value of the inputs utilized in making it up. As Quddus and Rashid (2000) point out, the concept of value addition takes on an additional significance in the case of exports, particularly in an industry which has to import many of its inputs, since this has a bearing on the country's foreign exchange earnings. It has been estimated that at the national level, the value added by the industry in terms of foreign exchange earnings has remained static at around 25–30 per cent for the last 20 years.[3] Weakness of backward linkages is one obvious reason. The country does not grow export-quality cotton or possess the natural resources for synthetic fibres used in clothing.

Raw materials have to be imported both for garments and the country's small textile industry, and accounted for around three-quarters of the import of total industrial raw materials in the 1990s (Bhattacharya and Rahman, 2000: 7). In fact, textile fabrics, a major input into the manufacture of woven garments, dominate these imports. While it is developing a local textile industry which could increase the value addition generated by garment production within the country, Bangladesh has no natural comparative advantage in this and the prices of its textiles are always likely to be higher than world averages because the raw materials have to be imported.

There are some exceptions to both these generalizations: some factories are moving into higher-value woven garments and in the 1990s there was a rapid growth in the production of knitwear garments where local value addition is much higher because only one backward linkage is needed (cotton to yarn), on average 50–60 per cent compared to 25–30 per cent for woven RMG.[4] Many of the factories producing higher-value items are based in the EPZs where direct contact with retailers and fashion houses have brought in new knowledge in marketing and fashion design and hence higher value addition in production. There is also some indirect evidence of increased process or manufacturing efficiency in knitwear factories producing trousers and jerseys, leading to cheaper products and increased market share. This is an indication of process upgrading and some movement up the manufacturing value chain, but does not indicate product upgrading.

An important point is that higher value items are generally more technology intensive and need better trained workers and supervisors; many joint venture firms in the EPZ and knitwear firms have foreign managers and supervisors. In addition, a much higher proportion of workers in these factories are male. Only 35 per cent of workers in the knitwear industry, which is more technology intensive than woven garments, are women (Chaudhuri-Zohir, 2000). This reflects the situation in other parts of the world where women lose out as manufacturing processes become more capital and/or skill intensive (Barrientos, Kabeer and Hossain, 2003) and is a point we will return to later.

4 The Ready-made Garment Commodity Chain

Product focus

The bulk of the RMG industry in Bangladesh thus specializes in low-value basic and casual wear products (woven trousers, shirts and blouses and knitwear T-shirts and jerseys) where it has to compete largely on the basis of its ability to produce reasonable quality goods at ever-decreasing prices.[5] Moreover, the industry is largely located at the lower end of the value chain for these products, essentially performing cut-make-trim functions.

The reasons for this are not difficult to understand. They reflect mutually interacting factors on both the demand and supply side. On the supply side, the conditions prevailing in Bangladesh mean that the direct costs of producing garments are only a small fraction of the total costs of doing business in the country. The Asia Foundation report offers a useful step-by-step breakdown of value addition in a typical shirt exported by Bangladesh to the US. The direct labour costs of making such a shirt are around US$0.16. The cost of buttons and other accessories is US$0.24 so that the total cost of the shirt when it leaves the factory is US$0.40. The price received at FOB (the point at which it leaves Chittagong port) is US$5.03. Duty and freight add 20 per cent, giving a LDP (landing duty paid) value in the US of US$6.04 for a shirt which is likely to retail at US$13 to US$14 in a US store. If the cost of fabric is factored into these calculations, and assumed to be around 60 per cent of the FOB value of US$5.03, then US$3 of the FOB value never reaches the garment factory, US$0.40 is the cost of direct labour and trim and there is an additional US$1.60 unaccounted for (Table 3).

Table 3: Breakdown of Cost of Cotton Shirt Exported to the US

Stage	Cost in US$	% of Retail Price	% of FOB Price	% of LDP Price	% of Retail Price
Labour	0.16	1.2	3.2		
Trim	0.24	1.8	4.8		
Cost at factory	0.40	3.0	8.0		
Fabric	3.02	23.2	60.0		
Other indirect costs	1.61	12.4	32.0		
Price at FOB	5.03	38.7	100.0	83.3	
Duty and freight	1.01	7.8		16.7	
Price at LDP	6.04	46.5		100.0	46.5
Retailing mark-up	6.96	53.5			53.5
Price at US retail	13.00	100.0			100.0

Source: Compiled from Asia Foundation, 2001
Only 3 per cent of total value addition to the US retail price of a cotton shirt takes place at the factory and a miniscule 1.2 per cent is from labour. The major value addition before shipment is from fabric (23.3 per cent of the retail price and 60 per cent of the FOB price), but this never reaches the factory because it is imported under the special bonded warehouse provision. Direct production cost (labour plus trim) comprises only 8 per cent of the FOB price compared to 32 per cent from indirect costs. Over half of value addition takes place in the US after landing and payment of duties.

The report suggests that some of this unaccounted for element represents the indirect costs of doing business in Bangladesh. The vast majority of factories are 'zero-service operations': apart from cut-make-trim operations, they have little else to offer the buyer in terms of design, marketing and sales services or quality assurance. These have to be assumed by the buyer and therefore cut into the profit margins of the manufacturer. In addition, there are the macro costs[6] of doing business in Bangladesh which are outside the control of the garment firms. These include the costs associated with shipping in raw materials and shipping out the finished garment: poor infrastructure, made worse by frequent flooding, congestion in the main port, frequent *hartals* (strikes), poor telecommunications, weak financial systems, uneven proficiency in the English language, unreliable and uncompetitively priced energy and so on. There is also the red tape and accompanying corruption (customs clearance and delivery to factories of imported materials can take three days) and 'miscellaneous expenditures'.

Given Bangladesh's distance from its main input and output markets, these various indirect costs take on even greater significance because of their implications for the lead times that producers need to turn around an order. According to one estimate, Bangladesh factories which rely on locally available fabric need 75–90 days between confirmation of a purchase order to the day of shipment, while those using imported fabrics need 120 days. In the rest of Asia, estimates vary between 45 to 60 days. This clearly restricts the kind of buyer that will deal with Bangladeshi entrepreneurs, particularly in an industry which is essentially buyer driven.

Box 2: Who Buys What in Bangladesh's Garment Industry

Unlike producer-driven industries in which supply factors largely determine the nature of demand, it is decisions made by the big buyers in the clothing commodity chain that shape the structure of global production (Quddus and Rashid, 2000). Buyers are an extremely heterogeneous group and include retailers and agents of retailers as well as other intermediaries representing the haute couture end of the market, expensive department stores, high street retail chains, fashion brands, mail order firms and so on. However, given the costs of doing business in Bangladesh, it is mainly the mass market retailers and low-end fashion buyers, mainly from the US, who can *afford* to work here. The buyers present in Bangladesh today represent a 'who's-who of the world's major volume retailers' – Wal-Mart, Gap, K-mart, Sears, J.C. Penney, Levi Strauss from the US, C&A, H&M, Marks and Spencer and a host of smaller brands from the EU (Asia Foundation, 2001:16). The Asia Foundation report comments: 'Their gigantic volumes mean the companies have the financial strength to continue to provide whatever facilities the factories are unable or unwilling to offer'. But there is a catch: 'those same volumes also give these buyers the leverage to dictate ever-lower prices'.

Factory owners in Bangladesh consequently find themselves trapped between the buyer-driven demands of a global industry characterized by season and fashion-related fluctuations and a domestic environment characterized by extreme unpredictability. They work in a climate of extreme uncertainty which is becoming more uncertain as competition gets more intense: interviews with a number of factory owners by the authors suggest the number of seasonal peaks in demand has increased from three to six and lead times have been cut back as the major retailers seek to download the risks of their business onto the factory owners.

The factory owners appear to bear a great deal of the risk. They have to pay for their fabric before they have received payment for the order. If the buyer is dissatisfied with the shipment or the shipment is too late, the firm may have to cut back on its price in order to ensure that it is sold and that they can meet their debts and pay their labour. On the other hand, there is no guarantee that the orders will come in on a regular basis. For the quota-regulated US market, quota buying and selling leads to high quota premiums (or the price of quota) which can increase vulnerability of both factory owners and workers. This is because factories that have taken orders with insufficient quota (in the hope of buying quota) may be forced to ship at a loss or abandon orders mid-way, a common occurrence (Asia Foundation, 2001:12). Moreover, to add to the uncertainties they face, employers who deal directly with buyers find that they are being cited ever-decreasing prices for their goods at a time when they are also under pressure to comply with the various codes of conduct that buyers are imposing in response to consumer pressure.

Table 4: Trend of RMG Exports to the US and EU in the 1990s

Year	Exports to the US (% of total exports)	Exports to the EU (% of total exports)	Combined share of US and EU exports (%)
1991–1992	49.14	46.42	95.56
1992–1993	48.72	45.69	94.41
1993–1994	38.08	55.43	93.51
1994–1995	45.15	49.36	94.51
1995–1996	39.33	55.17	94.50
1996–1997	41.49	54.11	95.50
1997–1998	–	–	–
1998–1999	43.24	52.38	95.65

Source: Export Promotion Bureau, Dhaka, and Bangladesh Garment Manufacturers and Exporters Association, cited in Khundker, 2002:74

Structure of the RMG industry and employment patterns

These factors help to explain the structure of the garment industry in Bangladesh and the informal character of much of its employment. The industry can be differentiated into a number of segments. The first tier factories at the formal end of the industry are epitomized by those in the EPZ: they have direct links with international buyers, modern equipment, better quality assurance, a large relatively skilled and educated workforce and generally better working conditions than the rest of the industry – although trade unions have been banned till recently within the EPZs. Second tier factories outside the EPZs also have a direct, often long-term, relationship with their buyers and hence some reliability in their orders. They vary in size from large to medium and also observe certain minimum labour standards, largely because of their dealings with buyers. There is, however, a third tier which merges imperceptibly with the informal economy. The size of this tier is not known but it is made up of small low-grade factories which have no direct relationship to buyers or the capacity to open a Letter of Credit. They work

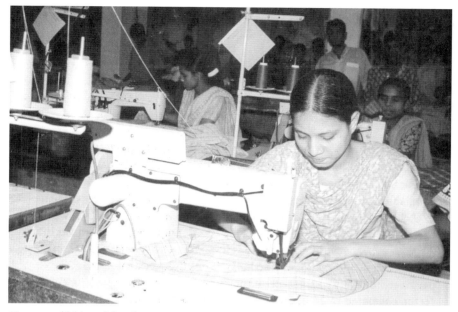

Women machinists work long hours.   PICTURE: ABDULLAH ZUBERI, *THE NEW AGE*

in small rented premises with 100 to 200 machines and largely rely on sub-contracted orders from the larger factories which have taken on too many orders or need to meet a deadline.

Apart from the 'bideshi' (EPZ) factories and a few 'bangla' factories outside which deal directly with buyers, the majority of employers appear to operate with an 'informal sector' mindset, adjusting their production to demand through a variety of means. Thus production lines are subcontracted or outsourced during peak season and shut down at other times. One survey found that three-quarters of the firms included were subcontracting out to other smaller firms, while more than half were subcontracting in.[7] Firms may also take on cheaper orders during the lean season to earn enough to pay their workers.

Work arrangements

The informal mindset of garment employers is also evident in the pursuit of a strategy of 'primitive accumulation' with regard to their workers, a strategy which requires them to maximize returns from the key factor of production under their control at the minimum possible cost. They hire workers with little or no education, provide them with minimum on-the-job-training, do not issue them with a contract as required by the law, keep them on temporary status regardless of how long they have been in the factory, provide few of

145

the benefits to which they are legally entitled and dismiss them without any notice. Hours worked in the garment industry are longer than elsewhere in the manufacturing sector, including the export manufacturing sector, and workers sometimes work all night to meet deadlines. And while their monthly take home pay is by no means the lowest in the formal manufacturing sector, given their overtime earnings, the hourly returns to their labour may be the lowest, given the long hours that have to be put in to earn it.

Box 3: Wages in the Bangladesh Ready-made Garment Sector

International comparisons suggest that wages paid in the RMG sector in Bangladesh are among the lowest in the world – US$0.15 an hour compared to US$0.30 in Nepal, US$0.35 in India, US$0.35 in China, US$0.45 in Sri Lanka and US$16 in the US (Khondkar, 2002). Employers have argued that wages are low because productivity is low. Productivity is indeed low in Bangladesh by international standards. It has been estimated that 25 person-minutes are required per basic product in the Bangladesh RMG sector, compared to 24 in Sri Lanka, 20.7 in the Republic of Korea, 19.7 in Hong Kong and 14 in the US. However, employers do little to change this scenario.

The alternative route to this strategy of 'primitive accumulation', i.e. paying labour an efficiency wage, observing 'normal' hours of work and investing in labour productivity, appears to have been ruled out by most employers on the grounds that irregularity in the orders they receive and the overall uncertainty of the industry preclude such investment. There is, of course, a further factor which may explain their reluctance – the availability of an apparently unlimited supply of female migrant labour willing and able to work the long hours demanded for little pay until it has to be replenished by fresh recruits from the countryside. As long as there is this reserve pool of labour willing to put up with the exploitative conditions associated with a strategy of primitive accumulation, employers have few incentives to change their strategy. However, while it is clear that women's comparative advantage for employers in a highly price-competitive, labour-intensive industry lies in the fact that they can be more easily exploited than men, what explains why women allow themselves to exploited in this way? In the next section, we examine some of the disadvantages within the labour market and the wider economy that account for this comparative advantage, as well as the extent to which the emergence of employment opportunities in the garment sector may have served to mitigate or exacerbate these disadvantages.

5 Women Workers in a Labour-surplus Economy

The impact of the export garment industry

Bangladesh continues to have a labour-surplus economy where the problem is less one of open unemployment than of disguised unemployment, under-employment and low returns to labour. Returns to female labour continue to be even lower than those to male labour because women have lower levels of education and are 'crowded' into a far more limited range of productive opportunities. Estimates by Rahman (2000) suggest male underemployment rates of 12 per cent in 1995–96 compared to 71 per cent for female, and male unemployment-equivalent rates of 8 per cent compared to 31 per cent for female. In other words there was, and continues to be, a large reserve pool of female labour, much of it located in the countryside.

While cultural norms, discrimination by employers and trade union practices all help to explain women's exclusion from the wider labour market, it was also reinforced in the past by a policy environment which protected employers from the consequences of such discrimination. Sheltered from global market forces by policies which promoted and protected domestic industry, competition within national labour markets was also suppressed, giving male workers privileged access to better paid formal employment. The participation of women in paid work was extremely low and confined to marginal informal activities which did not appear in the national statistics.

Studies made in the late 1970s – some around the time the first garment factories were being set up – saw little prospect of change in the barriers that women faced in accessing paid work. Reviewing the nature of patriarchal constraints in Bangladesh, one influential study pointed out: 'The systemic nature of patriarchy suggests that solutions to the problem of women's vulnerability and lack of income-earning opportunities will not be easily reached' (Cain et al., 1979:434). However, the advent of the export garment industry proved that patriarchal structures in Bangladesh were more flexible to the 'push' of poverty and the 'pull' of opportunity than the authors had feared. The industry's 'revealed preference' for female labour effected a very visible transformation in the gender composition of the country's labour force, both in terms of female rates of participation in paid work and its diversification into the industrial sector.

Whereas in 1951, nearly 90 per cent of employed men and women in Bangladesh worked in agriculture, by 1985–86, only 11 per cent of working women remained in agriculture compared to 63 per cent of working men (Ahmad, 1991:252). The urban manufacturing sector was a major factor behind this changing pattern of female labour force participation. Between 1974 and 1985–86, the percentage of working women in manufacturing rose from 4 to 55 per cent, while urban female labour force participation rose from around 12 per cent in 1983–84 to 20.5 per cent in 1995–96. While men continue to dominate the labour market – there were three men for every woman in 2000 – new labour market entrants are overwhelmingly female: for every new male worker joining the labour force, there are three women workers. Roughly one-quarter of female workers entering the labour market during the 1990s were employed in industry where they are to be primarily found in garment manufacturing, while the female share of new employment in industry was 39 per cent in the mid-1990s, rising to 60 per cent in 2000.[8] The result is a more pronounced 'feminization' of the labour force in urban areas where between the mid-1980s and mid-1990s the urban female labour force grew by one-third every year compared to a annual growth of only 9 per cent for the male labour force.[9]

The evidence strongly suggests that the garment industry is tapping into this reserve pool of female labour in the countryside.[10] The overwhelming majority of women in the garment industry are rural migrants and for the majority it is their first job. While studies carried out in the early phase of the industry's expansion suggested that some of the women joining the industry had been previously engaged in the kind of occupations traditionally associated with women, recent data suggest that the current generation of factory workers are new entrants into the labour force. Moreover, whereas earlier female migration had been primarily 'in association with' male family members seeking work, increasingly women are migrating into the cities on their own in search of work, and very often explicitly in search of garment work (Kabeer and Mahmud, 2004).

It is also clear that the garment industry is drawing from poorer (but by no means the poorest) sections of the rural population. Studies suggest that most migrants came from the higher density districts of Bangladesh which also supplied much of the male migration into Dhaka city (Newby, 1998). Studies also suggest that female migrants are much more likely than male migrants to be drawn from landless households (Feldman, 1993; Afsar, 2001). This is in keeping with the broader pattern in South Asia of a positive correlation between female participation in paid work and household poverty (Kabeer, 2003). Our own 2001 survey of working women in urban slum neighbourhoods (Kabeer and Mahmud, 2004) confirms this pattern for the majority of the garment workers who work in 'bangla' factories. They came from households with little or no land, prone to food-shortages during the year, many of which had no educated adult members. EPZ workers, who account for less than 5 per cent of employment in the export RMG sector, were considerably better off: they were more educated and were more likely to come from land-owning and food-secure households, while wage workers outside the export sector were generally poorer (Kabeer and Mahmud, 2004).

Women's employment in the export garment industry compared with other forms of work

Further insights into why women took up garment employment can be obtained by comparing their wages and working conditions with alternative forms of employment available to them. One study used wages and conditions in other manufacturing industries as the basis for comparison (Paul-Majumder and Begum, 2000). However, while it noted that gender inequalities in wages appeared to be greater in the garment sector than in other industries, it failed to note the far greater gender inequality in access to employment in the other industries, where men made up 85–93 per cent of the workforce. In other words, these are precisely the industries where exclusion of women in the past led to low rates of employment and their over-crowding in a limited number of occupations. A study by Bhattacharya and Rahman (1999) found not only that women constitute a higher percentage of workers in export industries generally, but that gender differentials in wages were generally lower in the export-oriented industrial sector than in other industries

A comparison between wages and working conditions in garment export industries and rural wage labour markets has greater validity because this is where most of the workers in the garment industry, who are recent rural migrants, might otherwise have sought work. From a macro-perspective, it appears that real wages in manufacturing activities steadily increased in the 1990s, while real wages in agriculture declined and real wages in service activities stagnated (Mahmud, 2002). If female wages were subject to similar trends to male wages, between the late 1980s and 2000 average female real wages increased only in formal manufacturing activities, which represented 20 per cent of female employment in 1999–2000. Since the male-female wage ratio for manufacturing wages has declined, the increase in real wages for female workers in formal manufacturing has been relatively greater, and this is particularly evident in the case of urban formal manufacturing employment.[11]

A microanalysis is provided by both Afsar (2001) and Rahman (2002). Afsar noted that 83 per cent of working women in rural areas are classified as unpaid family labour compared to 15 per cent of men. Of the remaining 17 per cent of women, 4 per cent are employees, 7 per cent are self-employed and 7 per cent are in casual daily labour. Men, in other words, dominate paid work in rural areas while women predominate in unpaid work. According to the Bangladesh Bureau of Statistics, a female day labourer earns 25 takas

(US$0.46) a day in rural areas, which is half of male wages in the rural informal economy, and 36 takas (US$0.66)in urban areas, which is half of male wages in urban areas.

Rahman cites evidence which suggests that the wage rates of unskilled male labour in the countryside were much higher than wages earned by an unskilled male worker in a garment factory, particularly if income from other sources typically earned by rural male labourers was added in. For men, therefore, there is a positive opportunity cost associated with taking up garment work. For women, on the other hand, garment factories offer higher wages than the wages that most would earn in the countryside, where alternative sources of employment are in any case limited. It also offered more than they would have earned in domestic service, the other main source of female employment in the urban economy. According to Afshar (2001), a domestic servant earned around 690 takas (US$12.7) a month (1996 figures) which was half the average wage of a worker in the RMG industry of 1,389 takas (US$25.7).

A survey carried out in 2001 (Kabeer and Mahmud, 2004) attempted a more systematic comparison of the wages and working conditions of women working in the export garment industry and women working in other forms of urban employment. It found that the better-off and more educated EPZ category were also most likely to work in conditions which approximated formal sector employment: they were more likely to be tested on entry, to be issued with a contract letter, to be given 'permanent' status (although even within the EPZ, only 30 per cent of those in our sample reported permanent status), to know about labour laws and to report a variety of benefits (including childcare, paid leave and medical facilities) than other garment workers. They are also likely to report higher incomes and work fewer hours.

However, even other garment workers who worked in the 'bangla' factories and accounted for the majority of the industry's workforce, while enjoying lower wages and poorer working conditions, were nevertheless better off by both criteria compared to other female wage workers in the urban economy. Moreover, while these other wage workers worked fewer hours than garment workers, this was very often a result of the far more casualized nature of their jobs and their inability to find work on a regular basis (Kabeer and Mahmud, 2004). Disadvantage thus takes different forms for different groups of poor working women in the urban economy.

While the majority of workers in the survey used their wages to meet various basic needs (food, rent, clothing, medicine), garment workers were more likely to save and to remit some of their income to families in the countryside. (Afshar found that the female garment workers in her study remitted more money home than male garment workers – around one-third and two-fifths of their monthly income, respectively.)

Income security

The single most important aspect of garment employment that women workers valued was that they earned a secure income. While their wages were not always paid on time, in contrast to many other forms of employment available to them, they were paid and so had a minimum degree of security. A survey of garment factory workers retrenched in the post-9/11 decline in orders found that the overwhelming majority who were still looking for employment (around 92 per cent of those interviewed) expressed a preference for garment employment, while around half of those who had already found employment would have preferred garment employment. As the report notes, higher and more stable incomes were the main reasons for their preference (Sidique, 2003).

However, if employers operate with 'informal economy' mindsets in relation to their workers, the women workers respond in kind. While they may be more prepared than men to accept the conditions which prevail in the factories – long hours sitting in one place doing the same repetitive tasks under the watchful eye of supervisors – most do not stay in any one factory for very long, changing jobs frequently in search of higher wages. Alternatively, they drop out for a period – because of illness in the family or to return temporarily to their village – and then take up factory employment again at a later stage. They do not necessarily expect to work in garment factories for a prolonged period. Indeed, given the toll taken on their health by long working hours, it would not be possible to undertake such work for an extended period of time. Our survey of working women found that on average women worked in the garment industry for five years.

Our findings also suggested that there is a strong life cycle element to women's livelihood strategies. It is largely young unmarried women or women starting out in their married lives who work in factories. As they get older, and their domestic responsibilities increase because of marriage or children, they drop out and seek work where conditions are flexible enough to combine work and domestic and childcare responsibilities (Kabeer and Mahmud, 2003).

Women with less education and savings end up in more casual forms of waged labour, either in domestic service, small workshops or construction work. Thus around 25 per cent of those who were currently in these kinds of occupations had been garment workers in the past. The better off among them, particularly those with savings, started up their own businesses: around 38 per cent of those who were currently self-employed had once been garment workers.

There is a great deal of debate as to whether access to relatively regular forms of paid work by women in a context in which they had previously been denied such access has 'empowered' them. Opinion on this depends on whether the focus is on the employers' perspective ('primitive accumulation and 'exploitative rents') and the wages and working conditions that go with it or on the workers' perspectives and how they view their choices. The general public in Bangladesh perceives that garment employers have been given considerable incentives and encouragement by the government to set up their factories but appear to be reluctant, except in the face of buyer pressure, to redistribute some of their profits to improve the working conditions of their workers.

From the point of view of women workers, it is clear that they do not see work in the garment industry as a humanly sustainable livelihood option in the long run. On the other hand, it has had significant effects in the personal arena of their lives, including in their capacity to negotiate with dominant family members, to postpone their age of marriage and to exercise greater choice in who they marry, to contribute to their families and thus to be perceived and valued as earning family members. What it has not done is to enable them to organize themselves as workers and to use their collective power to negotiate a better deal for themselves at work or in society at large.

Collective organization and workers' rights

While the trade unions blame garment employers for their hostility to their attempts to unionize workers, employers point to the long history of disruptive behaviour by trade unions in the public sector as their justification for keeping them out. Both versions are true. Employers are known to have used strong-arm tactics to intimidate anyone found to be attempting to unionize and they have succeeded in keeping the garment industry largely non-unionized.

On the other hand, the trade unions are not particularly representative of workers elsewhere in the economy. Indeed, it is estimated that they represent at most a third of formally employed workers (who themselves make up less than 10 per cent of the total workforce) and around 3 per cent of the total workforce in Bangladesh. This partly reflects the difficulties of organizing workers in an economy which is largely characterized by informal conditions of employment using organizational forms which were developed for more formal forms of employment in industrialized economies. The problems of organization are clearly exacerbated when the workers in question are young women who have only recently migrated from the countryside where there no history of trade union activity and where they have been under strict patriarchal control.

However, low levels of unionization also reflect the evolution of trade unionism in Bangladesh. Most trade unions belong to federations which are affiliated to the main political parties. The majority of trade union leaders attempt to perpetuate their leadership through their political connections, particularly when they are affiliated to the party in power, without attempting to seek the support of rank-and-file workers (Mondol, 2002; Taher, 1999; Hye, 1992). The politicized character of unions, their corrupt practices and disruptive behaviour partly justify the reluctance of employers to deal with them.

From the point of view of women workers, there are additional problems. The trade unions are overwhelmingly male dominated, reproducing within their leadership and rank-and-file membership the patriarchal attitudes of the wider society. Few have been willing to take up 'women's issues' seriously – harassment on the streets and within factories, proper toilet facilities, maternity leave and childcare. This appears to be changing, as a number of the more progressive unions have sought to set up 'women's wings' which deal more sensitively with women workers. There is evidence of a greater willingness on the part of women workers to engage in collective bargaining at the enterprise level or to engage in individual negotiations with management (Afshar, 2001). There may be also greater support from workers and management for enterprise-based unions which respond to the needs of workers within their factories rather than seeking to represent the interests of political parties.

6 Lessons Learned

Main findings

By way of conclusion, let us draw out some of the key lessons to be drawn from the Bangladesh experience in export-oriented garment manufacturing and consider some of the challenges that the industry faces. Firstly, the evidence strongly suggests that the industry has made a significant contribution not only to economic growth and export earnings in the country, but also to poverty reduction. Apart from the negligible proportion in the EPZs, the majority of its workers come from poorer households and the poorer districts of Bangladesh; they have low levels of education and their families are often landless and in food deficit for some of the year.

Secondly, it would appear that the garment industry is addressing the gender dimension of poverty by providing wage employment to a section of the labour force which has faced considerable discrimination and which was previously confined to the margins of the labour market and was part of an invisible reserve army of labour. The wages women are able to earn in the garment industry are higher than in the available alternative forms of employment; they enable them to support themselves and one other adult at levels of living above the poverty line. The fact that many workers remit part of their income to the countryside suggests that it is indeed being used to support their families. This ability to contribute to the family's standard of living appears to have had positive effects within the family, helping to transform women from dependents into economic actors and giving them a greater say in different aspects of their lives.

Thirdly, however, these jobs do not provide a long-term solution to female poverty. The garment industry has been notoriously footloose in global terms and the impending phasing out of the MFA makes its future in Bangladesh extremely uncertain. Clearly, the capacity of the industry to continue to generate employment is tied up with its capacity to survive. But the jobs are also not sustainable from the perspective of individual women. Extremely long hours doing the same repetitive tasks with little or no prospect of promotion mean that few workers last more than five years in the industry. In any case, most women cannot continue to work these hours once they have children to look after. Consequently, those who have some education or savings will take up self-employment of various kinds; others will take up waged employment outside the garment sector which pays less but allows greater flexibility in management of their time.

Fourthly, the advent of the garment industry has given rise to an unprecedented degree of attention to the question of the rights of women workers in Bangladesh. Although women have increasingly entered paid work, particularly since the 1970s, they worked largely in the informal economy and very little notice was taken of their pay and working conditions. There are a number of reasons for the intense scrutiny that the industry has received domestically and internationally. One is the visibility of its female workforce in a context where women used to be largely invisible. In addition, the public perception of garment employers is not favourable: they are seen as individuals who have amassed considerable wealth in a short time with support from the government, but who are unwilling to pay their fair share of taxes, to share their profits with their workers or to engage in any form of socially responsible behaviour. It is widely known that any improvements that have taken place in labour standards in the industry have reflected pressure from international buyers rather than enlightened self-interest on the part of employers.

However, pressure from buyers does not necessarily reflect greater self-enlightenment on their part, but is rather a result of international pressure, particularly from the trade union movement in the buyers' own countries, backed by consumer groups and student activists. But these groups are only interested in the export sector of the economy, the sector which competes with their jobs or provides the goods they consume. Moreover, while they have succeeded in improving labour standards in this sector, the improvements are largely confined to those factories with which buyers deal directly. Such top-down improvements in labour standards do little to contribute to workers' rights since they are the product of voluntary agreements between buyers and their suppliers. Indeed, most workers do not know that they have rights: only 23 per cent of workers in the EPZs, 18 per cent in the Desh garment factories and 3 per cent outside the industry had heard of the country's labour laws.

In a country like Bangladesh, where the interacting constraints of poverty and patriarchy have led women, particularly those from poorer households, to be perceived, and to perceive themselves, as second-class citizens, global attempts to improve labour standards in a small part of the economy by international buyers who are simultaneously cutting back on the prices they offer local producers hold out very little promise in the long run for promoting women's rights as workers and as citizens. The top-down imposition of standards may be better than having no standards at all, but it does not substitute for building workers' awareness and their capacity to represent their own interests with employers and the government.

There is a critical need for 'bottom-up' capacity building, but it is not clear how this can be done. Trade unions could have played a constructive role in this process but their adversarial tactics, politicized character and male dominance suggests that they will have to undergo considerable reform before they are able to do so: 'social responsibility' should be as much an obligation on the part of trade unions in Bangladesh as of employers. The organization of the poor in Bangladesh has been carried out more effectively by other civil society organizations, including developmental NGOs. The NGO sector is obviously not a homogeneous one, but most NGOs work with precisely those sections of the population that are ignored by the trade unions – the working poor in the informal economy, with a particular emphasis on women.

It is worth noting that in the consultations with the poor carried out in connection with the *World Development Report 2000*, consultations in urban areas suggested that of the formal institutions which impinged on the lives of the poor, it was the garment industry and the NGO sector that were seen as positive. In our survey, women associated with NGOs in the urban slums, who were mainly self-employed, were far more likely to vote in national and local elections than other women.

Most NGOs work in rural areas but the few that do work in urban areas and deal with garment workers have adopted a very different model of organization from that of trade unions. Some are service-oriented – organizing low-cost housing for workers or providing childcare facilities – but others provide legal education on their rights for workers in urban slum communities and legal support to take grievances to the labour courts. It is likely to be this painstaking building up of a sense of citizenship from the grassroots which will lead to more sustainable improvements in the terms and conditions in which the poor sell their labour in Bangladesh than can be achieved through a trade union movement that is out of touch with the lives of the majority of the country's workers who are located in the informal economy.

It is probable that much greater progress would have been made on the issue of workers' rights if more attention had been paid both to the content and enforcement of Bangladesh's labour legislation. There are far too few labour inspectors to bring any real pressure on enterprises to comply with legislation and those few are too busy collecting 'tolls' from factory owners to have time to check conditions. There are law courts to which workers and management can turn for adjudication of disputes but these are expensive and time-consuming. To some extent it is this failure to observe national laws that allows international buyers to insist on their own codes of conduct with local employers.

In addition, however, much of the labour legislation is not only irrelevant to the vast majority of the country's workers, it is also obsolete. Of 51 labour laws, 13 date back to the British period, 25 date to the period when Bangladesh was part of Pakistan and 13 have been passed since independence. The majority were thus formulated to protect privileged formal sector workers within the context of a protected domestic economy. A thorough review of labour legislation needs to be carried out so that it can be brought into line with the country's current realities and backed with the resources necessary to ensure compliance. A new labour code is being formulated by the Ministry of Labour with fairly wide-ranging consultations with labour organizations and trade unions. The experience of women workers in the RMG sector has informed many of the new provisions in the labour code but the weakness of the enforcement system remains the main barrier to implementation.

The future

The Bangladesh RMG industry is at a critical point in its history. The MFA is due to be phased out by the end of 2004 and the industry will have to compete in a world where the quotas which restrained the export growth of some of its competitors will no longer apply. Some observers believe that the industry needs to move into more value-added, higher-priced and higher fashion products which means investing in more technology-intensive processes. This may make sense from the point of view of individual manufacturers or groups of manufacturers.

However, not all sections of the industry have the capacity to upgrade; they can only survive if they continue to compete at the low-cost, low-value end of the industry. It may be possible to consider whether these segments could move in the future to closer markets in other parts of Asia where the demand for low-value products is likely to increase. Moving to markets closer to home also means that Bangladesh's long lead times may not be as problematic and may even be reduced.

Nor does the move into higher-value items necessarily make sense from the point of view of all sections of the workforce. Such a strategy is likely to lead to higher wages and better conditions in the industry, but it is also likely to be associated with a shift into more capital-intensive technology and reduced levels of employment. It is likely to lead to increased employment of educated (male) workers and reduced employment of less educated (female) workers. The example of the knitwear industry is illustrative.

There are other ways in which the garment industry could increase its share of value added without taking the hi-tech route, many of which would dramatically improve conditions for the country's industrialization. On the part of government, this would include improving infrastructure, for example conditions in Chittagong port, and reducing the level of corruption and red tape. On the part of employers, it would mean investing in quality assurance and workers' productivity.

However, whatever measures are taken by the industry, it is clear that its future is uncertain and that many women are likely to lose their jobs, while others will face more restricted options in the future. This puts two further policy considerations on the agenda. The first is the need to train women workers in those basic skills that will equip them to cope in a world where secure life-time employment is everywhere being displaced by shorter-term, and often short-lived, forms of employment. Bangladesh's comparative advantage may remain at the lower end of the value chain, given its levels of poverty, but certain basic skills, including legal literacy and knowledge of their rights, have become essential if its workers are to earn their living with dignity, cope with the decline in some opportunities and respond to the emergence of others. Some of this education has to begin at school; some of it can be carried out through NGOs, vocational training institutes and the efforts of trade unions.

The second consideration is the interdependence that exists between the formal and informal economy. This is particularly the case in a country like Bangladesh, where only a tiny proportion of the workforce is located in what was conventionally regarded as 'formal sector employment', and the vast majority are located on a continuum with highly casualised forms of work at the other end of the spectrum. Attempts to focus on labour standards only for those who are employed by the export sector – because of the international attention it has received – is detrimental to the vast majority of workers who have no labour standards and no form of protection to help them cope with unemployment or crisis. Far more attention needs to be given to the needs of these workers and more needs to be learned from safety net mechanisms which have worked for them: micro-insurance services and public works programmes. In the end, however, it will be the economy's capacity to generate employment opportunities for all which will serve as the most effective form of social protection in the long run.

Notes

1 Export incentives include special bonded warehouse facilities, back-to-back letters of credit (LCs), duty drawback, cash compensation of 25 per cent of FOB value of export and simplified export procedures. The dual exchange rate system of the 1980s was replaced by a unified system. The revised industrial policy of 1986 reduced the role of the public sector in manufacturing through denationalization and divestiture of state-owned enterprises and restricting future public investment to a few 'reserved' areas such as defence and armaments and nuclear power.

2 These included reduction of advance income tax deduction from 0.5 to 0.25 per cent of export earnings; an increase in the cash compensation scheme from 15 to 25 per cent; reduction of the tariff on the import of capital machinery from 7.5 to 0 per cent; differential rates of duty drawback replaced by a flat rate for a large number of imported inputs; relaxation of eligibility for duty drawback; interest rates on bank loans reduced slightly from 8–12 per cent to 8–10 per cent; reduction in the differences between incentives in EPZs and the DTA (domestic tariff area); operationalization of the duty drawback system and flexible exchange rate from managed 'float' now replaced by fully floating exchange rate.

3 In the late 1990s only 10–12 per cent of fabric used in the woven RMG industry came from local textile mills; this share may have increased slightly due to new investment in recent times (Bhattacharya and Rahman, 2000:16).

4 In knitwear value addition is higher, ranging between 40–60 per cent of the gross value of exports, but it is still lower that that of Bangladesh's competitors since Bangladesh has to rely to a larger extent on imported yarn (Bhattacharya and Rahman, 2000:16).

5 These items accounted for 80 per cent of all knitted exports and two-thirds of all woven exports in 1999. Other items include terry towels, infant playsuits, cotton bathrobes and cotton overalls (Asia Foundation, 2001:25–32).

6 The macro costs of doing business are invariably highest where direct labour costs are cheapest (Asia Foundation, 2001:9).

7 Larger firms send their own supervisors and managers to monitor quality in the smaller firms to which they subcontract.

8 The female share of incremental increase in the labour force has been rising over the years. According to official labour force surveys, the female share of incremental increase was 23 per cent between 1983–84 and 1989, rising to 48 per cent between 1989 and 1995–96. This figure was 72 per cent between 1995–96 and 1999–2000.

9 The female labour force participation rate grew from 7 to 22 per cent in rural areas and from 12 to 26 per cent in urban areas, but remained the same for men or even declined slightly in the recent past. During this period the female share of the labour force more than doubled from 9 to 22 per cent.

10 In the early 1990s the female population growth rate in urban areas was 14 per cent per annum compared to 10 per cent for males, resulting from the higher

female migration rate from rural areas compared to men. Women also have higher labour force participation rates in urban areas compared to rural areas, unlike men, and the female labour force in urban areas grew much faster compared to that in rural areas (Mahmud, 2004).

11 One estimate shows that the average weekly earnings (in 1985–86 prices) in the formal urban manufacturing sector increased from 273 takas (US$5) in 1983–84 to 418 (US$7.7) takas in 1995–96 for male workers and from 124 (US$2.3) to 241 takas (US$4.5) for female workers.

Currency: 1 taka = US$0.018

References

Afsar, R. (2000). 'Female Labour Migration and Urban Adaptation', Proceedings of a national seminar on the Growth of the Garment Industry in Bangladesh: Economic and Social Dimensions, BIDS and Oxfam, Bangladesh, Dhaka.

Afsar, R. (2001). 'Sociological Implications of Female Labour Migration in Bangladesh', in Sobhan, R. and Khundker, N. (eds), *Globalisation and Gender: Changing Patterns of Women's Employment in Bangladesh*, University Press Limited, Dhaka.

Arizpe, L. and Aranda, J. (1981). 'The "comparative advantages" of women's disadvantages. Women workers in the strawberry export agribusiness in Mexico', *Signs* 7(2): 453–73.

Asia Foundation (2001). *Bangladesh's Apparel Export Industry: Into the 21st Century – The Next Challenges*, Asia Foundation, Dhaka.

Barrientos, S., Kabeer, N. and Hossain, N. (2003). 'The gender dimensions of the globalization of production', background paper for the World Commission on the Social Dimensions of Globalisation, ILO, Geneva.

Bhattacharya, D. and Rahman, M. (1999). 'Female Employment under Export-propelled Industrialization: Prospects for Internalising Global Opportunities in the Bangladesh Apparel Sector', UNRISD Occasional Paper No. 10, UNRISD, Geneva.

Cain, M., Khanam, S.R. and Nahar, S. (1979). 'Class, patriarchy and women's work in Bangladesh', *Population and Development Review* 5(3): 405–38.

Bhattacharya, D. and Rahman, M. (2000). 'Bangladesh's apparel sector: Growth trends and the post-MFA challenges', Proceedings of a National Seminar on the Growth of the Garment Industry in Bangladesh: Economic and Social Dimensions, BIDS and Oxfam Bangladesh, Dhaka.

Chaudhuri-Zohir, S. (1998). 'Gender implications of industrial reforms and adjustment in the manufacturing sector of Bangladesh', unpublished PhD dissertation, University of Manchester, UK.

Chaudhuri-Zohir, S. (2000). 'Household Dynamics and Growth of Garment Industry in Bangladesh', Proceedings of a National Seminar on the Growth of the Garment Industry in Bangladesh: Economic and Social Dimensions, BIDS and Oxfam Bangladesh, Dhaka.

Dannecker, P. (2002). *Between Conformity and Resistance: Women Garment Workers in Bangladesh*, University Press Ltd., Dhaka.

Feldman, S. (1993). 'Contradictions of gender inequality: urban class formation in contemporary Bangladesh', in Clark, A.W. (ed.), *Gender and Political Economy: Explorations of South Asian Systems*, Oxford University Press, New Delhi.

Hossain, I. (2002). 'Export processing zones in Bangladesh and industrial relations', Chapter 7 in Muqtada, M. *et al.* (eds), *Bangladesh: Economic and Social Challenges of Globalisation*, study prepared for the ILO, Geneva, UPL, Dhaka.

Hye, M.A. (1992). 'Trade Unionism, Wages and Labour Productivity in the Manufacturing Sector of Bangladesh', BIDS Research Report No. 133, Bangladesh Institute of Development Studies, Dhaka.

Kabeer, N. (2000). *The Power to Choose: Bangladeshi Women and Labour Market Decisions in London and Dhaka*, Verso Publications, London.

Kabeer, N. (2004). 'Globalisation, labour standards and women's rights: dilemmas of collective (in)action in an interdependent world', *Feminist Economics* 10(1): 3–36.

Kabeer, N. and Mahmud, S. (2004). 'Globalization, Gender and Poverty: Bangladeshi Women Workers in Export and Local Markets, *Journal of International Development* 16(1): 93–109.

Khundker, N. (2002). 'Globalisation, Competitiveness and Job Quality in the Garment Industry in Bangladesh', Chapter 3 in Muqtada, M. *et al.* (eds), *Bangladesh: Economic and Social Challenges of Globalisation*, study prepared for the ILO Geneva, UPL, Dhaka.

Mahmud, S. (2003). 'Is Bangladesh Experiencing a Feminization of the Labour Force?', paper presented at the annual meeting of the Population Association of America, Minneapolis, US.

Mahmud, W. (1998). 'Macroeconomic Management and Reforms: Issues in Governance', in *A Review of Bangladesh's Development 1997*, Centre for Policy Dialogue, University Press Limited, Dhaka.

Mahmud, W. (2002). 'Macro Economics of Poverty Reduction: The Case of Bangladesh', paper prepared for UNDP, Dhaka.

Mahmud, W. (2003). 'Bangladesh: Development Challenges and Outcomes in the Context of Globalisation', paper presented at the conference on The Future of Globalisation: Explorations in Light of Recent Turbulences, Yale Centre for the Study of Globalisation and the World Bank, 10–11 October 2003, Yale University.

Mondol, A.H. (2002). 'Globalisation, Industrial Relations and Labour Policies: The Need for Renewed Agenda', Chapter 5 in Muqtada, M. *et al.* (eds), *Bangladesh: Economic and Social Challenges of Globalisation*, study prepared for the ILO Geneva, UPL, Dhaka.

Newby, M.H. (1998). 'Women in Bangladesh: a study of the effects of garment factory work on control over income and autonomy', PhD thesis, Department of Social Sciences, University of Southampton.

Paul-Majumder, P. and Begum, Anwara (2000). 'The Gender Differentiated Effects of the Growth of Export-oriented Manufacturing: A Case of the Ready-made

Garment Industry in Bangladesh', background paper, Policy Research Report on Gender and Development, World Bank, Washington DC.

Quddus, M. and Rashid, S. (2000). *Entrepreneurs and economic development: The remarkable story of garment exports from Bangladesh*, University Press Limited, Dhaka.

Rahman, R. I. (2002). 'Skill Development in Bangladesh: Responses to Globalisation', Chapter 4 in M Muqtada et al (eds.) Bangladesh: Economic and Social Challenges of Globalisation, Study prepared for the ILO Geneva, UPL, Dhaka.

Rashid, M. A. (2002). 'Globalisation, growth and employment', Chapter 2 in Muqtada, M. *et al.* (eds), *Bangladesh: Economic and Social Challenges of Globalisation*, study prepared for the ILO Geneva, UPL, Dhaka.

Sidique, K. (2003). 'Deceleration in the Export Sector of Bangladesh and Women Workers: Assessing Impacts and Identifying Coping Strategies', CPD Occasional Paper Series No. 26, Centre for Policy Dialogue, Dhaka.

Standing, G. (1999). *Global Labour Flexibility: Seeking Distributive Justice*, Macmillan, Basingstoke, UK.

Taher, M. A. (1999). 'Politicization of Trade Unions: Issues and Challenges in Bangladesh Perspective', *Indian Journal of Industrial Relations* 34 (4): 403–20.

On the Threshold of Informalization: Women Call Centre Workers in India

Swasti Mitter, Grace Fernandez and Shaiby Varghese

1 Introduction

The issue of offshore outsourcing of Information Technology Enabled Services (ITES), needed in areas such as customer care, data entry and medical transcriptions, has become central in the current discourse on the world trading order.[1] Most of the analysis, however, has focused on the implications of outsourcing for workers in the North and it has remained persistently gender neutral. This chapter aims to redress the balance by providing a perspective from the South and from the women involved. It does this in order to assess the opportunities and threats that the growing volume of offshore outsourcing of ITES from high-wage to low-wage countries poses for traditionally disadvantaged groups such as women in the poorer parts of the world. It highlights areas of policy intervention which could augment livelihood and employment opportunities for underprivileged women on a secure basis in the information economy. In the spirit of the UN Millennium Development Goals, which aim to reduce poverty and gender inequality, the chapter bases its arguments on a brief preliminary survey of the consequences of the relocation of customer care services to call centres in India, a country that is the prime receiver of outsourced ITES jobs. Call centres as an institution have been chosen not only because the centres have become an important focus of the North–South dialogue, but also because:

- women form the majority of call centre workers;
- the training required to be an operator in a call centre is not as expensive as the training needed to work in the software sector;

Opposite: *Call centre workers in India.* PICTURE: ICICI ONESOURCE

- with initiative and imagination on the part of policy-makers, NGOs and donor agencies, such training could be given to women and men from semi-urban and rural areas where poverty is generally more endemic than in the cities and towns.

The opportunities that call centre jobs open up for women and men in India, however, need to be assessed in the context of the vulnerability of these jobs in the face of:

- rapid technological changes that are likely to erode the relevance of the skills that women have acquired and can offer to call centres; and

- the growing protectionist lobby in the North against the offshore out-sourcing of customer services and other ITES work.

Export-oriented development, as epitomized by the booming ITES sector in general, and call centres in particular, thus presents aspects of informaliza-tion based on the latent insecurity in the sector. However, as this chapter argues, the skills and expertise acquired in the process can be extended to strengthen the information and communications technology (ICT) base of the national economy, geared to the needs of the local communities and not simply to the business needs of overseas clients. The best practice, in this con-text, will be to combine global knowledge with local expertise to alleviate the problems of inequality based on class privilege and gender. The strategic vision should be to link the global with the local so that women, together with other disadvantaged groups, can aspire to have sustainable employment.

The experience of India could have significant implications for other Commonwealth countries in the South and the factors underlying India's success, including the role of the government in creating a conducive environ-ment for the growth of employment opportunities, offer a basis for replicat-ing the Indian experience elsewhere.

It is within this framework that the chapter evaluates and assesses:

- the benefits and threats that offshore outsourcing of ITES jobs bring to women in the South;

- the informalization of employment that these new jobs imply;

- the possibilities of extending the benefits of these jobs to under-privileged women of the South;

- the roles that policy-makers can play in utilizing the potentials of service sector jobs for poverty reduction.

2 The Global Information Technology Enabled Services Industry: The International Story

In the 1980s and 1990s, the introduction of computer technology led to an effective fragmentation of production processes and facilitated the outsourcing of manufacturing jobs from high-wage countries to low-wage ones. Young women in developing countries, inside and outside export processing zones, were the major recipients of these jobs. The implications of global assembly lines, particularly in textiles, clothing and electronics, for the quality of women's working lives have been an important area of debate and discussion in policy circles and NGO networks. Similar and perhaps more dramatic changes are now taking place in the relocation of service sector jobs, again involving women in the developing world.

The relocation of service sector jobs mirrors the experience of 'runaway' manufacturing jobs and is a consequence of business strategies as well as of technological advances. The convergence of computer and communication technologies, culminating in networking technologies, has made it possible to digitize a vast amount of information that can be transported, processed and retrieved to and from a distant location at little cost. From a technical and productivity standpoint, an information-processing worker sitting 6,000 miles away might as well be in the next cubicle and on the local area network. In this scenario, with the cost of telephoning steadily falling, the advantages of relocating ICT-related and ICT-enabled jobs from the US or the UK to India, Malaysia or Ghana are obvious. It costs a US company $13,000 to hire a new graduate, with combined IT engineering and business skills, of the Indian Institute of Management, Ahmedabad. A Stanford University graduate with similar qualifications can demand somewhere in the region of $95,000. These are what the trade describes as world-class graduates (*Business*, September 2003:116), but the cost differentials are equally noticeable at the relatively low-skilled end of the information processing sector, as in customer care services, medical transcriptions work, processing of airline tickets, accounting and tax return forms. These are described generally as Information Technology Enabled Services and are opening up novel opportunities for women. The worldwide market for ITES is set to grow at a rate of 66 per cent per annum in the coming years and it has been estimated that it will be worth more than $500 billion in 2004 (Bhattacharya *et al.*, 2003). These services are a very important part of the Business-to-Business (B2B) component of e-commerce, arising out of what is described in trade journals as the offshoring of business process outsourcing (Mitter, 2004b). A large proportion of these new jobs are likely to be exported to low-wage countries. The logic is simple. The average annual wage of an employee in a call centre in the UK is £12,500 (US$23,000); the average annual wage of a similar employee in India is £1,200 (US$2,210) (*BBC News Online*, 15 December 2003).

Thus, globalization now offers women in some developing countries opportunities to find employment in the ITES sector, arising from offshore outsourcing by global corporations, on an unprecedented scale. Women also gain because these jobs are of much better quality than those previously on offer in export-oriented manufacturing. Yet there are reasons to be cautious. Call centres primarily cater for the needs of overseas companies which control the supply chain – including the final market as well as the technology. Strategic decisions are taken outside the host countries with national policy-makers and employees having little or no say. In order to encourage global companies to bring business and employment, policy-makers sometimes alter or modify national employment regulations and legislation, which may or may not be to the advantage of the employees.[2] In addition, relocation of service sector jobs raises demands for protectionism from the trade unions and the public in high-wage countries which increases volatility in the South.

It is against this background of unpredictability in the quantity and quality of export-oriented service sector jobs that national policy-makers need to ensure that women, a traditionally disadvantaged group, do not bear the brunt of sudden adjustments if foreign companies pull out and some or most of the jobs disappear.[3]

3 The Global ITES Industry: The India Story

Growth of ITES in India

At the beginning of the new millennium, the worldwide demand for ITES was projected to grow at the dramatic rate of 66 per cent per annum (*Communiqué India*, No. 2, February 2002); India considered that it had the potential to bid for a large part of this market.[4] In 1999, NASSCOM (National Association of Software and Services Companies), projected that by 2005 nearly 1.1 million Indian workers would be employed in ITES in India. By 2008, ICT services and back-office work in India is expected to swell five-fold to become a $57 billion annual export industry employing four million people and accounting for 7 per cent of India's GDP. India's export-oriented ICT services are expected to generate 20 million jobs by 2020 – a welcome prospect in a country where 200 million people will be entering the workforce during the same period (*Business Week*, 8 December 2003) and where the unemployment rate for young men and women is already high.

There are no gender-disaggregated statistics on employment in outsourced ITES in India, although according to the Deputy Director of the

---

Box 1: Gender Structure in Back-office Services

Routine: requiring only basic skills – women predominate

- Data capture and processing
- Customer call centres – for routine queries, order taking and referrals
- Hotel or rental car reservations
- Virtual service centres (e.g. home delivery pizza companies)

Discretionary: requiring technical training and problem solving – women predominate

- Data verification and repair (e.g. optically scanned documents)
- Claims processing
- Mailing list management
- Remote secretarial services.
- Customer call centres – account queries, after-sales support

Specialized: requiring specific expertise and managerial authority – men predominate

- Accounting, book keeping, payroll processing
- Electronic publishing
- Customer call centres – problem/website design and management
- Dispute resolution
- Technical transcription (e.g. medical, legal)
- Medical records management
- Technical online support
- Indexing and abstracting services
- Research and technical writing

Source: Adapted by Swasti Mitter from *I.T. Information Technology*, Vol. 11, No. 2, December 2001, EFY Enterprises Pvt Ltd, New Delhi

---

Confederation of Indian Industries (CII) at least 40 per cent of these newly created jobs are filled by women (Field Survey, 2002).[5] Prospects for women workers look good in this sector because the ITES segment of e-business is more resilient than the software sector. In the last few years volatility in the

US economy and on Wall Street has affected the volume of e-business in software. Even a NASDAQ-listed company such as Infosys, India's second largest listed exporter of software services, came under pressure as US clients sharply cut their spending on technology services (*Financial Times*, 11 April 2002). Yet Infosys has invested US$5 million in setting up a business process outsourcing (BPO) unit as it expects to receive a steady supply of back-office tasks such as bill processing.

ITES that refer to relocated back-office operations open up opportunities for women. Yet one should be cautious about the future. There are various types of back-office services, requiring different levels of skills from women and men, and there is a discernible trend to hire women in operations that require less complex skills (Box 1). Businesses in ITES are generally seen as low margin and high volume, requiring repetitive skills that are amenable to automation. Thus, while jobs may disappear in the next phase of technological change, this type of work currently provides much-needed cushioning to companies such as Infosys against recession in the US and other client countries.

An additional reason for caution is that, in addition to threats of redundancies as a result of technological changes, most ITES jobs are 'footloose' in nature, and there is growing competition among Commonwealth countries in the South to attract these jobs. African countries such as Ghana, which have made visible entries into the internet economy, are attracting some of the jobs that went previously to India. Wages in some African countries are much lower than those in India and the lower cost makes these countries attractive sites if the requisite environment and skills can be found for outsourcing companies in the US. The average wage of a data entry operator is US$480 per annum in Ghana; the wages for a worker with comparable skills is US$1,250 in India and US$25,000 in the US. These footloose jobs open up new opportunities and higher pay for women in Ghana, a country with a lower per capita income than India (*Business*, September 2003:159), but as with labour-intensive, export-oriented manufacturing jobs, there is reason to be concerned about the quality of work in what are sometimes referred to as 'electronic sweatshops' (Box 2).

India's comparative advantage

In spite of competition from other developing countries and the difficulties that global companies face in operating in India, it has been the most popular site of ITES outsourcing by US and UK based companies, particularly for call centres.[6] It is worth exploring the reasons for this.

India is a country of contrasts. Despite its presence in the global digital economy, it contains the largest number of poor people in the world. 300

Box 2: Do Run-away Jobs from India Create Electronic Sweatshops in Ghana?

If you are caught playing your radio too loudly in Times Square, selling ice cream while parked in a Harlem crosswalk or dumping your kitchen trash in Prospect Park, your ticket does not go to City Hall to be processed: it goes to Ghana. Just days after the tickets are written out on New York City streets, they are scanned and sent as digital photographs to computers in a small office in downtown Accra, Ghana's hot and crowded capital. From New York's perspective, it hardly matters whether the work is done in Africa or Delaware: the contract is simply a way to process the half-million environmental tickets the city hands out every year. It is good work, by Ghanaian standards. The typists earn 500,000 cedis a month (almost US$70) – three times the Ghanaian minimum wage and more than twice the average per capita income) to type the offender's name, address, fine and offence location into a searchable database that is sent back to New York. It can then be stored electronically and used to generate payment notices. The company's contract requires it to return the transcribed information with an error rate of no more than 1 per cent and within 48 hours of pick-up. The employees work in revolving eight-hour shifts that run 24 hours a day. They are immaculately dressed and sit silently at computer terminals, typing as fast as they can in a plain office. The workers get one 30-minute and two 10-minute breaks per shift to use the bathroom, eat and call friends. Their computers have no e-mail because it could be a distraction. Soon, workers will be paid by the keystroke, with deductions for errors. Data Management, the name of the office, is the largest internet centre in West Africa. Visitors at the internet centre downstairs jokingly call Data Management an 'electronic sweatshop'. But the jobs are so popular that dozens of people apply for each opening, even when the company does not advertise. And to many people in this city of open sewers and vast unemployment, the data entry operation represents a beacon of hope.

Source: Worth, 2002

million Indians subsist on less than $1 a day; more than one-third of India's 1.3 billion citizens are illiterate. At the same time India has certain features that make it a prime site for relocated service sector jobs. The relatively low cost of manpower makes India a very attractive base for sourcing cross-border IT-enabled services. India's large English-speaking, highly educated and low-wage talent pool has established itself as one of the fastest-growing outsourcing services markets in the world. A 12-hour time zone difference with the US and other markets for medical transcription or call centre services is also in India's favour. An article in *McKinsey Quarterly* in 2001 rated India as the highest preferred offshore service area among all countries. A recent survey by NASSCOM found that almost two out of five Fortune 500 companies currently outsource some of their software requirements to India. According to a study done by McKinsey, IT-enabled services offer an even better future than software and can generate substantial revenue and employment for India over the next four years.[7] In the UK, unions predict that up to 200,000 jobs in the finance sector will be moved offshore, mostly to India, as companies take advantage of India's cheaper labour costs. A. T. Kearney Inc. in the US predicts that 500,000 services jobs will go offshore by 2008. State governments in the US, like the private sector, increasingly use India to manage everything from accounting to food stamp programmes (*Business Week*, 2003:67).

Cheaper labour costs are only one reason for choosing India as a place to relocate services. India also offers a conducive environment which other developing countries do not have. There are more IT engineers in Bangalore (150,000) than in Silicon Valley (120,000), creating an enabling cyber culture. India now produces 2 million college graduates a year (a number which is expected to double by 2010), of whom 80 per cent are English-speaking (*Economist*, 13 December 2003). Another country, the Philippines, that is well equipped to compete produces only about 300,000 English-speaking graduates a year. India's main competitors are China and Malaysia. Currently the cost of operations in India is 37 per cent lower than in China and 17 per cent lower than in Malaysia, but China in particular is putting its resources into the quality of education so that it can remain competitive in the ITES sector.

In addition, government policies in India have helped to provide an enabling framework for the industry. By the late 1990s, recognition of the potential of the ICT industry had led to the establishment of the National Task Force on IT and Software Development, and the Ministry of Information Technology. The Export-Import (EXIM) Policy 2003 has removed some of the formalities that stood in the way of software exporting organizations; this has also helped ITES companies in the country (NASSCOM BPO *News Online*, April 2003).

In March 2003, the Indian Cabinet approved a proposal to ratify the ILO Night-work (Women) Convention to provide flexibility in the employment of women during night shifts, and the State of Maharashtra has enacted laws to remove restrictions on women working night shifts in the ITES industry provided some conditions are met (NASSCOM BPO *News Online*, June 2003).

The pioneers in India who first began to host outsourced services in the country got business from American Express and British Airways in the early 1980s. Some of the key multinationals that have already outsourced their work to India include HSBC, Standard Chartered Bank, Hewlett-Packard, Microsoft, DELL, American Express, Convergys and GE Capital. Norwich Union (Aviva) in the UK, which announced it was transferring a further 2,500 jobs to India, is just the latest in a long line of companies ranging from Abbey to Tesco, British Airways and National Rail Enquiries which have transferred sizeable parts of their operations to India. A NASSCOM survey of the ITES market covering 310 companies revealed that the average number of employees in a company in the ITES sector is 190, within which there was an enormous range from as few as four to as many as 16,000 workers.

A turning point in the industry came when GE Capital began to set up large call centres around Delhi in 1996, thus demonstrating that relocation could take place on a large scale and giving the centres a high visibility. Within ITES, customer care has emerged as the most important segment with call centres catering to customer queries from overseas countries booming in India, not only because of low wages, but also because of the availability of high quality workers. Nearly all Indian call centre workers have college degrees. In contrast, many of their American counterparts are high school graduates. More education can be helpful, as consumers increasingly need complex technical or financial information. In addition the attrition rate is much higher in the US compared with that in India, where call centre jobs are seen by men and women as lucrative, at least in the short run, and not a dead-end job as they are seen by employees in the UK and US.

Call centres in India

One of the most publicized types of relocation of ITES from developed to developing countries is in the area of customer care services. Call centres are characteristic institutions of the internet economy and represent distant and/or external sites of companies for answering customer business queries. Offshore call centres are located in low-wage, multilingual countries where overheads are relatively low. There are already more than 160,000 men and women on the payroll of Indian call centres in India; approximately 45 per cent of them are women. In some companies, the figure can be as high as 70 per cent. Companies are now scouring the towns and countryside away from the big cities to locate employees who can be trained for jobs in these centres. If the trend continues, women in India are likely to benefit, at least in terms of quantity of work. The question that needs to be addressed is that of the sustainability and desirability of these jobs.

> ### Box 3: Wipro Spectramind Pvt. Ltd – Case Study of a Company with Local Ownership
>
> The New Delhi-based company Wipro Spectramind Pvt. Ltd is owned mainly by Wipro, one of India's software giants, which has 96 per cent of the shares in the company. The other 4 per cent is owned by Spectramind's management. The company claims to be the first third party outsourcing company in India and also one of the main BPO companies in the country with five centres in different cities and a sixth about to be opened in Calcutta. The company undertakes a large number of jobs outsourced by various companies located in different parts of the world, mainly in the UK and US. Assignments include services at the lower end of the value chain such as medical transcription from dictaphones as well as higher-end services such as providing technical support and marketing products through voice processing.
>
> The company opened in 2000 with around 320 employees. Today there are 10,000 employees in the five centres, of whom 3,000 are employed in the Delhi centre. In Delhi, the ratio of female to male employees is 45:55 at the lower levels of the hierarchy and around 37:63 at higher levels. In Maharashtra the proportions are reversed, perhaps reflecting a more liberal society. All employees have a minimum qualification of graduation. Methods of recruitment include advertisement and campus recruitment. Candidates are screened, short-listed, and required to participate in group discussion and interview. Recruitment is followed by two months of rigorous training on accent, grammar and the culture of the client country. Employees are allocated responsibilities according to their performance during training. For senior managers, recruitment is done mainly through personal reference. Head-hunting by current employees is encouraged and a monetary incentive given for identifying suitable applicants. Advertisements are also placed on the company notice board so that employees with appropriate qualifications and experience can apply for promotion. The company prefers young people, who are expected to be more efficient and have better computer skills.

There has as yet been very little research on the business strategies and recruitment pattern of call centres. However, a brief survey undertaken by the authors in 2003 during the preparation of this chapter helps to provide some information. The survey covered two typical call centre companies in India, one a subcontractor and the other a subsidiary of an overseas company. This gives some indication of the growth of the call centre business and the impact of this on women (Boxes 3 and 4).

Box 4: MsourcE Corporation – Case Study of a Subsidiary of a Foreign Company

The Bangalore based company, MsourcE Corporation, is a subsidiary of Mphasis-BFL, itself a subsidiary of a leading US-based remote e-services company, .t. It was one of the first companies to establish a fully operational international call centre in India. It has two operations centres, one in Bangalore and the other one in Pune. MsourcE's main area of work is customer service, which is provided to foreign companies. It claims to provide high quality, value-added contact centre services and BPO services to Fortune 500 companies. MsourcE provides inbound and outbound voice services, as well as transaction processing and web-based services to many clients, including a US-based financial house and credit card company

The company started in 2000 with a small staff of 30 which has now grown to 3,200 people. More than 90 per cent of them are graduates and the remainder are postgraduates. Most of the employees are are from educated and socially and economically well-off families. Most of them are unmarried. The majority of employees are female, although only a few women work at managerial level, and most are in their early twenties. They generally work for up to two years and then look for better prospects. Most of the female staff leave the job after marriage.

Working conditions

Recruitment in the call centres surveyed is done through advertisements, campus interviews and agents. Graduates and talented undergraduates are recruited after resumé screening, telephone interview, group discussion, written test and interview. After recruitment employees are provided with training for a period of 80 days on language, accent and the culture of different countries and about their work/product. There are regular trainers for these purposes, many of whom have been trained abroad. Salaries are not fixed and are completely dependent on experience and performance. The average initial salary for customer service employees is approximately Rs.8,000 per month (approximately US$175). This increases to Rs.12,000 (US$262.5) per month within a year. Trainers get around Rs.15,000–18,000 (US$328–394) per month and managers get Rs.35,000–45,000 (US$766–985) per month. Employees are given incentives and extra remuneration from time to time through competitions and there are possibilities for employees to reach higher levels within the recruitment rank. The employees are generally given two days leave per month.

Box 5: Electronic Sweatshops: The Mixed Reaction to Call Centre Jobs in India

'But to tell you the truth, the work itself is very boring. There is nothing creative or challenging in the work itself. Sometimes, we wonder what are we doing here.'

'As compared to other factory jobs, getting 5,000 rupees as a start seems good. That is only till you have family responsibilities.'

'We work five days a week. The off-days may vary from one month to another. But that is fine. Besides, we have meetings of the teams every once a month. We can raise any issue we want to in these. Like if we have problems with taking leave or anything.'

'But the main thing is that all of us want to leave at some point; so there is not much of an interest in improving things. You talked about some organization or collective body of employees. No, we don't have any such thing. That is the reason. There is not that sort of interest.'

'I like the job, find it challenging and feel that this industry has given the younger generation, especially girls, a welcome opportunity to know about the world and also to be able to earn well. The job has given me a sense of freedom, especially in terms of money and the training received has given me a lot of self-confidence.'

Source: Gothoskar, 2000

In almost all call centres in India, there are activities round the clock in different shifts. There are, however, adequate breaks during the shifts. Companies such as MsourcE organize 'family days' where parents of young employees are invited to interact with management and discuss their problems. Parents are reassured that their daughters may be working unconventional hours, including night shifts, but are doing a perfectly safe, decent and socially accepted job.

Since the centres are open 24 hours a day, it is standard practice to have a doctor on call. Facilities including gymnasiums, reading rooms and internet browsing centres are often provided to help employees keep fit and relaxed. The major problem, attrition of employees, is handled by encouraging employees to participate in relaxation programmes. Companies worry about women leaving once they marry as shift work, particularly at night, is not seen as compatible with married life. There are additional anxieties about

Box 6: Hi, I'm in Bangalore (but I Dare not Tell)

With frosted glass and funky amber lights playing off the turquoise walls, the offices of Customer Asset look more like a Santa Fé diner than a telephone call centre in southern India. The cultural vertigo is complete when employees introduce themselves to a visitor.

'Hi, my name is Susan Sanders, and I'm from Chicago', said C. R. Suman, 22, who is in fact a native of Bangalore and fields calls from customers of a telecommunications company in the United States. Ms Suman's fluent English and broad vowels would pass muster in the stands at Wrigley Field. In case her callers ask personal questions, Ms Suman has conjured up a fictional American life, with parents Bob and Ann, brother Mark and a made-up business degree from the University of Illinois. 'We watch a lot of *Friends* and *Ally McBeal* to learn the right phrases', Ms Suman said. 'When people talk about their Bimmer, you have to know they mean a BMW.'

'Or when they say "No way, José", there is no José', added Ms Suman's co-worker, Nishara Anthony. Nishara Anthony and C. R. Suman seem all-American at work in Bangalore, India. Ms Anthony goes by the name Naomi Morrison and, if asked, says she comes from Perth Amboy, N.J. The point of this pretence is to convince Americans who dial toll-free numbers that the person on the other end of the line works right nearby — not 8,300 miles away, in a country where static-free calls used to be a novelty. Call centres are a booming business in India, as companies like General Electric and British Airways set up supermarket-size phone banks to handle a daily barrage of customer inquiries. The companies value India for its widespread use of English and low-cost labour.

Source: *New York Times*, 21 March 2001

losing trained employees who are often poached by rival companies.

With a buoyant demand for employees who are computer literate and speak English, call centre jobs present young women with opportunities that they have never experienced before. The salary of $200 to $400 a month may look small by American or British standards, but it can provide a high quality of life in India. The work environment also appears to be women-friendly and caring

However, there is a high attrition rate among young women, reflecting to a large extent the stress that they experience in call centre jobs. The work is also highly repetitive and leads to burn-out syndrome. It is understandable that the call centres are often described as 'electronic sweatshops'.

A serious problem in the export–oriented segment of the business is that employees generally have to pretend to be European or American in order to convince the customers that the answers are not coming from offshore countries and that their personal information is not sent outside their country of residence. The cultural schizophrenia that this pretence entails on the part of the employees (Box 6) has its cost.

Despite the concerns and stress, however, women employees generally appreciate the benefits of newly found opportunities and acknowledge the social and economic empowerment that these jobs have brought.

4 The future

Security of employment

The reasons for apprehension about call centre jobs relate mainly to their long-term sustainability. Although located in the formal sector, the newly-created jobs display characteristics that verge on the informal. Insecurity in employment arises not so much from the current conditions and contracts of employment. It is more to do with the fact that the business is controlled by global companies that could withdraw their custom without having to face resistance either from the employees or from the national government.

The call centre jobs, as we know them now, may disappear as changes in technology may soon alter drastically the volume and the nature of call centre service provisions. Instead of providing a central base, call centre services may be provided virtually, supported by fast data communication linkages among a network of home-based teleworkers with consequent erosion of employment rights. The deployment of a portfolio of web-based technologies (Internet, Intranet and Extranet) may also reduce the market for call centre service provisions. In banking, for example, customers may organise their own transactions with the computer of the main company without the intermediation of the call centre operators. In this new techno-environment, instead of focusing upon a single task, call centres will be engaged in multi-dimensional tasks. Women will need to have access to generic training in order to retain their share of the evolving call centre jobs of the future.

Employment in export-oriented services sectors, including in call centres, is also highly volatile, as it depends a great deal on the economic and political climate in the client countries. India is already at a cause for concern in the US where politicians are starting to view offshore outsourcing as the root of the jobless recovery[8] in the technology and services sectors. An outcry in Indiana recently prompted the state to cancel a $15 million IT contract with Tata Consulting Services. The telecom workers' union is raising concerns and the US Congress is probing whether the security of financial and medical records are at risk. The state legislature in New Jersey is proposing to make it compulsory for every call centre to identify its location and to give the caller the right to insist that her/his call be re-routed to a call centre in the US. There are similar protectionist pressures in the UK. As Norwich Union shed 2,350 jobs and exported the work to India, the Amicus trade union criticized the decision as despicable and vowed to fight it (*BBC News Online*, 11 December 2003). The UK Trade Secretary, Patricia Hewitt, announced on 6 December 2003 that she would be commissioning an independent inquiry into the implications of off-shoring (Connon, 2003).

More than a trickle down

Although call centres have brought much-needed employment opportunities for women in India, the informalization and potential disappearance of the jobs created warrants caution and action in India, and provides lessons for other Commonwealth countries. In particular, in the face of technological change, the movement of custom in search of lower wages and a protectionist global trading environment, it is important to think through strategies to limit the economic disempowerment of women, if and when these jobs disappear. An important strategy could be to use the current boom in outsourced work to create a climate of cyber culture where skills and expertise gained in providing services to overseas companies could be used to meet local needs on a sustainable basis. The spread of e-governance, as in Hyderabad, India, for example, opens up possibilities of improving productivity and employment opportunities of non-elite men and women in relatively simple information processing work.

The skills and expertise acquired through call centre jobs could also be used to promote self-employment. Familiarity with computer technologies and acquisition of expertise in the use of networking technologies in local communities could likewise enhance opportunities for marketing goods and services even from rural areas where the majority of the poor live. For example, the use of internet technology in monitoring the fluctuating price of soybeans in major markets has given farmers a competitive edge in trading in India (*New York Times*, 1 January 2004). Such success stories, based as they are on local experience, initiatives and needs, should not be difficult to replicate if interventions and assistance from government and donor agencies are provided in the area of infrastructure and technical training. However, the benefits of such interventions, in the absence of a gender focus, will elude women.

Finally, the benefits that globalization has brought or is likely to bring to the poor or underprivileged women and men of India are contingent on wider issues of education and life chances. Access to basic tools and networks is expensive and is thus beyond the means of the majority of India's one billion population. The cost of infrastructure, however, may not be the most restrictive factor. Some community projects, including one in West Vinod Nagar in Delhi, initiated for slum children by the Institute of Social Studies Trust[9] and supplied with computers by the Habitat Learning Centre,[10] reveal that it is the lack of literacy, particularly in English, rather than the cost and availability of tools, that is the real obstacle which prevents children from slums being connected to the network world. Average literacy rates in India are low at 65.4 per cent, and particularly low among women at 54.3 per cent (*2001 Census*). Gender disparity in literacy rates essentially reflects the overall gender inequalities in access to material resources. In the New Economy, the question of gender and class inequalities remains just as valid in assessing sustainability, replicability and indigenization of best practices as it was in the Old Economy. Policy-makers need to take this into account in formulating measures which deal with the benefits and costs of ITES jobs.

Notes

1   The ITES industry refers to services delivered over telecom networks or the Internet to a wide range of business areas. Most of the functions are human intensive where technology is used as a tool to provide the services. Because of their human-intensive nature, these processes and services can be outsourced in order to achieve a cost advantage without giving up quality. ITES covers mainly back-office operations like accounts, financial services, call centres, data processing, geographical information services, human resource processing, insurance claim processing, legal database processing and payroll processing.

2   For example, night shift work for women.

3   For a discussion of this fear see Mitter, 2004a.

4   According to NASSCOM's 2001–2002 data, the MNC segment emerged as an important contributor to total software and services revenue with a share of 27 per cent, of which 45 per cent is ITES services.

5   Interview by Swasti Mitter with Sushanto Sen, the Deputy Director of CII, India on 8 March 2002.

6   Call centres in India face challenges that need to be addressed in order to achieve sustainability. One major challenge for the industry is the attrition rate, which is lower than in the US or UK but at 30–35 per cent is still high, apparently due to stress or low levels of job commitment. Staff working at call centres tend to be young and aspire to further study and other professions. Most women leave the job after marriage – and most Indian women marry young. Company response to staff attrition has included recruitment from smaller towns and cities, the hiring of older staff who are more dependent on income from their jobs, provision of nearby housing to cut down on commuting time and stress and the provision of various in-house entertainment/relaxation programmes to deal with job stress.

   Another major challenge is meeting the high expectations of customers from different parts of the world. It has recently been reported that Dell, the world's largest computer seller, is scaling down technical support services in India because its corporate clients have complained about the poor level of service they were receiving. For the emerging management skills that the client company and the subsidiaries/subcontractors need to learn for successful quality control and transnational networking, see Bhattacharya *et al.*, 2003.

7   The UK trade union Amicus estimates that as many as 50,000 jobs have already been 'moved overseas', as the consultants term it. Employment consultants Addecco predict that by 2008, 200,000 more posts will follow – half the new call centre jobs it expects to be created by British companies over that period.

8   Jobless recovery happens when an economic upturn is not accompanied by a rise in employment. In the US in the last quarter of 2003, only 1,000 jobs were created in spite of an economic upturn. For the importance of ITES outsourcing to India in the current US Presidential campaign see, 'Bush Administration shows more support of free trade', *Online New York Times*, 31 April 2004; Finding lessons of outsourcing in 4 historical tales', *Wall Street Journal*, 29 March 2004.

9   For more information, see ISST's Community Centre: *http://www.isst-india.org/Outreach_FccCommC.htm*
10 Habitat Learning Centre is the innovation of India Habitat Centre, Delhi, to provide computer literacy to underprivileged children.

Sources of Information

Business journals and newspapers:
'The Outsourcing Solution', *Business*, September 2003, pp. 159–60.
'A talent hunter's guide to Business Schools', *Business*, September 2003, p. 116.
'The Rise of India and What It Means for America', *Business Week*, 8 December 2003, pp. 66–77.
'The Hidden Costs of Outsourcing', *Business Week*, 27 October 2003.
'All The World's A Call Centre', *Business Week*, 27 December 2003, *http://www.ebusinessweek.com/magazine/content/03_43/b3855070.htm*
'Call Centres are Bad for India', *BBC News Online*, 15 December 2003, *http://news.bbc.co.uk/2/hi/south_asia/3292619.stm*
BBC News, *World Edition Online*, 15 December 2003, *http://news.bbc.co.uk/2/hi/business/3255606.stm*
Connon, Heather (2003). 'Is It All Bad When UK Jobs Go to India?', *The Observer*, 7 December 7, reported in the Special Report on Globalisation, *Guardian Unlimited Online*, 16 January 2004.
Kapoor, Coomi, 'Doors Slammed on IT Experts', *The Star Online*, Malaysia, 2 June 2003.
'Relocating the Back Office', *The Economist*, 13 December 2003, pp. 65–67.
'Exim Policy 2003: A Bouquet of Incentives', NASSCOM BPO, *News Online*, April 2003, *http://www.nasscom.org/bponewsline/apr03/policy.asp*
'Night-shift Nod for Women: Cabinet Moves to Make Legal Provision', *The Telegraph*, Calcutta, 5 March 2003.
'Policy', NASSCOM BPO News Online, June 2003, *http://www.nasscom.org/bponewsline/june03/policy.asp*
Aggarwal, Balaka Baruah, 'Women Power Coming of Age, Courtesy ITES', *CIOL News Online*, 26 March 2003, *http://www.ciol.com/content/news/trends/103032601.asp*

Books and journal articles:
Bhattacharya, Somnath, Behara, Ravi S. and Gundersen, David E. (2003). 'Business risk perspectives on information systems outsourcing', *International Journal of Accounting Information Systems* 4:75–93.
Gothoskar, Sujata (2000). 'Teleworking and Gender: Emerging Issues', *Economic and Political Weekly* 35(26): 2293–98.
Hafkin, Nancy and Taggart, Nancy (2001). *Gender, Information Technology, and Developing Countries*, USAID, Washington.

Mitter, Swasti (2004a). 'Offshore Outsourcing of IT Enabled Services: Implications for Women', 4 March, *http://www.developmentgateway.org/node/133831/browser/?keyword%per cent5flist=277008&country%5flist=0*

Mitter, Swasti (2004b). 'Globalization, ICTs and Economic Empowerment: A Feminist Critique', *Gender Technology and Development* 8(1): 4–29.

Mitter, Swasti (2003). 'ICTs and Employment and Livelihood Opportunities of Women in South and Southeast Asia', *http://www.isst-india.org/Session III-Swasti.pdfv*

Mitter, Swasti (2000). 'Teleworking and Teletrade in India: Diverse Perspectives and Visions', *Economic and Political Weekly* 35(26): 2241–52.

Mitter, Swasti and Sen, A. (2000). 'Can Calcutta become another Bangalore', *Economic and Political Weekly* 35(26): 2263–68.

Mitter, Swasti and Efendioglu, Umit (1999). 'Is Asia the destination for 'runaway' information processing work? Implications for trade and employment', in Mitter, S. and Bastos, M.-I. (eds), *Europe and Developing Countries in the Globalised Information Economy: Employment and Distance Education*, Routledge, London and New York, pp. 9–27.

Worth, Robert (2002). 'In New York Tickets, Ghana Sees Orderly City', *New York Times*, 22 July 2002.

The Trade Policy Context

Sheila Page

Trading opportunities and the economic and policy changes that affect them have acquired greater importance in development strategies in recent years. This is not principally because of the growing share of trade in world output: that share has always been high for many developing countries. It is partly because of the change in development models, towards a focus on markets rather than governments to determine patterns of growth and development. But it is also because many of the countries which are still poor and seeking the first steps towards development are small, and therefore particularly dependent on external markets rather than domestic demand. Thus it is increasingly necessary for producers to understand external markets and how they are changing.

At the national policy level, there is increased awareness on the part of governments in many developing countries (including Ghana, South Africa, Bangladesh and India) of the importance of trade policy. They no longer simply accept special, preferential access from developed countries; they are trying to change policy through participation in the WTO and also in regional arrangements, both among developing countries and with developed countries. A similar awareness of the impact of trade policy is increasingly necessary for producers.

Although India and South Africa have substantial domestic markets, four of the case studies in this book are from countries where domestic demand is too low to support a national market-based strategy (Bangladesh, Ghana, Mozambique and Samoa). Two of the initiatives are clear responses to changed trading opportunities: call centres in India are a response to the technological and organizational changes which allow the supply of services at a distance; and the growth of garment manufacture in Bangladesh is a response to policies which have given it an advantage in developed country markets. Two others are examples of long-established exports – cocoa from Ghana and fruit from South Africa. But Ghanaian cocoa producers have attempted to find a new place in the market, based on fair trade, so that also is a response to change. The examples of cashew, in Mozambique, and coconut, in Samoa, are different in that they are more 'supply-driven'; here the initiatives stem from national or group objectives – the entrepreneurs appear to have looked at the markets only after they had decided on what to produce.[1] If they now find that they face disadvantages of cost and scale (as in coconut), this is a risky strategy.

The trading system continues to present barriers to producers in developing countries. The clearest example of this in this book is the protection of dairy and sugar products which deters Ghanaian cocoa producers from moving directly into production of chocolate; but call centres and fruit producers also fear protection. The examples of cocoa production and garment manufacture show how some producers react to obstacles. While the cocoa producers have found ways to get around the protection (by taking a share of a company producing chocolate within Europe), the garment producers have exploited the protection against other countries. They are now aware of the threat from the ending of the Multifibre Arrangement which gave them that opportunity, and some producers in Bangladesh are actively planning for the changed environment. Both past and current strategies have been encouraged by government policy. Policies other than those on trade can also be an obstacle to producers. The high dependence of Samoa on aid and remittances, which is noted in the case study, suggests that any exports will face difficulties as these inflows of funds cause Samoa's exchange rate to be high and its exports to be less competitive. The cashew processors' activities in Mozambique are constrained by high interest rates.

This chapter will attempt to look at how the current situation and policy environment are likely to change and how this could affect the initiatives described in this book, as well as other potential exporters in developing countries. It will examine both the direct effects which policy changes may have on these products and the indirect effects, which may alter the relative advantages of different types of export.

1 New Economic Opportunities by Sector

That the demand for traditional commodities grows slowly, and that therefore their prices are likely to be depressed, has been well known in development analysis for over half a century. The conventional advice is that countries should diversify away from traditional exports of raw commodities like cocoa, coconuts or cashews. One strand of advice suggests moving into 'value-added' products based on these, as some of the producers who are the subject of this book have done, with fair trade cocoa, coconut oil products and processed cashew nuts; but the strategy which has been followed by many successful countries has been to move into new goods based on a reassessment of countries' comparative advantages. For many of the Asian countries, this meant moving into labour-intensive sectors, whether process-ing goods, as in the ready-made garment industry in Bangladesh, or supply-ing services, as in Indian call centres. In the 1980s, a third form of diversifi-cation, into new horticultural goods like South African fruit, was suggested, but this has never been more than a small part of countries' strategies.

Traditional commodities

While the negative forces, relatively slowly growing demand and increasing efficiency of production, often by new suppliers, continue to depress long-term expectations for the prices of traditional commodities, there are occa-sional reversals. In the past, these have been because of wars or exceptional growth periods in developed countries; a new factor is emerging at present – the emergence of China as a major importer. For many commodities, China has little production of its own. Its rapid growth has required massive imports, leading to significant shifts in the direction of trade and in world commodity prices. In the first quarter of 2004, the index of all non-fuel com-modity prices was 25 per cent above its 2001 level, and for the two basic commodities represented here, cocoa and coconut oil, prices in the first quar-ter of 2004 were almost 50 per cent and 100 per cent higher than in 2001. These peaks need to be kept in perspective. The price of cocoa was 30 per cent lower in 2000 than in 1990, and the price of coconut oil and the average price for all commodities are still below their 1995 levels. As past experience suggests that it is only a rapid increase in demand, not continuing high demand, that raises commodity prices above their trend path, even if China continues to grow, a levelling off would be expected and any deceleration would lead to price falls. Nevertheless, this recent reminder that prices can go up as well as down indicates that value-added commodity products will not always have a strong advantage over traditional commodities.

Agricultural commodity prices may also perform better than trend over the next few years if there is reform of the highly protected regimes in the EU, Japan and the US. A combination of high barriers to imports and subsidies that hold their own domestic production well above economic levels have kept world demand for agricultural commodities from the rest of the world below its market level. This has depressed prices. The estimates that have been made of the effect of US and EU subsidies on cotton prices suggest that they could be 20 per cent higher in the absence of subsidies (Gillson *et al.*,

2004). A change in agricultural policy would not affect tropical commodities like cocoa and coconut oil directly, but in some developing countries it might lead to a shift back to the commodities that are now subsidized. Like the effect of Chinese demand, this modifies, rather than reverses, the rule that 'commodity prices fall'. The combination of these two forces, however, suggests that the arguments for shifting away from traditional commodities will become weaker in the current decade.

The cocoa production described in the chapter on Ghana is principally for traditional export, and this part of the output may therefore gain. Although the price guarantees and any premium on the price received because of the fair trade element may appear small by comparison, they are nevertheless very important for the farmers involved. In the longer term, the question that needs to be asked is whether the demand for fair trade cocoa will expand sufficiently rapidly (or whether the producers of fair trade products can market the concept to make the demand expand sufficiently rapidly) to counter the trend fall in basic commodity prices. For coconut oil, the same question must be asked about the demand for organic products, but the Samoan producers are perhaps less likely to gain from any uplift in prices because of their small-scale and weaker market power (in contrast, the cocoa study notes the way that Ghana has used its market position).

New or non-traditional commodities

Pineapple and prawns in the 1980s, and flowers and fruit in the 1990s, have seemed to offer the best of both worlds: high prices, because unlike traditional commodities they have a high income elasticity, and an easy transition for farmers who need to move out of commodities. The first caveat to these examples is that in no country are they a large-scale export. (In Kenya, where flowers and fruit have been frequently studied, they are around 5 per cent of exports.) Second, most of them can be, and now are, produced in a number of countries, so that while their prices may fall less rapidly than those of commodities for which demand is rising slowly, they still fall. And finally, as will be discussed below (and as is noted in the chapter on South African fruit), there are increasingly onerous barriers in the form of both government and private sector standards. As with any demand-driven and competing product, producers must continually innovate in the product and constantly reduce costs to meet new competition.

Processing traditional commodities

Whether this is a sensible route towards diversification depends partly on the relative cost of transport of the raw and processed goods. For a few commodities and countries, the choice may also be made for industrialization policy reasons: if processing offers access to technological or organizational learning that will have significant effects on a country's economic development. But in most cases, the choice depends mainly on whether a country which has the conditions that give it a comparative advantage in production also has these for processing. For many commodities, the conditions are very different, so that Bangladesh, for example, like many other developing countries, processes its garments using imported textiles. Although it produces some fibres, the intermediate stage of producing textiles is highly capital and technology intensive, so it specializes in the labour-intensive stages of growing cotton and making clothes. Changing ways of organizing production, such as the satellite production discussed in the study on Mozambique, can create the conditions for successful processing, and the growing experience of different ways of subcontracting production may offer increasing opportunities of this type.

The example of the Kuapa Kokoo Cooperative from Ghana taking a direct share in a chocolate production company in its European market is another case where changing organization increases the opportunities for a developing country to process its raw materials. The high barriers to milk and sugar, and therefore to chocolate which contains them, have deterred the processing of cocoa in developing countries, but by locating the processing within Europe, Kuapa Kokoo has overcome this barrier (and probably also reduced its vulnerability to unreasonable EU food standards).[2] This provides income to Ghana through profits rather than wages, but this income can also be used to increase employment. It is likely that innovations and improvements in how firms can organize their production at a distance will increase these opportunities, but producers should never assume that processing is the logical step.

Manufacturing

This is the traditional route to increased income and development, and the growth in demand for basic goods such as the apparel produced in Bangladesh, combined with increased awareness by developed country importers of the significant labour cost advantages of producing in developing countries, has led to large shifts of some products and some stages of production from developed to developing countries. The study of Bangladesh illustrates both the opportunities and the limitations of this pattern. The shift has increased the number of workers, including many women, who receive wage incomes, but the constraints caused by production conditions in Bangladesh has made it difficult to find opportunities to move to more value-added products. This type of opportunity is likely to continue to be available in new areas of production, as well as in those where it is already strong, but it requires countries (or entrepreneurs within them) to identify new opportunities that are often unrelated to its commodity resources (Bangladesh makes apparel from East Asian fabric, not its own cotton or jute; Malaysia processes integrated circuits, not rubber). These activities are, therefore, the opposite of the Samoan or South African examples, where existing products are being used.

Services

Although the share of services in world trade has not yet risen as strongly as it has in most national economies, they are an important export for developing countries, and this share is likely to rise faster in the future for the same reasons as it has nationally – demand for services increases faster than income. Tourism, for example, now has a higher share of world trade than cars or oil, and it is particularly important for many small and poor countries. The high labour intensity of most services makes them obvious sectors for India to exploit. The fall in the cost of communications and electronic technology which has permitted the emergence of call centres as an 'export opportunity' may not continue at its recent rate, but most types of company and service product have not yet adopted the technologies now available, so that this is likely to remain a major area of growing opportunities. Although, as with the transfer of jobs in manufacturing to developing countries, the initial organization is centralized, the same potential to reorganize and decentralize could allow these opportunities also to go to smaller groups and countries.

2 Changing Trade Policies

Until the 1970s, most developing countries did not actively promote their exports through international trade policy. Their traditional products normally faced low, if any, tariffs or barriers, except for a few such as dairy products and sugar, which faced apparently immutable barriers. Their new products usually faced low barriers in their principal markets because of preferences offered by developed countries to their traditional suppliers (extended to more countries by the Generalised System of Preferences in the 1970s); services were not yet on the horizon. Of the products described here, only fruit and coconut oil appear to face some tariff barriers. In the 1960s, countries which had active trade policies to promote development were more likely to be promoting production for domestic consumption by controlling imports than following an export-led policy.

The change in approach towards export strategies, combined with a reversal in the early 1970s of the generally liberalizing approach of developed countries, which increased protection in clothing and other manufactures where developing countries were starting to be successful, led to a change to a more active trade policy: first in the largest or most successful exporters (India and Bangladesh among those described here, followed by South Africa in the 1990s when it ceased to be under sanctions), and then in the others (Ghana and Mozambique in the last four to five years). Both governments and producers now not only are more interested in knowing how other countries' policies will affect them, but try to alter policies through multilateral and regional agreements. The study of Bangladesh notes that the shift to garment production came about because of policy changes in other countries (the quotas imposed by developed countries on other producers) and in Bangladesh (trade liberalization), as well as changes in technology.

Multilateral policy

The growing influence of developing countries in the WTO has already had an impact on some of the exports discussed here. In the Uruguay Round of negotiations, which concluded in 1994, it was agreed that the system of quotas for exports from the most efficient developing country producers of garments and textiles, the Multifibre Arrangement, would be ended, but with a ten-year adjustment period. This reflected the interests of the stronger producers, including India and the East Asian countries; the slow phase-out was a concession to the interests of those countries which, like Bangladesh, had benefited from not facing quotas. Developing countries also then began the process of bringing agriculture under multilateral disciplines; it seems increasingly possible, if not yet likely, that they will secure further reforms in a renewed Doha Round. These would, as discussed above, increase the share of developing countries in world trade in the currently restricted products, and increase the returns which they obtain. This could affect the products analyzed here by providing alternative opportunities.

Preferential arrangements

In the 1990s, developed countries appeared to be moving away from offering preferential treatment to imports from developing countries. They started to negotiate reciprocal trading arrangements (for example NAFTA and the EU Agreement with South Africa), and the Uruguay Round WTO settlement offered little in new special treatment for developing countries. Since then, however, preferences have come back into fashion. The EU allows all imports from least developed countries (LDCs), including Bangladesh, Mozambique and Samoa, without tariff or quota barriers (sugar, rice and bananas have transition periods). Until at least 2008, it also has virtually no restrictions (except on sugar, rice and bananas which are the sensitive agricultural products) on imports from the ACP countries, which include Ghana, Mozambique and Samoa). The US has offered new opportunities to most African countries under the African Growth and Opportunity Act – with exclusions for countries judged not to be acceptable on human rights grounds. The most striking increases have been in clothing, particularly in the small low-income countries, because the US has allowed these to continue to use imported fabric. Other developing countries such as India, together with East Asia and much of Latin America, face varying barriers in their export markets. South Africa benefits as an African country from AGOA, although under WTO definitions it is 'developed' (by its own choice). It seems likely that LDCs, at least, will retain a favoured position. Therefore countries that do have major preferential privileges, including the four discussed here, can use them as an additional 'advantage' in trade. However so far, of the cases discussed in this book, only Bangladeshi apparel is an example of this.

Regional arrangements

Most developing countries are now also members of regional trading arrangements, but not all of these have a significant impact on trade and it is notable that none of the producers discussed in this book appears to rely on these for its exports. However, for small producers of the type discussed here regional opportunities, even without strong links in a formal regional arrangement, may be important, as they do not need large export markets and may find regional neighbours more familiar and therefore easier to deal with. But it is not clear that there will be increased opportunities from stronger regional arrangements, and their future is uncertain. In the past, proposals for regional agreements have tended to emerge at times when multilateral trade negotiations were not happening or appeared to be stalled; but then they recede. The exceptions are groups which have a clear political, social or security interest in a long-term relationship, as well as an economic motivation. This matters because any economic reason for a region is likely to hold at least equally strongly for multilateral liberalization. It is regions with non-economic foundations that can overcome the sectoral, protectionist interests which impede multilateral liberalization. The 2003–2004 cycle of disillusion with the WTO after Cancún, followed by failure of the apparent regional substitutes (notably the Free Trade Area of the Americas, but the EU's negotiations with ACP regions are also going slowly), followed by a renewed effort at multilateral negotiations was unusually rapid, suggesting that regions may be attracting little support.

Rules and disputes

The Uruguay Round strengthened the enforcement provisions of the WTO by removing countries' right to refuse consent to a ruling (the old rules had required consensus), and the increased attention to rules in trade has increased interest in using the provisions. To the extent that this makes the trading system more predictable and less subject to arbitrary actions, particularly by the major traders, it makes exporting easier for all small producers. But there are also some potential direct effects on producers of the type described in this book.

Brazil has made the first successful (subject to appeal) challenge to agricultural subsidies – against the US on cotton. While there are both legal and practical obstacles to generalizing this case to all subsidies by all producers (different types of subsidies, the costs of litigation, the real possibility that losers, or potential losers, will bargain and 'settle out of court'), this judgment, in parallel with the impact of developing countries in negotiations, weakens the long-term prospects for subsidies.

There have been several disputes about what type of differential treatment countries can offer to either regional partners or countries receiving preferences. On regions, the decisions have tended to restrict countries' ability to increase barriers to countries outside the region in order to favour members, weakening the role of regions. On preferences, however, the most recent judgement, in a case brought by India against EU preferences that discriminated against it, appears to open up new scope for preferences. It suggests that while purely discretionary choice of beneficiaries is not allowed (so India won that case), transparent and clearly defined discrimination may be. This could legitimate special help for groups such as small islands (this would not directly help Samoa as it already receives help as a LDC), and could possibly allow special treatment for particular types of product. The EU's General Preferences give extra preference for sustainably produced tropical timber and to countries meeting core labour standards. If these, or standards of other types, such as fair trade or organic production, were made less discretionary, they might meet the new interpretation. Decisions in WTO disputes need not follow precedents, however, and this is a controversial decision, so any implications can only be speculative.

The 'outsourcing' of services, of the type found in the Indian call centre sector, has attracted opposition in some developed countries, notably the US. Some of the proposed measures to stop it, including discrimination by local governments against companies who outsource any of their activities, may be contrary to US commitments under the WTO. The dispute procedure might be used to protect India from such policies.

Private standards

The growing role of supermarkets in setting standards for products is particularly emphasized in the study of fruit workers in South Africa; this role of retailers in developed countries is also important in other areas, notably textiles and garments. It is also significant in services – standards for tourism and tour companies are already affecting developing country producers, and those for financial services could affect activities like call centres. Producers will need not only to meet these, as they need to meet any market requirement, but to find ways of negotiating on them, as they can be set without consulting suppliers. They are not official, so there is no direct recourse either to government-to-government negotiations or dispute procedures. The response of Ghana to a different problem, the concentration of market power in cocoa in a few buyers, i.e. taking a united national approach to selling to increase its own market power, is one possible remedy. Working with European producers, as in the Kuapa Kokoo investment, is another. Cross-national alliances of similar producers could be another. All the producers will need to find permanent systems, rather than relying on *ad hoc* responses.

3 Trade, Poverty and Gender

The case studies suggest that an informed view of external markets and trade policies can increase the likelihood of success. But they look only at the direct effects of trade on poverty and the opportunities for women. It is important to remember that what happens in trade is likely to be much less important for reducing poverty than the other national policy and economic conditions that influence how opportunities from trade are transmitted to different groups within the economy. On the other hand, the indirect effects of trade can allow a government which is committed to reducing poverty and increasing opportunities for women to do so, even if there is no direct link through production. This focus on direct effects may be valid when governments do not have the capacity to redistribute income if the country decides that immediate poverty reduction is more important than longer-term gains. But even direct poverty-reducing trade may not produce a favourable outcome if the government does not want to improve income distribution. If manufacture of chocolate in Europe is more efficient than in Ghana, given technical and policy conditions, either the company or the government can, through taxation, redistribute the profits to improve the incomes of the poor within Ghana. An alternative remedy for the concentration of income from cashew nuts exports in the hands of traders would be to tax them. Providing good social conditions for the poor in South Africa can be done directly, rather than through rules on labour. Governments must choose the most efficient combination of direct and indirect strategies to meet their objectives.

Notes

1   Although production and processing of cashews in Mozambique for the world market was encouraged in the 1960s and 1970s.
2   Other developing countries are also setting up processing companies in the EU and the US.

References

Gillson, Ian, Poulton, Colin, Balcombe, Kelvin and Page, Sheila (2004). 'Understanding the impact of cotton subsidies on developing countries and poor people in those countries', Report to the Department for International Development, UK, March.

Page, Sheila with Caroline Ashley, Dills Roe and Dorothea Meyer (2004). 'Tourism and the poor: analysing and interpreting tourism statistics from a poverty perspective', Working Paper forthcoming in *Pro-Poor Tourism* series.

Page, Sheila and Hewitt, Adrian (2001). *World commodity prices: still a problem for developing countries?*, Overseas Development Institute, London.

Lessons Learned

Marilyn Carr

The purpose of this concluding chapter is to undertake a review of benefits resulting from implementation of the six initiatives described in this book and of the strategies used to achieve them.

The chapter is divided into three sections. These are:

- **Benefits** – which looks at the positive impact of trade liberalization on low-income women producers and workers, and also at some of the problems being encountered;

- **Implementation** – which looks at the policy environment, and examines and compares some of the strategies used by different agencies to assist low-income women producers and workers;

- **Replicability and sustainability** – which looks towards the future and makes some suggestions to Commonwealth governments and other stakeholders based on good ideas arising from the review of the case studies.

1 Benefits

All the initiatives described in the case studies have created a significant number of earning opportunities for women and for men. The numbers of women involved vary from a few hundred in Samoa and Mozambique to over a hundred thousand in South Africa and India, and well over a million in Bangladesh. The proportion of those involved in the initiatives who are women also varies from 30 per cent in Ghana to over 90 per cent in Bangladesh. There is quite a significant difference between those initiatives which deal with independent producers and those which deal with wage workers. The latter reach much greater numbers of women and also tend to involve a higher percentage of women.

There have been direct economic benefits resulting from profits, fair trade bonus payments and wages. In the case of Ghana, a figure for profits from sale of the commercially traded cocoa is not available, but US$1 million was paid into the Kuapa Kokoo Trust Fund from fair trade bonuses between 1993 and 2000. In Samoa, the total profits from the oil processing businesses are unknown, but it has been estimated that families receive four times as much income from selling virgin oil as from copra and that the weekly earnings from one business are between US$240 and US$400 – compared with an average annual per capita income of US$1,420. A lot more could be earned if processors worked for a full working week.

In Mozambique, many women have access to cashew nut trees and earn income from selling traditionally processed cashews in the local market. They also sell to traders for export, but although prices have gone up, it seems to be the traders who have retained most of the increased profits. Women also have jobs in the new processing factories where they can earn from 100,000–300,000 meticais (US$5–15). Higher wages of up to 700,000 meticais (US$35) are earned only by men. This compares with the average rural agricultural wage of 560,000 meticais (US$28). Despite the low wages, these jobs are highly sought after and prized. In the case of South African fruit farms, contract workers' earnings range from $38.60 to $115.79 per month, compared to a wage of $57 per month needed to put an average household above the poverty line.

In Bangladesh, although wages in the ready-made garment sector are among the lowest in the world (US$0.15 per hour as compared with US$0.35 in India and US$0.45 in Sri Lanka), they are nevertheless very welcome to the thousands of women who otherwise would have no earnings at all. And in India, the average wage for women in call centres is US$200–400 per month, which is quite high in a country where the average daily wage is less than US$1 per day.[1]

In addition to these direct economic benefits, a number of indirect economic benefits and non-economic benefits have also arisen from the initiatives. These include community development projects, raising of women's self-esteem and status, raised morale and sense of independence, newly acquired skills and building of civil society organizations. Thus, in Ghana, women cocoa farmers have been involved in building their own cooperative and are visible in all positions, including society presidents and board members of totally owned companies and experience a significant degree of representation. They have also been able to welcome foreign visitors and to travel overseas to talk about their work, which increases their self-esteem and knowledge. In addition, they are the main beneficiaries of the bonus payments received from that portion of their cocoa which is fair traded; this is invested in women's enterprises and community development projects such as hand-dug wells, corn mills and schools which meet some of women's priority needs. Free health care has also been provided to 100,000 people. Of course, further improvements could be made. For example, the objective of having two women members on every farmers' committee has still to be met, and there is some way to go in raising the number of women members.

In Samoa, as the new oil processing enterprises have been introduced through a Women's NGO (WIBDI), women's status has increased as they are seen as being the ones who have brought these new opportunities to their villages. Women manage all but three of the cooperatives, and although the male head of household controls the distribution of money, some women have been able to set up a savings account through WIBDI which gives them a source of cash they can spend without consulting their husbands. In addition, women have received both technical and business training. But the marketing and production of value-added products have been problematic.

In South Africa, changes in national legislation have led to women in permanent jobs being issued with contracts in their own right (as opposed to being employed on the basis of their spouse's employment). Packing is becoming a more important activity because of the demands of UK supermarkets and this is predominantly done by women who are well paid; some farms are breaking down the division of labour between women and men by introducing multi-skilled teams of which both are a part. However, the new legislation has led to the shedding of some on-farm women workers as a cost-saving measure, with the result that they are now forced to accept more precarious off-farm work with lower pay and fewer benefits.

In Bangladesh, women in export-oriented garment industries earn more and have better working conditions than those working in domestic industries, although they still work long hours in very harsh conditions. Many have migrated from rural areas and send remittances back to their families which raises their status. Finally, in India, many relatively well-paid jobs have been created for young women in call centres who would otherwise have been unemployed. They too report that this has raised their status and self-esteem.

In addition to the benefits outlined above, socio-cultural factors – both positive and negative – have had a role to play in the way in which the initiatives have been developed and implemented. In Samoa, the cultural environment has specifically required that both women and men be included in the oil processing enterprises and that cooperatives be formed on the basis of extended family groups rather than the community in general. Production in the enterprises is limited, however, because people tend to work only when they need money rather than on a regular basis. In South Africa, the paternalist relationships which existed between growers and women workers before apartheid have now been reinvented in the contract sector, with women being highly dependent on their contractor to provide transport, access to credit and assistance with financial and personal difficulties. In Bangladesh, cultural norms, as well as employer discrimination and trade union practices, help to explain women's exclusion from the wider labour market and therefore their willingness to work in garment factories for very low wages. And in India, despite changes in labour legislation which allow women to work night shifts, parental pressure acts as a constraint on their employment, and anti-social hours make it difficult for women to continue to work in call centres once they marry.

2 Implementation Strategies

A major objective of this book is to present policy-makers and other stake-holders with good examples of successful strategies for assisting independent producers to link with global markets and for creating jobs for women in export industries. It is therefore useful to say something about the strategies used in the six initiatives described.

Favourable policy environment
By and large, the initiatives have arisen in response to some major inter-national and/or national policy change related to exports. Thus, in Ghana and Mozambique the initiatives arose in response to liberalization in the 1990s that was part of structural adjustment programmes which resulted in the disbanding of government marketing mechanisms and/or factories. In South Africa also, the government marketing mechanism was disbanded as a result of liberalization in the 1990s. As a result, individual fruit growers were exposed to the direct forces of global competition and international quality standards, including standards on employment for fruit workers. In Samoa, it was the combination of a series of cyclones, combined with a long run of low international prices for copra and coconut oil, which led to the collapse of the coconut sector and prompted WIBDI to find an alternative niche mar-ket for specialized organic products. In Bangladesh, the massive growth in the garment export industry was largely a response to the imposition of quotas and the search by Korea and other countries for quota-free locations where they could set up garment assembly plants. Finally, in India, the creation of thousands of jobs for women in the export of services can be traced to rapid technological change at the global level which is speeding up the relocation of service sector jobs from high-wage to low-wage countries.

While trade liberalization policies have resulted in initiatives which have delivered both economic and other benefits for significant numbers of women, some trade policies can present barriers once these initiatives have been established. As was seen in the chapter on the trade policy context, protection of dairy and sugar products in EU markets has been a factor in Ghanaian cocoa producers moving directly into the production of chocolate in Europe. While Bangladesh has so far benefited from exploiting protection against other countries, it will suffer badly from the end of the quota system when the Multifibre Arrangement is phased out in 2005. Trade policy can also be used to try to support local industry and employment – as with the raising of export taxes on cashew nuts in Mozambique to try to support the growth of local processing industries.

However, trade policy is only one of a set of economic policies and programmes that governments have put in place to promote development and the case studies show that many policies have been very supportive of the initiatives. For example, in both Ghana and Mozambique the government has offered support in terms of guaranteeing loans or providing low interest loans to the private sector. Ghana has a strong market support system as the government only partially liberalized the Cocoa Board, which still provides export marketing and quality control services. However, Mozambique has a very weak marketing infrastructure which impedes the marketing of cashew kernels. In Samoa, the government has strong policies favouring the diversification of commercial agriculture, the revitalization of susbsistence agriculture and the active role of women in development; more recently, it has become interested in and commissioned research on organic agriculture. In South Africa, the national legislation introduced after the end of apartheid is more progressive than international codes of conduct imposed by UK supermarkets, and the government is pursuing a path of increased labour regulation at a time when most countries are deregulating in response to the pressures of global competition. In Bangladesh, following the imposition of quotas, the government undertook a series of economic reforms to open up its economy, including direct export incentives; it is now in the process of developing a new labour code which has been informed to a certain extent by the experiences of women workers in the RMG sector. And in India, the government has changed labour laws to remove restrictions on women working on night shifts so that they can work in call centres more easily.

Without support such as this, many of the initiatives would not have achieved as much as they have. Again, however, there is still room for improvement. For example, although both South Africa and Bangladesh have (or will have) new labour legislation, both case studies point to the fact that there are insufficient labour inspectors to enforce legislation effectively. Thus, positive policies by themselves are not sufficient; there also needs to be a means of implementing them.

Production systems: global value chains

The case studies have placed considerable emphasis on global value chains and the use of these chains in analyzing how the gains from globalization can be further spread to marginal producers and workers in terms of altering the balance of power, access and returns. A global value chain is the network that links the design, production and marketing processes that result in a commodity or product. Such chains link individual workers and enterprises, often operating under both formal and informal arrangements, spread across several countries and linked to one another within the global economy.

Global value chain analysis was developed primarily within the manufacturing sector where there are two types of chains: producer-driven and buyer-driven. Producer-driven chains are those in which large, usually transnational, manufacturers play the central role in coordinating production networks, including backward and forward linkages. This is characteristic of capital- and technology-intensive industries such as automobiles. Buyer-driven chains refer to those industries in which large retailers, branded marketers and branded manufacturers play a pivotal role in setting up decentralized production networks in a variety of exporting countries, typically located in the South. This pattern of trade-led industrialization has become common in labour-intensive consumer goods industries such as garment manufacture (Gerrefi, 1999). Global value chain analysis is now being extended to horticulture and traditional primary commodities through the introduction, for example, of trader-driven chains (Gibbon, 2001). It can therefore be applied to most of the case studies in the book and has been used to map out where low-income women fit into the chain and how they can increase their power and returns within it.

In Ghana, Kuapa Kokoo buys cocoa from its large network of 45,000 farmers and sells it through the Ghana Cocoa Export Board to the International Cocoa Organization in London. The ICCO then sells the cocoa to the three or four giant agribusinesses which process raw materials for the equally large chocolate manufacturers. Just three firms in the US and the UK control 75 per cent of the chocolate market. As the Export Board still exists, and since it handles such large quantities of cocoa (including that from Kuapa Kokoo), it is able to negotiate a good price on the London market. In addition, Kuapa Kokoo, as well as being a buying company, has now been assisted (with funds from DfID) to set up its own chocolate company in the UK as a joint venture. Thus its members have effectively moved along the value chain from being producers to being buyers and retailers as well.

In Samoa, all the produce for the export market is sold through one channel – the Pacific Coconut Oil Company which was established by

WIBDI and has recently been sold to a private buyer in New Zealand with Samoan family connections. This is a very small chain, but as we have seen still lends itself to useful mapping.

In Mozambique, most cashew nuts are shipped to India for processing. Eight or ten traders control exports and have a large network of small traders who buy the nuts for them from the smallholders. Prices are set by international markets through Indian processors, but even with price increases the traders retain most of the profits. In this case, a buyer-driven chain (which goes from the Indian processors to the Northern retailers) is combined with a trader-driven chain[2] which links smallholders with exporters. The two factories described in the case study which were recently established to process cashew nuts in Mozambique each sell directly to single buyers – one in the US and the other in Rotterdam. The latter was found with the help of SNV in the Netherlands. In this second factory, efforts are being made to shorten the marketing chain at the provincial level, including through the introduction of satellite processing units. This should help provide greater returns to smallholder producers and processing workers, but there are still constraints posed by extremely powerful Northern actors in the chain.

In South Africa, 34 per cent of fruit exports go to the UK where supermarkets are the main buyers representing over 89 per cent of the retail market (with the big four representing 50 per cent). Supermarkets formally operate through the open market but in reality have tightly integrated global value chains through which they source fruit and demand stringent quality and production conditions. As we have seen, it is the strong relationship with UK supermarkets which has led to the implementation of international codes of conduct for workers. As with national legislation, however, the codes are not well monitored.

Ready-made garments for export represent the ultimate in buyer-driven global value chains. Large retailers in the North outsource production to manufacturers in the South, where wage rates are much lower. There are basically three tiers of firms producing garments in Bangladesh. First, there are the firms in export processing zones which have direct links with international buyers, and have modern equipment and better working conditions. Second, there are large and medium-sized firms outside the EPZs which also have direct links with the buyers and maintain reasonable labour standards because of these links. And third, there are a large number of very small firms in the informal economy with which large firms place subcontracts. About three-quarters of the large firms subcontract in this way. Competition is fierce and this keeps production and labour costs low – especially because Bangladesh produces mainly low-value basic and casual wear products where it has to compete largely on the basis of its ability to produce reasonable quality goods at ever-decreasing prices. Finally, in India, export of information services is controlled by a few multinationals; this industry is joining garment manufacture in the 'race to the bottom' in which companies move their business from one country to another in search of the lowest wages.

A major use of global value chain analysis is to highlight inequalities in the chains and also to identify where positive interventions to decrease inequalities can be made and by whom. Typically, local producers and workers in supply chains account for less than 10 per cent of total costs. Thus, as is seen in the Bangladesh case study, wage costs amount to $0.16 for making a shirt that retails in the US for $13. Consumers in the North and producers and workers themselves need to have access to this type of information. Tracing appropriate points of intervention is also important. In garment manufacturing, it may be impossible for owners of small workshops to pay their workers higher wages because they have minimal profit margins themselves as a result of pressures from further up the chain. However, it would be quite feasible for Northern retailers to add a tiny amount to the sales price of garments with little hardship to consumers and great benefit to workers (McCormick and Schmitz, 2002). This type of analysis is beginning to be used by those involved in fair or ethical trade initiatives who are interested in fairer prices for local producers or in better working conditions for wage workers.

These different models of production, with their different ownership and marketing arrangements, help us to better understand the role of low-income women involved in producing for the global market. There is a need to produce more case studies which cover different arrangements, countries and sectors.

Market access: fair trade and ethical trade

Several different marketing strategies are illustrated by the case studies. An important one is fair trade. This is the model used in Ghana. Samoa is also about to be registered. In Ghana 3 per cent of Kuapa Kokoo's cocoa production is fair traded, which may not seem significant but which the farmers themselves find enormously beneficial because of the $150 per tonne fair trade 'bonus'. While there is no one definition or business model of fair trade, a fair trade approach usually includes the following key practices: (a) direct purchase from producers; (b) transparent and long-term trading partnerships; (c) cooperation, not competition; (d) agreed minimum prices, usually set above market minimums; (e) focus on development and technical assistance via the payment to suppliers of an agreed social premium; and (f) provision of market information to producers (Barratt Brown, 1993). As these practices show, fair trade is about more than buyers paying a higher price for a good than it would otherwise pay on the open market or ensuring that minimum standards of work conditions are complied with. The essence of fair trade is about empowering producers by making them partners in the supply chain. It is this approach that enables fair trade to offer consumers, businesses and citizens a practical way to improve the situation of producers in the South.

Although the market for fair trade goods in the North is relatively small, it is growing very rapidly with sales in the US and Europe growing by 30 per cent in 2003 to $400 million (*Guardian*, 28 February 2004).

In the case of Samoa, market contacts in Australia and New Zealand were made with the assistance of the Internet, this being the only initiative which seems to have used new information and communications technologies as a marketing tool. Organic virgin coconut oil was carefully chosen as being a product for which Samoa could find a market, as it lends itself to small batch production and therefore gives no advantage to larger coconut oil producers like those in the Philippines. WIBDI set up its own marketing outlet for the oil but used a buying agent. However, marketing was not proceeding as well as expected and so WIBDI sold the company to a private entrepreneur in New Zealand. There is currently no local market for the oil in Samoa itself as people prefer imported oils based on other products. However, WIBDI is mounting information campaigns to try to bring about a change in consumer tastes. Organic certification has been achieved and subsequently sales expanded; fair trade certification is also being negotiated.

In Mozambique, the social entrepreneur on whose factory the case study is mainly based found his market with the help of SNV, the Netherlands based-NGO which also assisted Kuapa Kokoo. All his cashews now go to one buyer in Rotterdam. Otherwise, marketing could have been very difficult because of the weak marketing infrastructure in the country. All Mozambique's cashew nuts are organic and given the booming market for organic products in Western Europe this could be a new opportunity. However, again the marketing infrastructure is too weak to develop the necessary links.

While these three case studies follow a fair trade approach, the South African case study is an example of ethical trade. Fair trade and ethical trade are both about improving the lives of people who supply products into international markets. As outlined above, fair trade works with producer businesses and enables access to new markets and buyers under terms that are mutually acceptable. Ethical trade, on the other hand, is mainly driven by the concerns of brand image in the destination market. It concentrates on ensuring that employees in established supplier companies are working in conditions that match or exceed a minimum standard so that companies which sell the products are reassured that supplier employees are not being exploited

(Redfern and Snedker, 2002). Marketing in South Africa is done through developing linkages with UK supermarkets which belong to the Ethical Trade Initiative and which tightly govern the production chain, including implementation of ETI's code of conduct in respect of the workers employed by their suppliers. In addition to implementation of codes of conduct, supermarkets demand very high quality products and will agree on prices only after a consignment has been delivered so that its quality can be checked. This means that there is considerable risk for the producer. Many buyers are prepared to be part of a supermarket chain, however, because prices are higher than in the free market and are also more stable.

There is a large and growing literature on ethical trade and codes of conduct. Some agree that in the era of globalization and trade liberalization, voluntary codes have the advantage of extending the application of labour standards across national boundaries and governmental jurisdictions, and along international corporate supply chains, but are sceptical about their usefulness, particularly if there is no provision for independent verification. They agree, however, that codes can reinforce the regulatory role of the state, as is happening in South Africa (Jeffcot and Yanz, 2000). Others query why so many codes leave out the principles of freedom of association and collective bargaining which are fundamental to trade union development and functioning (Diller, 1999).[3]

Technology and competitiveness

The case studies bring up some interesting ways in which technology has been either used or ignored in relation to competitiveness. The first of these also relates to choice of technology and employment. It is frequently assumed that increased output and export earnings are only possible with the use of capital-intensive technology and large-scale production. However, two of the case studies show that this is not necessarily so and that it is possible to compete in export markets with the use of more labour-intensive technologies and smaller-scale production. Thus, in Samoa, the use of small-scale oil expelling technology enables rural people to run village level enterprises and still compete in export markets. This is because with current technology virgin coconut oil can only be produced in small quantities, so that Samoa can compete with larger countries in the region which cannot at the moment benefit from economies of scale. In 2001, Samoa did in fact produce more organic virgin coconut oil than the Philippines.[4] Similarly, in Mozambique, one of the two cashew nut processing factories is using semi-mechanical labour-intensive technology imported from India with good results in export markets as this causes less breakages and produces more of the whole nuts than the larger-scale technology.

Secondly, in the fiercely competitive world of garment manufacturing, Bangladesh has followed the policy of competing through paying very low wages. The case study points out that the alternative would be to diversify into higher value products, but rather than this meaning higher wages for women, it could mean that they would be replaced by men who have the necessary skills to operate the more advanced technology involved. Indeed, this has already happened in the knitwear sector of the industry. Thus, while technology can sometimes be the source of income, it can also be the cause of women being displaced if they are not given the skills training required to use it.

Thirdly, the case study from India is a perfect example the 'third technological revolution' which involves the convergence of computer and communications technologies, culminating in networking technologies which have made it possible to digitize a large amount of information that can be transported, processed and retrieved to and from a distant location at little cost. As the authors point out, the relocation of service sector jobs mirrors the experiences of the effective fragmentation of production processes in the 1980s and 1990s which was based on the introduction of computer technology and facilitated the outsourcing of manufacturing jobs from high-wage to low-wage countries. As with manufacturing jobs, however, there are benefits and costs for women. Jobs are being created in India now, but continued technological development could easily make existing skills redundant (for example through a move to voice recognition services); jobs are also at risk as companies move to competing countries with lower wages.

Organization

As we have seen, the case studies cover a range of organizational strategies and the issues raised by the studies describing independent producers differ considerably from those involving wage workers. The former include a large cooperative in Ghana which buys cocoa from its members, has a very complex membership structure and provides a number of services for its members. In Samoa there are small producer-based cooperatives which are family based and which are provided with a range of services by a women's NGO. The Mozambique case study introduces us to very small 'satellite' cashew processing units which supply a local small-scale processing factory. Although the first of these units are being tested out with entrepreneurs in charge, eventually it is envisaged that they will be community/cooperatively owned and operated.

Over the years, cooperatives have had a mixed history, but generally they have fallen out of favour. According to the ILO, this is because 'in many countries, state-controlled 'cooperatives' failed to mobilize members ... and the cooperative vision of enlarging the economic power of individual members through membership-driven entrepreneurship was devalued and discredited'. It goes on to say:

> Cooperatives are a very significant part of the global economy. Ranging from small-scale to multi-million dollar businesses across the globe, they are estimated to employ more than 100 million women and men and have more than 800 million individual members. Because cooperatives are owned by those who use their services, their decisions balance the need for profitability with the wider interests of the community. They also foster economic fairness by ensuring equal access to markets and services for their members, with membership being free and open.   ILO, 2003

This would very much seem to fit in with our cooperative models, although in the case of Ghana the involvement of fair trade organizations has probably strengthened Kuapa's business approach.

With wage workers, the issues relate much more to organizing to bargain for better wages and working conditions. In none of the three cases are women workers members of unions and there appears to be no other form of organization through which women can make their voice heard. Indeed, in EPZs in Bangladesh, organizing has been generally forbidden in most factories, while in South Africa women's increasing off-farm status makes it difficult for unions to recruit them as members. In any case, only 2 to 8 per cent of the agricultural workforce are unionized, and many rural unions are male-dominated and do not respond to women's needs. Even women and men working in the more formal call centres in India are not unionized or formally organized, and women in particular seem to be unconcerned about this as they stay for such a short time in employment.

Action is possible here both at the national and international level. Both South Africa and Bangladesh have, or are introducing, new national labour legislation but have a major problem with implementation as there are so few labour inspectors. Trade unions should also have a role to play here. Although our case studies paint a bleak picture of trade unions, it should be noted that globally the union movement is changing. According to a recent DfID report:

> In part, this is reflected in the development of new forms of labour organization such as the Self Employed Women's Association in India. But there are also many examples of traditional unions re-thinking their approach to previously unprotected sectors of the workforce. For example, in South Africa, unions played the lead role in a campaign to extend the provisions of the basic Conditions of Employment Act and the Unemployment Insurance Fund to domestic workers – a vulnerable and predominantly female section of the workforce   DfID, 2004

Such interventions should be encouraged.[5] Similarly, those concerned with fair trade and ethical trade in the North, as well as consumers associations, can put pressure on growers and companies.

Institutions

Finally, many types of agencies have been involved in supporting market access and fair prices for local producers, and fair wages and benefits for local wage workers. In addition to the government ministries and departments involved in economic, trade and labour policies, these include United Nations agencies such as UNDP, UNIFEM, FAO and UNV; bilateral agencies such as DfID and NZAID; international NGOs such as SNV, Tehnoserve and Oxfam; fair trade and ethical trade organizations such as Twin Trading and the Ethical Trade Initiative; academic and research institutions such as the Australian National University; national and regional NGOs such as WIBDI and ECOWOMAN; government agencies such as the Ghana Cocoa Export Board and the Mozambique Institute for the Promotion of Cashews; and various parts of the private sector including small businesses in Mozambique, fruit growers in South Africa, supermarkets in the UK and the many multinational corporations and national firms involved in the garment and services export industries in Bangladesh and India. Unions have been mentioned very little and then only in the Mozambique, South Africa and Bangladesh studies.

As was seen in the policy section of this chapter, governments have played a major role in all six cases studies, through the implementation of trade or other economic policies, institutional support to production and/or export marketing, assistance with finance for setting up cooperatives or private companies or changes to labour legislation.

As for other agencies, there is a clear split between the independent producer initiatives and the ones involving wage workers. In the former, international NGOs and fair trade organizations have been to the fore, with some private sector involvement. Much of the success of these initiatives can be credited to the strong business orientation of the agencies involved and, with the exception of Mozambique, their strong gender orientation. In this type of initiative there are often no business-oriented agencies involved at all or there is tension between the fair trade agencies and the NGOs; but this does not seem to have happened in these cases.

In the initiatives involving wage workers, the orientation has been almost totally private sector with some limited involvement of unions and ethical trade organizations. Although large numbers of women are involved in all these cases, there has been little or no attempt to ensure that women receive the same treatment or wages as men. The exception to this is India, where there seems to be no difference in wages between men and women working in call centres. Conditions in export industries do seem to be better than else-where because of the links with international buyers who exert pressure on their suppliers to observe at least some minimum standards.

3 Replicability and Sustainability

So what of the future? We have looked at six case studies with interesting organizational models and features. But can they be replicated or scaled up, and are they and the markets they are linked with sustainable? Finally, what are the recommendations for the future in terms of support from decision makers and other stakeholders?

Replicability

There is every indication that replication is already underway in a number of the initiatives. In Ghana, Kuapa Kokoo is helping to set up a sister coopera-tive called Sompa so that even more farmers can benefit from their own mar-keting system. It is in touch with other West African cocoa producing countries in an attempt to share its experience and offer assistance, and in the North it is seeking new markets through its chocolate company in the UK. According to a recent DfID publication, things look encouraging in terms of getting blanket penetration of fair trade products across mainstream distributors. For example, the Co-op Group in the UK, which is supplied by the Day Chocolate Company, converted its entire own-brand block chocolate range to fair trade in November 2002 with very promising results. Despite having to make a small retail price increase on the new range, sales of the Co-op's own brand chocolate were up by 25 per cent (*Developments*, 2004). This obviously augurs well not only for Kuapa Kokoo members (who play their own role in trying to increase the share of fair trade), but also for many local producers throughout the developing world. However, there are still doubts as to whether fair trade can ever be effectively mainstreamed. According a recent ILO report:

> While greater penetration into mainstream markets is arguably the only way forward ... it must be recognized that mainstream businesses demand a dif-ferent approach to the ATO niche. In most companies, buyers will not toler-ate late delivery and poor communication or changes in an arrangement, Therefore, there is a risk that the gain of a broader distribution of benefits resulting through the supply of greater volumes will be countered by a lessen-ing of the quality of those benefits.   Redfern and Snedker, 2002

In Samoa, the technology on which the village oil production enterprises are based came from Fiji and there is every indication that it could now be trans-ferred to other countries in the Pacific. In Mozambique, the 'satellite' model is being set up specifically with replication in mind.

Few developing countries have the breadth of labour regulation and protection that now exists in South Africa; in fact, pressures of global competition and economic liberalization are encouraging many countries to relax labour market regulations rather than tighten them. However, many women workers in countries such as Kenya and Zambia are also concentrated in insecure forms of employment and are lower down the employment hierarchy than men; they face the same problems as South African women and could potentially benefit from the South African experience. Finally, the replicability of garment factories and call centres is well proven as they are already proliferating, but questions obviously exist about the type of 'immiserizing' growth involved in such industries which is driving wages down as companies move around the globe in search of lower wages.

Sustainability

Replicability is one thing, but are these initiatives sustainable in the long-term, given all the changes taking place in global markets? The previous chapter covered some of these issues, but it is worth repeating the major question here: are the income opportunities created sustainable?

In all cases, there is the important question of maintaining competitiveness. As was argued in the previous chapter, given the slow growth of demand for traditional commodities and accompanying depressed prices, it is often recommended that producers move into value-added products based on these commodities or into new markets such as horticultural exports and labour-intensive garment and service export industries. All the initiatives discussed have done this in some form or another, but they still face competition from other countries. This is a real threat for Samoa, which is surrounded by other coconut growing countries that could easily take over its niche market for organic virgin coconut oil and associated products. Mozambique faces competition in the export of cashew nut kernels from new entrants to the market such as Vietnam, which is now the world's second biggest producer of cashew nuts after India and, unlike Mozambique, has massive government spending on research and development. As the authors of this case study conclude, it could well be in Mozambique's interest to look at local and regional markets such as neighbouring South Africa. South Africa itself faces competition in fruit exports from Chile and New Zealand, with China beginning to enter the market as a major fruit exporter. Bangladesh will face enormous competition in ready-made garments from a range of countries once the Multifibre Arrangement comes to an end in 2005. And India already faces competition from English-speaking countries in Africa, where there is a cheaper labour force anxious for jobs in data entry and call centres.[6]

As we saw earlier, technological development and transfer can in some cases increase competitiveness, and there is undoubtedly a need for more R&D which is aimed at assisting small producers and employers to upgrade or diversify and seek other ways to deal with rapidly changing global markets. But the main need is for appropriate trade policies. As was seen in the previous chapter, a number of recent changes in trade policy have been supportive of developing country exports. For example, if discrimination against companies which outsource activities is found contrary to US commitments under the WTO, then this could protect India from such policies. However, in a situation of increased global competitiveness, it is difficult to achieve a situation where all the countries win all the time. As the ILO puts it: 'The rising tide of trade has not been sufficient to lift all boats'. The phasing out of the MFA, which will help India and East Asian countries but hurt Bangladesh, is a perfect example of this. As the Bangladesh case study says, there will definitely be redundancies in Bangladesh. Now is the time to start planning – either by finding alternative markets in Asia or by diversifying and upgrading, but at the same time training women in new skills – so that hardship is kept to a minimum when the time comes.

Suggestions for the future

What then can we say about the future? Obviously, there is a need to examine policies and programmes which can continue to support and increase the involvement of women in global markets and export industries. There is also a need to protect access to markets, while at the same time trying to protect and improve labour standards. There are, of course, already a large number of actors involved in issues of gender, trade and employment, but not all of them have a focus on, or indeed an understanding of, the existing and potential contributions of local women producers and workers to export earnings. Nor has the impact of national economic policies and programmes on the distribution of benefits from trade been sufficiently discussed. Since many of the women we are talking about are among the poorest sectors of the population, the impact of trade liberalization on poverty reduction will be severely constrained if polices and programmes of the type described in the case studies are not more widely developed and implemented.

Ideas for Policies and Programmes

The case studies in this book offer many good ideas for policies and programmes which can be implemented by governments and other stakeholders. In summary, these include:

General

- Trade policy is an important development tool, but it should be viewed as only one of a set of economic policies required to create employment and reduce poverty.

- Trade policy should be reviewed to ensure that it does not contradict other economic policies which aim specifically to support employment creation and poverty reduction.

- Trade and other economic policies should be reviewed from a gender and pro-poor perspective to ensure that low-income women producers and workers are able to contribute to, and benefit from, export initiatives.

Independent Producers

- Independent producers need strong market support in the face of volatile global markets and fluctuating prices. The example of Ghana is a good one. By keeping some of the more important and less bureaucratic functions under government control after liberalization, exporting was made much easier for Kuapa Kokoo. In contrast, small producers in Samoa and Mozambique suffer from lack of a strong marketing structure and lose opportunities as a consequence.

- Fair trade has worked well in Ghana (and many other countries) and should be pursued more widely. The combination of a strong business emphasis and a sound development and gender approach seems to work very effectively. The Kuapa approach itself should be transferred to and supported in other countries. In addition, measures to mainstream fair trade should be promoted.

- Support is needed to increase access by independent producers and their associations to ICTs which can be used (as in Samoa) to find market contacts and information on market prices. Women need to have equal access with men to ICTs.

- The Mozambique experience suggests that for some commodities in some countries, local and regional markets should be given more emphasis than international markets. It also suggests that production of commodities will not be responsive to price increases alone, but that it also requires technical assistance which reaches women as well as men.

Ideas for Policies and Programmes (continued)

- Independent women and men producers need to have land or property rights which can be used as collateral to obtain loans to start cooperatives or enterprises.

- There is a need for increased R&D which is geared specifically to ensuring that technological solutions are available to small producers and businesses which need to diversify because of increased market competition. Special attention should be given to the needs of women producers.

Wage Workers

- New labour codes should replace outdated ones and follow the Bangladesh example in being informed by the experiences of low-income women workers. In addition, as in the South African experience, labour legislation needs to extend beyond permanent workers with contracts (who tend to be men); more labour inspectors are needed to ensure that such legislation is enforced.

- The South African experience shows that national labour legislation, if it is effectively implemented, is more efficient than codes of conduct, which are purely voluntary and not well monitored. However, codes of conduct can be useful in supporting national legislation.

- The Bangladesh experience tells us that upgrading technology in order to compete globally can cause the displacement of women in labour-intensive industries and that women should be given more training opportunities so that they can participate fully in situations where industries need to be upgraded and/or diversify to maintain competitiveness.

- Programmes to make people aware of their legal rights are essential for low-income women wage workers so that they learn about their rights and can organize to demand them in an effective way; new labour movements and sympathetic trade unions should be encouraged to reach out to them.

Notes

1   Of course, benefits cannot be measured only by income. For example, global markets provide an opportunity for specialization in the production of goods, which is pro-poor, especially in labour abundant countries. But specialization also brings risks and uncertainty and, some believe, could threaten food security. The opening up of markets has also led to increasing price fluctuations which the rural poor find difficult to deal with unless they are collectively organized to negotiate in markets (PRUS Notes No. 2, June 2001).

2   The Ghana example is different in that Kuapa Kokoo controls its own collection chain and still goes through the Government Export Board which maintains quality and negotiates on its behalf.

3   These were found in only 15 per cent of a survey of 215 codes.

4   Personal correspondence with WIBDI.

5   It should be noted, however, that while some studies show that the higher labour standards which result from union action have no relationship with sectoral trade patterns or export performance, other studies find that they can diminish the comparative advantage of developing countries in labour-intensive goods such as garments (DfID, 2004).

6   Although we are dealing here with export initiatives, it should be remembered that in many of these countries there are also many producers and enterprises which are being negatively affected by import competition with the result that they also need assistance to upgrade or diversify in the face of lost markets.

References

Barratt Brown, Michael (1993). *Fair Trade: Reform and Realities in the International Trading System*, Zed Books, London.

Department for International Development (2004). *Developments – The International Development Magazine*, DfID, London.

Department for International Development (2004). *Labour Standards and Poverty Reduction*, DfID, London.

Diller, Janelle (1999). 'A Social Conscience in the Market Place? Labour Dimensions of Codes of Conduct, Social Labelling and Investor Initiatives', *International Labour Review*, 138 (2).

Gereffi, Gary (1999). 'International Trade and Industrial Upgrading in the Apparel Commodity Chain', *Journal of International Economics*, Duke University, Durham, North Carolina.

Gibbon, Peter (2001). 'Upgrading Primary Production: A Global Commodity Chain Approach', *World Development* 29 (2).

ILO (2003). *Working Out of Poverty*, Report for 2003 International Labour Conference, ILO, Geneva.

Jeffcott B., and Yanz, L. (2000). *Codes of Conduct: Government Regulation and Worker Organizing*, Maquila Solidarity Network.

McCormick, Dorothy and Schmitz, Hubert (2002). *Manual for Value Chain Research on Homeworkers in the Garment Industry*, WIEGO/IDS, Sussex.

Poverty Research Unit at Sussex (2001). *PRUS Notes: Globalization and Poverty*, No. 2, June, University of Sussex, Brighton, UK.

Redfern, Andy and Snedker, Paul (2002). 'Creating Market Opportunities for Small Enterprises: Experiences of the Fair Trade Movement', SEED Working Paper No. 30, ILO, Geneva.

About the Contributors

Luis Artur is a lecturer and researcher in the Faculty of Agronomy and Forestry, Eduardo Mondlane University, Maputo, Mozambique. He holds an MSc in the Management of Agricultural Knowledge Systems from Waginingen University, The Netherlands. He participated in the liberalization, gender and livelihoods study of the cashew sector in Mozambique and has has co-authored International Institute for Environment and Development (IIED) working papers arising from the project. His research interests include changes in livelihoods due to new technologies and disasters.

Carla Braga is a lecturer and researcher in social anthropology at Eduardo Mondlane University, Maputo, Mozambique, and a gender specialist who has published on women and natural resources in Africa. She is presently doing a Master's course at State University of New York, researching HIV/AIDS and its impact at community level. She has published in the fields of gender in relation to land tenure and NGOs. She was previously an associate researcher with the Women and Law in Southern Africa Research Trust in Mozambique. She has also lived in Chile, where she was active in the women's rights movement.

Stephanie Barrientos is a Fellow at the Institute of Development Studies, University of Sussex. She gained her BA and PhD in Political Economy at the University of Kent. She has researched and published widely on gender and development in Africa and Latin America, globalization and informal work, ethical trade and international labour standards. She coordinated a DfID-funded project on 'Ethical Trade in African Horticulture – Gender, Rights and Participation' (2002–2004), and is coordinating the Ethical Trading Initiative Impact Assessment (2003–2005). She has advised a number of NGOs and international organizations on issues concerning gender, agribusiness, ethical trade and impact assessment, including the ILO, UNIDO, UNCTAD, the World Bank, DfID, Oxfam and Christian Aid. She is co-convener of the DSA Study Group on Corporate Social Responsibility. For more information on her publications and consultancy work see *http://www.ids.ac.uk*.

Marilyn Carr is a Research Associate at the Institute of Development Studies, University of Sussex and Director of the Global Markets Programme of Women in Informal Employment: Globalizing and Organizing (WIEGO). She has a BA in African and Asian Studies, a D.Phil in Development Economics from the University of Sussex and an MSc in Economics from the London School of Economics. She has been Senior Economist with the Intermediate Technology Development Group in the UK, Senior Economic Adviser for the United Nations Development Fund for Women (UNIFEM), based in New York and Harare, and Regional Adviser on Small Enterprises and Appropriate Technology for the Women's Centre of the UN Economic Commission for Africa in Addis Ababa. She has held fellowships at the Radcliffe Institute for Advanced Studies at Harvard University, the International Development Research

Centre (IDRC) in Ottawa and the IIED in London. She has researched and published widely on gender and the informal economy, small business development and rural industrialization, and gender, science and technology.

John Cretney is a former Chief Executive of the Nelson Marlborough Institute of Technology based in New Zealand. After completing a PhD in chemistry at the University of Canterbury, he pursued a career in education management. He has also served on the boards of a number of New Zealand national bodies related to tertiary vocational education. He now undertakes consultancy and advisory work, with a focus on the Pacific, including organizational review work and researching Pacific-related issues.

Grace Fernandez has a BA in Sociology and is trained in computer applications. She has been with the Institute of Social Studies Trust, Bangalore, since 1989 and is currently administrator of the Bangalore Office. Her areas of interest include poverty, health and HIV/AIDS.

Naila Kabeer is Professorial Fellow at the Institute of Development Studies, University of Sussex. She carries out research, training and advisory work in the field of gender, poverty, labour markets and livelihoods and has published extensively on these topics. Her most recent books include *The Power to Choose: Bangladeshi Women and Labour Market Decisions in London and Dhaka*, Verso Press, which deals with Bangladeshi women workers in the global garment industry, and *Mainstreaming Gender Equality in Poverty Eradication and the Millennium Development Goals*, published by the Commonwealth Secretariat. She is currently the Kerstin Hesselgrens Guest Professor at the University of Goteborg.

Nazneen Kanji is a Senior Research Associate at the IIED. She has been involved in gender and development work for the past 20 years and has extensive experience in Africa and South and Central Asia. She has studied the effects of economic and social policy change at the household level and has undertaken poverty and livelihood assessments in urban and rural contexts, and written widely on these issues. Her current research interests include land and livelihoods and the effect of trade liberalization on gender and livelihoods, including in the cashew sectors in India and Mozambique.

Andrienetta Kritzinger is Professor in the Department of Sociology at the University of Stellenbosch where she gained her DPhil. Her main areas of research and teaching are in gender studies, sociology of work, youth studies and rural sociology. She has published locally and internationally, and her most recent publications are on globalization, gender and changing labour arrangements in export fruit farming. Since 1994 she has conducted extensive research into the labour situation on South African export fruit farms, with a special focus on gender relations and the agricultural labour market. She participated in the DfID's Globalisation and Poverty Programme, collaborating with Stephanie Barrientos on South African horticulture. She is currently doing work on the contracting sector in South African export fruit.

Haruna Maamah is the Chief Executive Officer of ECAM Consultancy, consulting on economic, agricultural and institutional reforms. Prior to this he was the Coordinator, Cocoa Sector Reform Secretariat and the Chief Economist, Policy Analysis Division of Ghana's Ministry of Finance and Economic Planning. He has been on the boards of many companies, including COCOBOD, and has been a consultant to international, multilateral and bilateral organizations.

Jacqui MacDonald is the Chair of the Day Chocolate Company and was the Director of the Resource Centre for the Social Dimensions of Business Practice. She is currently an Associate of the Co-operative College in the UK, the European Regional Representative for Verité (Verification in Trade and Ethics) and an Associate Director of the Prince of Wales International Business Leaders Forum. As General Manager, Fair Trade, she played a key role in creating The Body Shop International's cornerstone strategies, as well as its Statement on Human Rights and Trading Charter, and she established and expanded its Community Trade Programme.

Simeen Mahmud studied statistics at Dhaka University and medical demography at the London School of Hygiene and Tropical Medicine. She joined the Bangladesh Institute of Development Studies after completing her Master's degree and is currently Senior Research Fellow in the Population Studies Division. She was a MacArthur Fellow at the Harvard Centre for Population and Development in 1993. Her past research has been on demographic estimation methods, women's work, status and fertility, micro-credit and its impact on women, and group behaviour. Currently, she is working on social policy with a focus on health and education, issues of citizenship, participation and accountability, demographic transition under poverty, and globalization and its implications for women workers in the export sector.

Swasti Mitter is currently an independent scholar and international consultant in the field of ICT and the economic empowerment of women. She was previously Professor of Gender and Technology at the University of Brighton, UK. She has also held visiting fellowships at the Center for the Study of Women, UCLA and at the Science and Technology Policy Research Unit at the University of Sussex. Between 1994 and 2000, she was Deputy Director of the United Nations University Institute of New Technologies, where she initiated a series of research projects on the impact of new technologies on women's employment. She has written numerous publications in the field of globalization, gender and new technology, and has contributed as a consultant to the work of a wide range of UN agencies and academic institutions on gender and ICT.

Frema Osei-Opare is an independent development consultant. Her work has focused on supporting marginalized groups in improving their economic, social and political position. In particular, her work covers research and advocacy concerning national and international policy issues affecting poverty alleviation. Her experience in development work is varied. She joined SNV, a Dutch development organization where her work included support for the Kuapa Kokoo programme, and she was the Country Director for ActionAid Ghana, an International NGO, from 1998 to 2003.

Sheila Page has been a Research Fellow, Overseas Development Institute, London, since 1982. Previously she was at Queen Elizabeth House, Oxford and the National Institute of Economic and Social Research. Her current research interests include how and why developing countries participate in international negotiations, and regional trading arrangements among developing countries and between developing and developed countries. She has written widely on the issues of world trade and on trade and finance in developing countries.

Hester Rossouw received an Honours degree in Sociology from the University of Stellenbosch in 1991. She works as a researcher and has researched and published on poverty and social protection in South Africa, as well as on South African agriculture. She specializes in looking at employment trends in the agricultural sector and working conditions on farms. She also works part-time as a social auditor for the Wine Industry Ethical Trade Association.

Adimaimalaga Tafuna'i is a founding member of WIBDI and served as Vice-President until taking over as Executive Director in 1998. After working for many years in the medical field, she became interested in development after working for eight years with the US Peace Corps. In 2002 she was chosen as one of four fellows by the Commonwealth Foundation and wrote a chapter for a book, *Empowerment of NGOs in the Pacific*. She currently serves as treasurer for both the Samoa Umbrella for NGOs and the Pacific Island Association of NGOs. She represents WIBDI on a number of government boards and committees in Samoa.

Pauline Tiffen is a business and financial adviser specializing in work with smallholders engaged in producing commodities and cash crops for developed country markets. She was involved in the start-up of Kuapa Kokoo and has also worked directly with many other small-scale farmers and cooperatives in East Africa and Latin America. She is currently an adviser to the Commodity Risk Management Group at the World Bank and Associate Director of the US Fair Trade Federation.

Shaiby Varghese has worked as a Programme Associate in the Institute for Social Studies Trust in Delhi since March 2003. She previously worked with *Vikalpa*, the academic journal of the Indian Institute of Management, Ahmedabad. She has a Master's degree in Economics from the MS University of Baroda and specializes in gender and development.

Carin Vijfhuizen is a rural development sociologist and gender specialist and is currently attached to Wageningen University and Research Centre in The Netherlands. She worked for 14 years at universities and in projects in Zambia, Zimbabwe and Mozambique) and recentlycoordinated the IIED/UEM project in Mozambique on Liberalization, Gender and Livelihoods: A Study of the Cashew Sector. Her research interests include rural livelihoods, gender identity and gender analysis of land and water rights in irrigation schemes. She has published on issues of gender and development and natural resource use.